INFANT RESEARCH AND ADULT TREATMENT

CO-CONSTRUCTING INTERACTIONS

Beatrice Beebe

Frank M. Lachmann

THE ANALYTIC PRESS

2002   Hillsdale, NJ   London

Published by The Analytic Press, Inc.
101 West Street, Hillsdale, NJ 07642
www.analyticpress.com

Typeset in Weiss by CompuDesign, Charlottesville, VA

Library of Congress Cataloging-in-Publication Data

Beebe, Beatrice, 1946–
    Infant research and adult treatment: co-constructing
interactions / Beatrice Beebe, Frank M. Lachmann.
        p.   cm.
    Includes bibliographical references and index.
    ISBN 0-88163-245-7
    1. Psychotherapist and patient—Case studies.
    2. Psychotherapy—Case studies.   I. Lachmann, Frank M.
    II. Title.

RC480.8 .B44 2001
616.89'14—dc21

                                                        2002033495

Printed in the United States of America

10   9   8   7   6   5   4   3

CONTENTS

Contents

ACKNOWLEDGMENTS

Not only is this book the result of an ongoing dialogue between us, but it is also based on an ongoing dialogue with our students, our colleagues, and our patients. We would like to thank the psychoanalytic communities that have encouraged our fascination with the relevance of infant research for psychoanalysis: for both of us, the New York University Postdoctoral Program in Psychotherapy and Psychoanalysis and the Institute for the Psychoanalytic Study of Subjectivity. In addition, for Beatrice Beebe, the Columbia Psychoanalytic Center; and, for Frank Lachmann, the Postgraduate Center.

We are grateful to the mothers and infants who gave generously of their time to make this research possible. All the infant research took place at New York State Psychiatric Institute, Columbia University, together with Joseph Jaffe, M.D. and Stanley Feldstein, Ph.D., lifelong collaborators of Beatrice Beebe. Dr. Stephen Ruffins is a member of Dr. Beebe's research team.

Dr. Beebe's research students who coded videotapes second-by-second and participated in the interpretation of the data were essential collaborators in this work: Rhonda Davis, Helen Dimitriodes, Nancy Freeman, Psy.D., Donna Demitri Friedman, MSW, Patty Goodman, Psy.D., Michaela Hager-Budny, Sarah Hahn-Burke, Psy.D., Liz Helbraun, Ph.D., Allyson Hentel, M.A., Tammy Kaminer, Ph.D., Sandra Triggs Kano, Limor Kaufman-Balamuth, Ph.D., Kristen

Kelly, Marina Koulomzin, Psy.D., Greg Kushnick, Paulette Landesman, MSW, Tina Lupi, MSW, Lisa Marquette, Ph.D., Irena Milentijevic, Psy.D., Jillian Miller, Alan Phalan, Ph.D., Danielle Kramer Phalen, Ph.D., Jill Putterman, Ph.D., Jane Roth, M.S.W., and Shanee Stepakoff, Ph.D. We thank the volunteers who helped make everything happen: Ron Avirom, Ph.D., Emma Barnstable, Lisa Braun, Emily Brodie, Emlyn Capili, Lauren Cooper, Terri Chmurak, Clare Davidson, Julia Dizenko, Lauren Ellman, Carlin Flora, Leah Feuerstein, Yael Hait, Jennifer Kohns, Eva Kourniotis, Catherine Man, Sara Markese, Allison Mercado, Debra Posner, Nancy Richardson, Michael Ritter, Alison Rodin, Ilana Rosenberg, Ronit Roth, Nick Seivert, Sonia Sonpal, Marina Tasopoulos, Tracey Toon, and Lillia Treyger.

Thanks to Samuel Anderson, Ph.D., Howard Andrews, Ph.D., Anni Bergman, Ph.D., Sidney Blatt, Ph.D., Phyllis Cohen, Ph.D., Marvin Hurvich, Ph.D., Sharon Koffman, Ph.D., Ilene Lefcourt, Jennifer Lyne, Wordy Olesker, Ph.D., and Donald Ross, Ph.D., who consulted on various phases of the research.

Parts of this book are based on or excerpted from earlier work: chapter 1 was partially drawn from Lachmann and Beebe (1983); chapter 2, partially drawn from Beebe, Jaffe, and Lachmann (1992); chapter 3, from Lachmann and Beebe (1996b); chapters 4 and 5, from Beebe, Lachmann, and Jaffe (1997); chapter 6, from Beebe and Lachmann (1998); chapter 7, from Beebe and Lachmann (1994); chapter 8, from Lachmann and Beebe (1996a); and chapter 9, from Beebe et al. (2000).

We thank John Kerr, who was an inspired and dedicated editor, as well as Eleanor Starke Kobrin, Paul Stepansky, and the staff of The Analytic Press.

PREFACE

For the past 30 years we have been engaged with one another, and with our colleagues, seeking to integrate infant research and adult treatment. In the course of this dialogue we have taken ideas from each realm and examined their relevance for the other. Although empirical evidence from infant research and the adult psychoanalytic process are different realms of discourse, nevertheless, each is germane to the other. Psychoanalysis has influenced our approach to infant research, and infant research has influenced our understanding of psychoanalysis.

Although there are many domains within infant research, in this book we address only one, the second-by-second analysis of face-to-face interactions. This focus omits consideration of such related issues as the regulation of sleep-, wake-, feeding-, and alone-states. However, face-to-face interaction research is specifically relevant to psychoanalysis because it describes the origin of relatedness and patterns of nonverbal communication that continue to operate in similar forms across the lifespan. Although most research in this domain examines mother and infant, the work we present is generally applicable to fathers and infants as well.

Face-to-face research has provided a view of early interactions as subtle, complex, and fascinating—a far cry from the psychoanalytic view of the "global undifferentiated" infant that prevailed when we started our collaboration. This research shows that interactions of face, voice, and orientation between mother and infant are "co-constructed." Although both partners contribute to the organization of the ongoing exchange, their contributions are not necessarily similar or equal. This research reveals how the mind is organized in interaction.

Infant research can be used to imagine the patient's early history and provides many more metaphors and scenarios than previously available. However, that has not been our main purpose in this book. Instead, we have used infant research to conceptualize the nonverbal and implicit interactive process itself within psychoanalysis. The usual level of psychoanalytic discourse entails an explicit, verbal, and symbolic narrative; but an interactive process that is implicit and nonverbal proceeds in parallel.

A shift toward interactive models and systems thinking can be found in the thinking of various psychoanalytic theorists throughout the 20th century. What is new in contemporary psychoanalytic views is the increasing centrality of the interactive process itself. This recent shift has been limited primarily to the verbal domain and associated feeling, reveries, and subjective states. In infant research, however, interactive models and systems thinking have long been used to describe the nonverbal domain of implicit communication through face, voice, and orientation.

In the course of this book we follow the story of how infant research has changed the way we think about psychoanalysis. In the first chapter we review the changes in our thinking across the three decades of our relationship by examining the case of Burton. This treatment forged the foundation of our collaboration during our first 10 years together. The contrast between our understanding of the case then and now illustrates the ways in which concepts from infant research can expand clinical understanding.

Our view shares much with current relational psychoanalysis, particularly the work of Stephen Mitchell and Lewis Aron. Like Mitchell, we are interested in studying the array of patient–analyst interactions. Our view is also consistent with Aron's (1996) definition of relational psychoanalysis as based on the "notion that mind is inherently dyadic, social, interactional, and interpersonal" (p. x). At the center of the relational view, Aron showcases the inevitability of a reciprocal, two-way influence process and the co-construction of meaning between patient and analyst. This position is at the center of our thinking as well. We are naturally pleased that Aron cites infant research and our papers (Beebe and Lachmann, 1988a, b; Beebe, Jaffe, and Lachmann, 1992) as having contributed to his conceptualizations. Our work can be differentiated from current relational psychoanalysis by our emphasis on systems approaches, our explication of the nonverbal dimensions of co-construction, and our use of the array of interaction patterns demonstrated by infant research to illuminate organizing principles of interaction in psychoanalysis.

Our view also holds much in common with that of Robert Stolorow, Bernard Brandchaft, and George Atwood (1987; Stolorow and Atwood, 1992) and Donna Orange (in press) in their description of the intersubjective field as a continuous, reciprocal mutual influence system in which each partner is contextualized by the other. Our views have cross-fertilized each other. In fact, we spent the year of 1995 in many transcontinental telephone calls with Stolorow discussing Thelen and Smith's (1994) approach to systems theory. These conversations resulted in further articulations of systems views (Stolorow, 1997; Lachmann, 1998; Beebe et al., 2000). With respect to both the relational theories of Aron, Mitchell, and others, and the intersubjective perspective of Stolorow and colleagues, our work further articulates the complexity and range of the organization of the reciprocal, mutual influence process.

In chapter 1 we discuss the treatment of Burton where our paths originally crossed. We use his case to illustrate how our thinking has changed across the last three decades. In chapter 2 we lay out the dyadic systems approach to interaction that underlies our work. In chapter 3 we plunge the reader into the case of Karen. Here we illustrate how we use a dyadic systems theory and introduce our fundamental organizing principles of interaction, self- and interactive regulation.

In chapter 4, tackling more technical aspects of infant research, we present an overview of the perceptual and cognitive capacities that the infant employs in organizing his experience. The infant uses these capacities to organize presymbolic representations, based on expectations of how action sequences of self- and interactive regulation unfold. Once we grasp these extraordinary early infant capacities, we see that the first year, even the first half-year, is a period with its own organization and importance, rather than a "preamble" to later symbolic development.

In chapter 5 we illustrate various patterns of interactive regulation during face-to-face play in the early months of life. These patterns yield further organizing principles of interaction, such as vocal rhythm coordination, facial mirroring, chase and dodge, and disruption and repair. These interaction patterns provide key parallels to nonverbal patterns in adult treatment. Using the experimental research reviewed in chapter 4, we argue that the infant represents these various patterns in a presymbolic format. This integration of perceptual and cognitive research, with the description of various early interaction patterns, forms the basis for our view of the origins of self- and object representations. We use a dynamic, transformational process view of representation, based on the expected moment-to-moment interplay of the two partners, which explicitly avoids a discrete, static individualistic view of representation (see Orange, in press).

In chapter 6 we return to adult treatment and the co-construction of inner and relational processes. We argue that the dyadic process reorganizes both inner and relational processes in analyst–patient, as well as adult–infant, interactions. Reciprocally, changes in self-regulation in either partner can alter the interactive process.

In chapter 7 we revisit one of the basic themes of the book—how the mind is organized in interaction. We turn once again to the subject of presymbolic representation and suggest three general organizing principles: ongoing regulation, disruption and repair, and heightened affective moments. These "three principles of salience" simultaneously illuminate the origins of representation and internalization in the first year. Chapter 8 illustrates the three principles of salience with a psychoanalytic case.

Chapter 9 proposes an interactive model of the mind for adult treatment. Our purpose is to reframe psychoanalysis within a systems view of interaction consistent with infant and adult research. This view changes our ideas about such fundamental concepts as the nature of interaction itself; how patterns of interactive expectations are formed and transformed; how verbal and nonverbal communication is integrated; and how the nature of self and other, internalization, and mutuality versus autonomy must be redefined. Although it is beyond the scope of this book, we want to note that there are multiple ways in which our view of an interactive model of mind intersects with relational, intersubjective, and self-psychological theorists in psychoanalysis (see for example Basch, 1988; Benjamin, 1988; Bromberg, 1998, Ehrenberg, 1992; Fosshage, 2000; Hoffman, 1998; Lichtenberg, 1989; Slavin and Kriegman, 1998; Stern et al., 1998).

The payoff of the infant research that we present, however, goes beyond its application to adult treatment and an interactive model of mind. It provides a systematic view of the origins of the processes of relatedness itself.

1

BURTON, THEN AND NOW

This book is a joint effort, literally co-constructed. It is a dialogue between us and a dialogue between psychoanalysis and infant research. We begin with the treatment of Burton which became the foundation of our collaboration as it got underway in 1972. We present Burton in the way we understood him at the time (Lachmann and Beebe, 1983) and then we revisit the case in the light of our study of infant research.

The Burton case illuminates the theme of the book, the ways that new knowledge about human development can expand clinical understanding and therapeutic intervention. The contrast between our understanding of the case then and now illustrates the revolution that our field has been living through since the publication of Daniel Stern's (1985) *The Interpersonal World of the Infant*.

This book is written in the "we" voice. Allow us to introduce ourselves, however, by describing our separate backgrounds and how we came to collaborate. I (Frank Lachmann) was a supervisor of psychology graduate students at a university mental health clinic for just one year, 1972 to 1973. For an hour and a half each week, three graduate students and I discussed one case treated by each of the students. One of the students was Beatrice Beebe.

In 1972 I had been in practice for a number of years and taught ego psychology at the Postgraduate Center for Mental Health in New York City. I had been particularly influenced by the work of

Edith Jacobson. I was also participating in a study group led by Martin Bergmann, where I had become acquainted with the work of Heinz Kohut, especially as it contrasted with the work of Otto Kernberg. Looking back, I can see that my ego-psychoanalytic theoretical bent was slowly bending. I was becoming interested in diverse ideas that ultimately would turn out to be difficult to reconcile with my classical psychoanalytic background. But in 1972 the schisms had not yet appeared, and I was as convinced as anyone of the soundness of the basic Freudian paradigm as articulated by Arlow and Brenner, and Jacobson.

What I liked about Edith Jacobson's (1964) *Self and the Object World* was the thrust of her developmental perspective—ever-upward, striving toward greater autonomy and independence. Looking back, I can see that all my psychoanalytic influences were one-person psychologies—psychopathology resided in the patient. As an analyst I was the kind of onlooker who would be able to free the patient's encumbered developmental strivings by addressing unconscious conflicts. Given new opportunities for growth, belated developmental steps could then take place.

My formal psychoanalytic training at the Postgraduate Center spanned the years from 1960 to 1964. For my first analytic case, I treated a very difficult patient, a suicidal, depressed, bisexual man with an intense, conflicted erotic transference. The analysis lasted 10 years and was extraordinarily challenging, personally and theoretically. The classical analytic technique that I had been taught was of little help when this man spent a weekend leaning out of his window wondering whether or not to jump. During my training, the input of supervisors exacerbated my problems with the patient and his problems with himself. Finally, I found a supervisor, Asya Kadis, who was able to understand the patient. She saw this man's desperate efforts to connect with me, rather than his more superficial attempts to ward me off and resist or "destroy" me. This way of looking at the transference made an enormous difference to my way of being with the patient and to the patient's ability to be with himself. This experience also veered me toward a model of treatment that focused on the patient's self-protective strivings.

With all this in mind, I listened to the cases brought to me by the student therapists at Teachers College. Beatrice Beebe had been assigned a patient who was even more "outrageous" and difficult than the one I had treated in my training. In retrospect, I think I was intrigued by the opportunity to provide for this patient and this therapist what had taken me several years to find. I felt that I had learned how to work with one very difficult patient, and learned, too, what not to do. Here was an opportunity to test out what I had learned.

I (Beatrice Beebe) began graduate school in 1968 at Teacher's College, Columbia University in a joint program of developmental and clinical psychology. Heinz Werner, Jean Piaget, and constructivist views of development were my earliest influences. In 1969 I met Daniel Stern in my search for someone doing research on early emotional development. I wanted to study mother–infant "reciprocity." Looking back, I do not think I knew what that concept meant to me, but I know I had these words in mind when I began graduate school. Stern was filming mothers and infant twins in their homes, and he took several graduate students with him. I remember one particular day when I played with a baby whose face was full of joy. As I watched her face responding to mine, going up and up and up, tears came to my eyes. I was so moved by how closely she tracked my face and by her bursting into a sunbeam. It was that day that I decided to do my dissertation with Stern, examining that very process of positive facial affect, how it builds to a crescendo, ebbs, and resurges.

Herbert Birch was at Teachers College at that time. My idea for a dissertation—an in-depth case study of one mother–infant pair, a frame-by-frame analysis of positive affect—was very different from the *Zeitgeist* of that era. Nevertheless, Birch championed it, making it possible for me to work with Dan Stern. Birch patiently taught me how to think about data and how to evaluate what infants might actually perceive. While I was still in the early stages of analyzing the data for my dissertation, Birch died, a great blow to me.

Stern led a group of infant researchers that included Joe Jaffe and Steve Bennett. We met weekly, with Stern giving exciting accounts of conferences he had attended, as the study of mother–infant face-to-face interaction was just beginning. Stern's first paper, "A Microanalysis of Mother–Infant Interaction," came out in 1971. The data for the analyses lined his office wall. We were thrilled to see the intricate ways in which mothers and infants interacted, especially since psychoanalysis in that era saw infants as much less complex, active, and social than we do now. Dan Stern's way of thinking about mother–infant interaction shaped my research career. Steve Bennett later sat with me as I analyzed the "chase and dodge" film during my postdoctoral fellowship with Dan Stern. Joe Jaffe became a lifetime collaborator.

Meanwhile, I had to figure out the clinical side of my training. From 1971 to 1972 I went to Yale for my clinical internship. There I met Sid Blatt. He was extremely receptive to my background in the ideas of Werner and Piaget and to my interest in self- and object representations. With him I pursued the question of the origins of self- and object representations, which has remained one of my central interests. I saw a range of rather disturbed adult outpatients at Yale, and I treated one psychotic depressed inpatient under Blatt's supervision.

My supervision with Blatt prepared me to meet Burton, the patient assigned to me at the Teachers College Clinic. Without the work I had done with Blatt I would not have had the common language that Frank and I recognized in each other at the beginning of the group supervision. To the dismay of the other two students, Frank and I actually believed that this extremely disturbed Columbia sophomore could be treated psychoanalytically.

Over the following eight years, my treatment of Burton continued in private supervision with Frank. Sometimes I was frightened by this patient's suicidal struggle, but I was always sure of Frank's deep involvement and confidence in me. Out of this supervisory relationship was forged a bond between Frank and me that was to outlast the supervision and provide the foundation for the years of collaboration that continue.

Burton became the subject of our first joint publication (Lachmann and Beebe, 1983). As we now review our report of his treatment, we see that our language and concepts would be radically different today. Our description of the treatment was limited to the patient's experience and to the therapist's verbal intepretations. We left out of our original account the intensity of the therapist's involvement with Burton, especially the agonized moments when Burton was suicidal or out of reach.

The theory we followed in the treatment of Burton focused on the consolidation of the self. We believed that separation issues occupied a central position in Burton's difficulties in the structuralization of the self. His pathology was seen as a result of merger wishes with consequent difficulties with separation. We assumed that the sense of self consolidates along three dimensions: (1) self–object differentiation, (2) the capacity to tolerate positive and negative affects, and (3) the experience of continuity over time, an essential ingredient of self- and object constancy. Whereas the term differentiation was used to refer to the process through which self and object were distinguished, separation was used to refer to the ability to maintain this distinction. Separation resulted in a diminution of an imperative need for the object's actual presence.

We also held that a consolidated sense of self was a prerequisite for the emergence of psychological conflict. Psychopathology that reflected difficulties in the structuralization of self-experience was distinguished from psychopathology that reflected a self in conflict (Stolorow and Lachmann, 1980). In Burton's treatment, especially in the later stages, we tracked the oscillations of pathology as one kind was, at times, more salient than the other. Early in the treatment, we viewed the pathology as based on deficits in structuralizations.

We used these theoretical constructs as our response to an ever-present danger of "fragmentation" in Burton's sense of self. We believed that, through an emphasis on these dimensions of experience, Burton would gradually be able to address his conflicts and defenses. And to some extent our expectations were borne out, although it took many years. During the treatment, we used the notion of "increments of separation" (Lachmann, Beebe, and Stolorow, 1987) as a theoretical touchstone to afford Burton a safety zone in which to organize his continual back-and-forth fluctuations into manageable proportions. Reciprocally, we viewed any retreat from a particular step of separation not as necessarily equivalent to a remerger with the feared and enticing mother, but rather as part of an oscillation. We believed that this line of interpretation would gradually enable him to modify his all-or-none fantasy that to separate meant isolation or death. This slow process was assumed to establish psychic structure by minute transformations.

Burton began his treatment as a patient at the university clinic and followed me (Beatrice) wherever I worked for the next 10 years. In the ninth year, a major consolidation of his personality took place. The severe pathology that had characterized him since early childhood diminished markedly. When we wrote up the ninth year of his three-session-per-week treatment, we named him Burton. Only an actor such as Richard Burton could play the role of such a volatile, tempestuous man. In a similar spirit, we named his first wife Liz and his second wife Sybille.

Burton began treatment, his fifth attempt at therapy, at the age of 20, as a college sophomore. He felt that life was not worth living; he complained of his self-destructiveness; and he catalogued an extensive involvement with drugs (LSD, ritalin), periodic alcoholism, stealing (for which he had already spent a month in jail), and persistent suicidal ideation. He heard a persecutory voice located "in the back of my mind" criticizing him, mocking him, and telling him to kill himself. He described difficulties in concentration, racing thoughts, lapses of memory, and out-of-body experiences. He felt that he was losing his sense of being alive, and he believed that he had a terminal disease. His sense of time was severely distorted—time was either speeding up or in danger of stopping. He made daredevil forays into dangerous neighborhoods, carrying a gun, planning to fight the drug dealers who supplied heroin to Liz, his girlfriend, whom he married in the third year of his treatment.

Whenever Liz rejected him, took drugs, or disappeared all night, Burton would simultaneously want to murder her and kill himself. He would then become dangerously suicidal. When Liz left him, in the seventh year of his treatment, Burton was hospitalized (his third hospitalization in the course of the treatment) for a severe depression that continued for a full year after the hospitalization. Burton, however, was able to use his ideal as a scholar to force himself to ignore urgent impulses to reconnect with Liz. They were divorced the following year.

Burton's strengths were also extremely impressive. He had a rich imagination, outstanding intellectual ability, a sensitive capacity for self-reflection, and intense concern for his friends. He consistently maintained a high academic standing and was able to pursue graduate work throughout the treatment. The vitality of his struggle suggested a passionate commitment to life.

At the start of the ninth year of the therapy, Burton was consciously attempting to become less preoccupied with Liz. By this time he was already living with Sybille, whom he later married. As we enter the clinical material at this time in the ninth year, Burton had begun to miss sessions for four weeks in a row. Burton thought that, by rejecting the therapist's help and missing sessions, he was stopping the process of tearing himself away from Liz. He began to panic, to feel that he had lost himself, that he had lost Liz, and that both he and Liz were evil. He made elaborate plans to shoot himself. His pull to reconnect with Liz was interpreted as a remnant of his early merger with his sadistic, abusive mother. The interpretations at that time addressed the many meanings of separation.

Much work had already been done on his relationship with his mother. Early in the treatment he had described, "We are like Siamese twins; both of us would die if we were separated." He had recalled a repetitive early nightmare of being locked in a coffin, with his mother outside—or vice versa. Separation meant being killed and killing. Burton recounted, "My mother would freak out for days, going crazy, nothing could stop her. I know what it's like to love someone who is determined to annihilate herself. When Liz would get self-destructive, I'd feel I'm getting shut out, killed. She's killing me, I'll kill her." Burton's fundamental metaphor was that separation meant death.

Lengthy reconstruction of his early relationship with his mother revealed memories of her as grossly inconsistent, alternately all-good or murderous, sexually seductive and then abruptly abusive.

The repetitive nightmare in which either Burton or his mother was locked in a coffin at night with the other outside captured his simultaneous suicidal and homicidal preoccupations and the fluid interchangeability between images of himself and his mother as killer and victim. Such memories as these were used in the crucial ninth year to remind Burton how much of his relationship to Liz reevoked his early relationship with his mother, so that at times he found it nearly impossible to distinguish the two sets of experiences.

Burton now began to experience himself more directly as evil and murderous for even thinking about separating from Liz. He was convinced that his relationship with his new girl friend, Sybille, was a betrayal of Liz. It was at this point in the treatment that Burton was first able to recover memories of his father's lifelong affair and his rage at his father for betraying his mother. Much previous work had already been done on his relationship with his father, for example, working through his memories of his father's beating him in the crib, his identification with his father's depression, and oedipal themes. This new material, however, ushered in a crucial missing link in the conflictual identification with his father, namely, his father as someone who had separated from and betrayed his mother.

To the extent that the identification with his father was paramount, the material increasingly lent itself to interpretation along conflict and defense lines. Interpretations were offered to Burton that he felt that he had betrayed Liz by the new relationship with Sybille, just as he felt that his father had betrayed his mother with his relationship to his mistress. In competition with his father, he had to be both more faithful than his father and the betrayed one, the abandoned one. Thus, he placed himself in his mother's position rather than being the one who left. Burton's ability to maintain cohesion and to experience conflict was fragile, however. What had begun as a bond of fidelity to his mother quickly evolved once more into a merger in which Burton experienced himself as all too similar to his abandoned, betrayed, helpless mother. In response to interpretations concerning his conflictual identification with his father, Burton reported a dream in which he stabbed his father to death because his father had been deceitful. At this point fears that separation would mean death again emerged.

In a rising panic, Burton attempted to convince me that he would die without Liz. The swings toward and away from Liz escalated. He needed to see Liz to repair the rift and to save her. Simultaneously, he announced his decision to accept a divorce from her. He still felt enraged and wished to kill her: "I miss her, I hate her. I want to get rid of her. I want to run back to her."

His functioning became disorganized: "I can't handle business. I can't get my books to the library. My apartment is a mess. My life is falling apart. I am not living, without Liz. This is not separation; this is the end." This disorganization culminated in a suicidal state reviving a merger with his mother as dying: "This is a subjective car accident. It's like my mother dying. I want to blow my brains out. I want to lose myself now."

Frank and I understood this process as an indication of the tenuousness of Burton's self-structure. He was unable to tolerate such intense affects. The self–object distinction was lost, and he reentered a merged state with Liz essentially similar to that which he had had with his mother. Homicide and suicide were interchangeable. Both he and his mother were dying. He was both killer and victim. Yet interpretations of his inability to tolerate these intense affects and his loss of the germinal self–object distinction only resulted in his losing himself further and becoming overtly suicidal. In contrast to the back-and-forth oscillation that characterized much of this period, at this point Burton temporarily lost this flexibility. I (Beatrice) accepted this dramatic reversal of the prior fleeting increments of separation as part of the process.

The vanishing time dimension inherent in the merger state was reintroduced by my pointing out to Burton that he imagined being trapped in the feared state forever. These interpretations enabled Burton to progress from his suicidal and merged position to an acceptance of a more differentiated and dependent state. He felt unable to take care of himself and overtly acknowledged his need for me. He dreamed of a woman who let him suck her breasts, whom he identified with me. He used these images to comfort himself in the face of the dread of murderous separation. He reintegrated various qualities of himself, not only as aggressive but also as needy, able to be comforted, and having sexual feelings. Burton's movement was articulated as an increment of separation toward a richer, more articulated self-experience. In this period we (Frank and Beatrice) understood the merger to be transformed into an object-related dependency with some self–object differentiation.

During much of the treatment, Burton's positive, idealized transference was in the background. Interpretations of this transference were kept to a minimum since we (Frank and Beatrice) understood it to be necessary for the process of treatment. At the start of the ninth year, when Burton began to miss sessions, the transference shifted into the foreground and began to be the subject of interpretation. At this point in the treatment, the work on the transference-dream of the woman who let him suck her breasts allowed Burton to use his overt acknowledgment of need as a way of transforming symbiotic-like longings into object-related dependency and a crucial new ability to be comforted.

These developments in Burton's integration of various qualities of himself enabled him to sustain feelings (rage, sexuality, dependence, fear of loss) that had previously been managed through remerger with his mother and Liz. At this point in the treatment, Burton was enraged about his sexual dependence on Liz and felt panicked that the loss of this relationship would mean the loss of his sexuality. He said, "I'm losing a part of myself; I'm resisting it. I feel like an abandoned child. I feel wronged. I can't give her up; I feel chained to a dead person." These thoughts were connected to Burton's early dreams in which either he or his mother was locked in a coffin with the other outside and with his lifelong dread that moving away from his mother would result in both dying. Burton appreciated that he was condensing his experiences with Liz and his mother, and said, "I can't take all my experiences so seriously."

Disentangling his sexuality from Liz, resigning himself to her loss, and recognizing that the depth of his loss experience was based on his experience with his mother were all major moves in the differentiation and separation process. Yet Burton again became suicidally depressed. He felt that his "whole existence was falling apart" and that he was evil. He was, however, able to take comfort in his closeness with me (Beatrice), although he experienced this closeness as another step away from Liz and as a betrayal of her. The suicidal depression was interpreted as a retaliatory torture of himself for the moves away from Liz and a wish to undo the considerable progress he had made.

Burton was able to use the interpretation of his suicidal depression as retaliatory torture. In a chagrined manner he summarized, "It is my resistance to getting better." We viewed this episode within a conflict-defense model. The interpretation of undoing was successful owing to an increasing self–object differentiation, which was already manifest in his nascent ability to experience and tolerate a dependent transference. The success of this interpretive strategy was apparent in Burton's own suggestion that his reaction was "resistance," which indicated a sense of himself as an agent capable of resisting. Despite continued depression, this work enabled him to go on with his graduate work, an accomplishment of which he was quite proud.

In the session that followed this intervention, Burton spontaneously acknowledged the defensive aspect of his "going crazy" and his "responsibility in choosing not to go crazy." This recognition was seen as a striking reconsolidation on his own, between sessions, in experiencing himself as a responsible agent and by tolerating his anxiety. As Burton progressively saw himself as successful and powerful in his work, with each academic success he experienced an onslaught of urges to sabotage or undo his work.

A core consolidation of the self (defined as distinctness of his image of self from that of the other) was established following the work on his father and the work on separating from his therapist. Burton no longer felt merged with his "evil" mother. Burton said, "I do feel I can survive and survive well. I feel lucky and happy in many ways. I feel good about myself, honest. But I also know there will always be times when I want to destroy myself." His progress in the three dimensions we had defined at the outset—differentiation of self and other, the ability to tolerate intense affects, and a sense of continuity over time—were now manifest in several salient ways. He was increasingly able to imagine his relationship with his therapist between sessions. He was able to revive memories of prior times without fear of being drawn back into experiences of himself as a killer, as identified with Jack the Ripper, as a psychotic, hospitalized adolescent, as belonging in jail, or as merged with his ex-wife or mother.

It has now been two decades since the termination of Burton's ten-year treatment. During these years Burton has retained intermittent contact with me (Beatrice) and has pursued no other therapy, with the exception of medication. In some of his telephone calls he was in crisis, and in others he was "checking in." There were long periods of no contact. In recent years, a brief telephone call has been scheduled once a week. Every few months I receive a warm card from him. Despite periods of intense depression and work inhibition, Burton is flourishing as a loving husband to Sybille, a warm and dedicated father, and an outstanding and productive member of his intellectual community.

Burton and the Systems Model

In reconceptualizing the treatment of Burton, we now bring into the foreground dimensions of the therapeutic exchange that were previously in the background. Although these dimensions were not conceptualized at the time of our original publication (Lachmann and Beebe, 1983), we now consider them to be critical aspects of the therapeutic action.

In the discussion to follow, we focus on various interrelated critiques of our former thinking: (1) the central concern with structure formation and structural deficit reflected a one-person view of psychological organization; (2) the model of development focused on separation; (3) the emphasis on the repetition of archaic attachments neglected the transformations of these attachments; (4) the weight given the verbal narrative and interpretation neglected the therapeutic action of the ongoing nonverbal exchange; (5) the use of a unidirectional model emphasized the influence of the therapist on the patient, neglecting the influence of the patient on the therapist.

Our understanding is now based on a systems view. In the following chapters we describe a systems view that is relevant to both early development and adult treatment, drawing implications essential to therapeutic intervention. For the moment, however, we shall describe the shifts in our thinking that altered our understanding of Burton and his treatment.

Our treatment of Burton had pursued the analysis of structural deficits and the promotion of structure formation. Consistent with a systems model, rather than looking at psychopathology as deficits in organization, we believe that every experience is organized in some way. Instead of the concept of psychic structure, we prefer "patterns of experience" that are *in process*, that is, organizations that may transform. In fact, we have gone so far as to change our original term "interaction structure" to "interaction pattern" to avoid the static implications of the concept of structure. Patterns of experience are initially organized in infancy as *expectancies of sequences of reciprocal exchanges*, and associated self-regulatory styles. This reciprocal, or bidirectional, influence, in which each partner contributes to the ongoing exchange, is termed "co-construction." Our emphasis on both self- and interactive regulation incorporates one- and two-person views of the system.

What difference does the concept of expectancies make in our understanding of the treatment of Burton? Expectancies have been included among the "nonspecific" or "noninterpretive" factors in psychoanalysis. Instead, we view the nonconfirmation of traumatic expectations as carrying a specific therapeutic action. Burton expected criticism, mocking, abuse, abandonment, explosions, and sexual overstimulation, as well as an immediate supply of nurturance (drugs, alcohol). That his therapist did not fulfill any of these expectations not only provided a "background of safety" (Sandler, 1987), but also "perturbed the system" (Thelen and Smith, 1994), thus making other interactions possible.

The concept of expectancies shifts the focus to the *process* in which patterns of interaction became organized in the patient's history and are becoming organized in the treatment relationship. In this process, each partner comes to expect patterns of response where each affects and is affected by the other with a certain timing and emotional tone. And simultaneously each partner experiences a range of ease or discomfort in being able to regulate arousal and inner states, one critical aspect of self-regulation. We term these patterns "expectancies of regulation" and "expectancies of misregulation." This emphasis on process facilitates an integration of the nonverbal dimensions of the exchange with the more customary verbal focus.

Although Burton's expectations of misregulation rigidly organized his childhood and dominated his relationships as an adult, they did not dominate the transference. On the contrary, he established a tender, warm, openly affectionate relationship with his therapist. He had had a very nurturing grandmother whom he loved intensely, and presumably this relationship provided a model and a hope that he brought to the transference. Moreover, despite the violent and at times highly sexually charged relationship with his mother, she had a very generous, loving side, and she believed in him. However, at times this tender and warm aspect of his relatedness to me (Beatrice) existed side by side with a cold, unreachable withdrawal or a charged, suicidal preoccupation.

In restrospect, in line with our changed understanding, we now ask how the patterns of his experience were reorganized. How did his expectancies of self- and interactive regulation change? And how did the "internalizations" of our original formulation actually work? Here we draw on our contention that internalization proceeds hand in hand with the organization of representations (patterns of expectancies). In development as well as in treatment, both partners jointly construct dyadic modes of regulation that include patterns of both self- and interactive regulation. We have built on Schafer's (1968) position that regulatory interactions are interiorized. Generating, elaborating, anticipating, and representing the self- and interactive regulations that are jointly constructed constitute the organizing process. And so, in Burton's case, the interactions in the analytic process gradually altered the nature of Burton's self-regulation processes. He became able to think, anticipate, soothe, and enliven himself without drugs or alcohol. Increasingly he was able to restrain himself from engaging in dangerous activities. Reciprocally these changes in his self-regulation patterns facilitated further transformations in the ways we interacted.

Our original concept of increments of separation can now be translated from a one-person view into a dyadic systems model. We initially used the concept to address a process that we believed occurred within Burton. We now suggest that a fascinating and complex interactive pattern of disruption and repair was being established.

Both Burton and I (Beatrice) became increasingly capable of contributing the repair process. When a crisis occurred, we learned to slow the process down, to make room for reversals, denials, and undoings; and we came to expect that we would eventually put the process back on track. Thus, the typical ways in which disruption and repair patterns proceeded came to be expected and represented by both of us. These expectations gradually reorganized Burton's inner regulation and simultaneously I (Beatrice) grew calmer. Thus the interactive exchange shifted for both analyst and patient.

In reconceptualizing Burton, our (Beatrice's and Frank's) developmental model has shifted from separation-individuation to attachment-individuation. Mahler's (Mahler, Pine, and Bergman, 1975) phase of symbiosis assumed a positive relatedness without self and object boundaries in the early months of life. She viewed the infant as differentiating representations of self and other in the second year, in the context of the increased physical separation of the toddler. The toddler's ambivalence about separation and differentiation, together with an increasing cognitive awareness of separateness, leads to a "rapprochement crisis," described as a normal stage of alternating avoidance and pursuit of contact comfort with the mother. In Burton's treatment, our concept of increments of separation was influenced by this view.

In contrast, Bowlby (1969) conceptualized the task of the first year and a half as establishing a secure attachment relationship. Building on Bowlby, Karlen Lyons-Ruth (1991) critiqued Mahler et al.'s (1975) description of ambivalence about contact as normative for the rapprochement period. Instead, she argued, such ambivalence or avoidance over contact is a mark of an insecure attachment. Lyons-Ruth suggested that we reframe the first two years of life as an attachment-individuation process rather than as an attachment-separation process. The toddler's optimal development includes affection, using the parent as a resource for help, vigorous pursuit of contact-comfort with a parent when under stress, and the assertion of initiative and opposition without fear of rejection. Thus the child's developmental process should be assessed by the degree to which patterns of affect regulation remain warm and mutual. At the same time, they should facilitate the child's pursuit of goals and initiative. This model of development emphasizes assertive relatedness rather than separation to achieve autonomy.

Although our theoretical model at the time of Burton's therapy emphasized separation, in retrospect we observe that we did continuously direct our attention to Burton's attachment to the analyst. Influenced by Kohut (1971), we were alert to instances where the tie was threatened or disrupted, and we tried to repair it. Attachment, however, was certainly in the background, and separation in the foreground, in our treatment of Burton.

Burton's attachment to Beatrice was continually and profoundly threatened by the everpresent lure of suicide. From what we understood about Burton's early life, his ability to turn to his parents in times of stress was impaired both by his parents' unavailability and aggression and by the extent of his terror and rage. Instead, he had turned to drugs, fighting, and extreme physical feats. In the treatment, it took many years before the attachment was experienced as "secure" by both Burton and his analyst.

At the time of the treatment, we (Frank and Beatrice) recognized Burton's attachment to Beatrice, but we did not explicitly conceptualize the role of Beatrice's powerful investment in Burton. This is a key aspect of therapeutic action in the treatment of the difficult-to-treat patient (Martin Bergmann, April 2, 1990, personal communication). Similarly, we conceptualized the analyst's influence on the patient, but we did not address the patient's reciprocal influence on the analyst. Thus, in the arenas both of attachment and of interpersonal influence, only half the system was addressed. That is, we did not think in a more inclusive bidirectional way about attachment and influence in the co-constructed treatment relationship.

Burton's influence on me (Beatrice) was present in the treatment, but not in the conceptualizations with Frank. I liked Burton and I showed it. I did not feel threatened by his rapid, intense, positive transference at the beginning of the treatment. I found him extremely interesting. As the treatment advanced, however, his level of distress and agitation increased; he did more and more dangerous things; he was frequently suicidal; and there were long periods when he was profoundly unreachable. At times I felt agonized about him.

From my own background, I expected of myself an unwavering capacity to tolerate his intense distress. When he was unreachable for a session, I worked very hard to connect with him. I always expected that he and I would find a way and that he would eventually respond to me. I was very anxious about his suicidal states, but I did not consider the possibility that he was untreatable. I was absolutely determined to find a way to make our connection work for him.

When my anxiety about Burton's suicidal states mounted, we (Frank and Beatrice) worked on facing the possibility that he could kill himself and what it would mean to me if he did. This process with Frank was essential to my ability to tolerate the stormy periods. We hospitalized Burton three times in this process. Frank had his own determination to demonstrate that this patient could be psychoanalytically treated. So, for different reasons, we were united in this premise.

Nonetheless, the nature of my influence was conceptualized solely in terms of interpretation. In so doing, Frank and I neglected the ongoing, moment-by-moment participation of the analyst in the co-construction of the relatedness. In contrast, we now formulate treatment as a co-constructed interactive process at every moment. In this process the narrative dynamic issues and the moment-by-moment negotiation of relatedness fluctuate between foreground and background.

I recall a poignant late-afternoon session with Burton when the daylight was beginning to fade. Neither Burton nor I made a move to switch on the light in the room. We entered a slow, near-reverie state, barely talking. We each sensed the other's calming down, and we were both quite content with our silence. For a very long time neither of us wanted to disturb it. Although Burton and I have never explicitly talked about this session, it marked a shift in our ability

to be together in a calmer way. This change was all the more striking in the context of his usually frenetic, urgent, impulsive, wildly
emotional states of mind. Simultaneously, it marked a shift away
from my anxious, agonized concern.

A systems perspective on Burton's treatment actually comprises
three people: Burton, Beatrice, and Frank. Burton had a profound
impact on both of us. We admired his extraordinary intellect, his
creativity and energy, his generosity of spirit, and the intensity of
his struggle.

Using the original separation-individuation model, the treatment emphasized Burton's attempts to separate from Liz. Burton
wanted to be able to live apart from her. His ability to establish a
sense of himself as able to survive and worthy of surviving without
her was a key focus. Interpretations emphasized his renunciation of
his responsibility for her fate. He feared that she would die or kill
herself if he left her. This struggle was connected to a similar difficulty in separating from his mother.

The treatment emphasized the repetition of his relationship with
his mother in his relationship with Liz. In retrospect, we prefer a
model that conceptualizes the interplay between repetition and
transformation. The relationship with Liz was a repetition in the
ways in which Burton made dramatically explicit his childhood sense
of his mother as dangerous and evil. However, in his relationship
to Liz Burton also made numerous attempts to transform his destructive tie to his mother. There were many tender and loving moments
with Liz, and he made consistent efforts to "save" her from depression and drug use. Although we were aware of these transformational efforts, the therapeutic efforts did not sufficently reflect them.
Nevertheless, despite his best efforts, he could not integrate and
transform the passionate hatred that characterized many of their
interactions into a less stormy love.

Through the work in the transference, however, Burton developed an expectation that an energetic and vital relationship could
be safe rather than murderous, pleasurable rather than overwhelm-
ing, ongoing and predictable rather than prone to rapidly fluctuat-
ing moods and disruptions. In this process, the passion of his

previous relationships was both preserved and transformed. When he met Sybille, he found an intense, passionately loving, intelligent woman working in a field related to that of his therapist. In his later years, despite occasional intense conflicts, Burton was able to transform his relationship with his mother into a warm and relatively harmonious one.

In our reconceptualization of the treatment of Burton, we have previewed our systems model. In the next chapter we turn to a detailed examination of this model, how it has been influenced by infant research, and its applicability to adult treatment.

CHAPTER

2

A DYADIC SYSTEMS VIEW

During Burton's treatment, the developmental views of Jacobson, Kohut, and Mahler were essential in our conceptualization of his chaotic experience. I (Beatrice), however, increasingly felt that I was living in two different worlds: one view of development as I sat with my patients and a totally different view of development as I did infant research. So, after Frank and I wrote up the ninth year of Burton's treatment, we took a year off to study infant research together. I continued to spend half my time doing infant research with Daniel Stern, and later Joseph Jaffe, at New York State Psychiatric Institute. Frank and I decided that together we would study the course on infant social development that I had been teaching at Ferkauf Graduate School of Psychology. I now had a way of reciprocating Frank's years of supervision, and we now had a new forum for continuing our intellectual development. In our dialogue attempting to relate infant research to psychoanalytic treatment, we educated each other.

I (Frank) was intrigued by the possibility of using infant research as a new port of entry into psychoanalysis, not from the couch, not from pathology, but through the eyes of many ingenious researchers who studied normal babies and what they could do. I found in the research an opportunity to revive my interest in research that I had held from high school, college, and graduate school. As we examined the studies, I came upon a picture of early development that was radically at variance with the psychoanalytic view. The empirical infant was an extraordinary phenomenon.

We became increasingly impressed by the role that dyadic interaction played in the early organization of experience. This remarkable infant was involved in a reciprocal, split-second, mutually adjusting system with a caregiver. At the same time, this infant had hitherto unsuspected capacities to regulate his own state. The various ways in which inner state and interactive process were linked in infant research defined an array of organizing principles of interactions. We began to draw on empirical infant studies to expand our understanding of patient–analyst interaction (see, e.g., Beebe and Lachmann, 1994, 1998; Lachmann and Beebe, 1996a, b).

Sander's (1977) work on the role of interactive regulation in the organization of sleep–wake cycles in the early weeks of life guided our thinking about the integration of self- and interactive regulation. In reviewing the literature, we noted that behaviors used to illustrate self-regulation could just as easily be examined for their role in influencing, and being influenced by, the partner and vice versa. This intimate connection between self- and interactive regulation became the core of our "systems" view of the dyad. That year of discussions set the foundation for our collaboration on the relevance of infant research for psychoanalysis. Over the past two decades we have continued these discussions for two hours weekly, generating the views that we are presenting here.

Much previous work on the relevance of infant research for psychoanalysis has focused on the infant origins of adult psychopathology. Our interest in writing this book is quite different. We are interested in infant research as it may illuminate basic processes of interaction. Thus our concern is psychoanalytic *process*. A systems model of the dyad sets the stage for our study of the intimate connections between self- and interactive regulation, which we will apply to the psychoanalytic process.

The real payoff from infant research comes as a surprise. It is fruitful in psychoanalysis not because earlier states may be recapitulated in adult treatment, as speculated by older theories, although this might occur. Instead, infant research is most fruitful because the basic processes of interaction at the nonverbal level remain so similar across the life span.

Systems theory provides an integrated way of understanding the data of infant research. These data make the most sense when they are viewed as an interlocking dyadic system of infant and parent. In this chapter we present this systems view in broad orienting terms. It is like learning a new language, very different from the one we customarily use in psychoanalytic discourse.

A systems view influences our understanding of therapeutic process in powerful ways. For example, empirical infant research describes patterns of interaction that enable clinicians to observe the nonverbal processes that lie beyond the usual verbal exchange. Especially with "difficult-to-treat" patients, this attention to the interactive process itself, analogous to frame-by-frame analysis, makes a critical contribution to therapeutic leverage. The co-construction of interactive patterns and self-regulatory ranges, unique to each dyad, is central to this approach.

Systems Models

Efforts at conceptualizing systems views are evident in both infant research and psychoanalysis. Each field, however, has come from the opposite bias. Infant research on social development has been preoccupied with interactive regulation, as opposed to self-regulation, since the early 1970s. With the exception of Sander (1977, 1985, 1995), who always emphasized both self- and interactive regulation, infant researchers have only in the last decade begun carefully to examine self-regulation processes and their integration with interactive regulation (see, e.g., Tronick, 1988, 1989; Tronick and Cohn, 1989; Fox, 1994; Shore, 1994, 1997; Thompson, 1994; Weinberg et al., 1999). Tronick has been at the forefront of this integration. In contrast, psychoanalysis has historically been concerned with the organization of inner states. Only recently have psychoanalysts seriously examined interaction in the dyad (Gill, 1982; Hoffman, 1983; Benjamin, 1990; Harris, 1991; Beebe et al., 1992; Ehrenberg, 1992; Stolorow and Atwood, 1992; Mitchell, 1993; Sucharov, 1994;

Greenberg, 1995; Aron, 1996; Stolorow, 1997; Shane, Shane, and Gales, 1998).

Approaches that integrate the contribution of the individual and that of the dyad to the organization of behavior and experience can be considered systems models. Although Piaget (1937) and Werner (1948) did not use the term systems theory, their emphasis on the continuous interaction of the organism and environment contained many of the central ideas of systems theory. Developments in many areas have moved from an individual-centered approach and linear views of causality toward systems and field approaches (Badalamenti and Langs, 1990, 1992; von Bertalanffy, 1968; Iberall and McCulloch, 1969; Kohlberg, 1969; Lewin, 1937; Sameroff, 1983; Thelen and Smith, 1994).

Systems theory (field theory) was conceptualized in physiology, physics, and biology. Von Bertalanffy (1968) was a leading figure who conceptualized theoretical biology as a theory of open and closed systems. His fundamental interest was the self-organization of the organism as it developed in the direction of increased integrity and self-direction. Although the organism was engaged in continuous transaction with the environment, von Bertalanffy's emphasis was on the use of transactions to maintain the self-regulation process.

Psychology was influenced by both physics and theoretical biology in its development of systems views. Lewin (1937) and Morris (1934), notable in the Chicago school of social psychologists, had an impact on Sullivan (1953), who drew on systems views in developing his interpersonal field theory. In his 1964 paper, *The Illusion of Personal Individuality*, Sullivan argued that a person has as many identitites as human relationships. Thus, the individual organization is continually shaped by the dyadic context.

Sullivan was active in the Washington School of Psychiatry and Chestnut Lodge, where he was influential in the work of Fromm-Reichmann and David and Margaret Rioch, as well as of Loewald. Rioch and Weinstein (1964) edited a book that discussed a central statement of systems theory by James Miller. Miller argued that there were essential similarities in information processing across cells, neurons, organs, organisms, humans, groups, and social organizations. Each level has its own unique characteristics, but all are living sytems open to energy and information. They maintain themselves in a changing environment by regulating inputs and outputs of matter, energy, or information and by preserving internal steady states of critical variables through the governance of subsystems. These living systems also share similarities in the way they respond to overload or "underload" of information, both of which can lead to pathology of the system.

In England, working with very different influences, Winnicott (1957, 1965) also developed a systems approach, illustrated by his famous concept that there is no such thing as a baby, but rather a mother–baby unit. In different ways, both Sullivan and Winnicott carefully conceptualized the contributions of both partners in the dyad. However, even as systems views filtered into clinical practice, the focus generally remained on the individual rather than on the dyad.

In developmental research, despite the increasing emphasis on systems views, more attention was given to the influence of the parent than to the influence of the child. Not until the early 1970s did infant research begin actively to endorse a fully bidirectional view of each partner's contribution to the organization of the dyad (Bell, 1968, 1970, 1971; Lewis and Rosenblum, 1974). In developmental psychology, three interacting units constitute the system: the parent as a self-organizing, self-regulating unit; the child as a self-organizing, self-regulating unit, and the parent–child dyad as an interactive field with a unique organization of its own. None of these three units can be fully described without reference to the other two.

Systems approaches shifted our thinking from a one-way to a two-way concept of interpersonal regulation in the dyad. In a bidirectional system, each person's behavior is *predictable* from (not "caused" by) that of the other. We are both influencing, and being influenced by, our partner's words and actions. Particularly at the nonverbal level, mother and infant, as well as analyst and patient, participate in a moment-by-moment coordination of the rhythms of behavior. This is the fundamental nature of social behavior. Each partner has continuous rhythms of behavior, for example, sound and silence, movement and hold. Even the moments of verbal or gestural "silence" are communicative. The rhythms of behavior of two partners are always coordinated in some way, usually outside awareness.

The capacity to enter into split-second facial or vocal exchanges is robust in infancy as well as adulthood and is probably highly adaptive in evolution. These split-second exchanges have also been documented in the facial-visual exhanges of monkeys (Chevalnier-Skolnikoff, 1976). Eibl-Eibesfeldt (1970) filmed lovers flirting on park benches while unaware of his camera. Microanalysis of the film revealed split-second responsivity of face, gaze, and head orientation between the lovers. Thus, much of the organization of nonverbal communication remains similar across the life span.

Although bidirectional influence is a central meaning of our term co-construction, we use this concept in a second way as well: the interactive- and self-regulation processes influence each other. Fogel (1993a, b) integrates both of these processes noting that all behavior unfolds in the individual while, at the same time, it is continuously modifying and being modified by the changing behavior of the partner.

In the empirical infant literature, studies of interactive regulation and self-regulation have tended to exclude each other (see, as important exceptions, Sander, 1977; Tronick, 1989). But we are always monitoring and regulating our inner state at the same time as we are tracking our partner's words and actions. Feeling anxious, agitated, or low will bear upon the way we affect, and are affected by, our partner. And vice versa: if the interaction is unpleasant, we will have difficulty staying calm.

Thus, a theory of interaction must specify how each person is affected by his own behavior—that is, self-regulation—and by the partner's behavior—that is, interactive regulation (Thomas and Martin, 1976; Thomas and Malone, 1979). Each person must both monitor the partner (influence and be influenced) and at the same time regulate his own state. Self- and interactive regulation are concurrent and reciprocal processes (Gianino and Tronick, 1988). Each affects the success of the other. They are optimally in dynamic balance with flexibility to move back and forth. Although this theory is now well articulated, neither infant research nor psycho-analysis (but see Aron, 1996), however, has taken full advantage of its implications.

Definitions of Self- and Interactive Regulation

When we discuss interactive regulation we use the terms mutual reg-ulation, bidirectional regulation, and co-constructed regulation inter-changeably. These terms *do not imply mutuality*. They mean that contingencies flow in both directions between partners. That is, the behavior of each partner is contingent on, "influenced" by, or pre-dicted by, that of the other. One or the other direction of bidirec-tional influence is usually emphasized. However, the person experiences both influencing and being influenced by the partner. The solid lines in Figure 1 illustrate the continuous reciprocal effects of self- and interactive regulation processes in a systems model. The dotted lines parallel to the solid lines indicate the history of these regulations. Figure 2 illustrates that all modalities contribute to the bidirectional exchange between mother and infant.

Infant
Self-Regulation

Interactive
Regulation

Mother
Self-Regulation

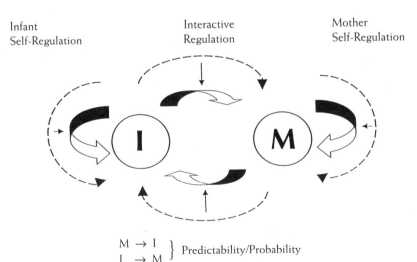

M → I
I → M } Predictability/Probability

Figure 1. Systems Model of Interaction. Arrows indicate predictability ("coordi-nation" or "influence") between partners. Dotted arrows represent the history of the pattern of predictability.

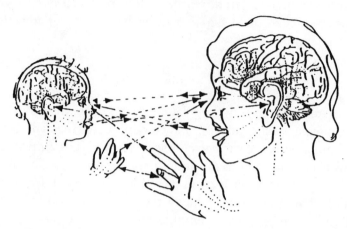

Figure 2. The Modalities of Mother–Infant Bidirectional Exchange. From Trevarthen (1989). Reproduced by permission.

These terms *do not imply symmetry*: each partner may influence the other in different ways and to unequal degrees. *Nor is a causal model* implied. Regulation is defined by probabilities that one partner's behavior is predictable from that of the other. *Nor is a positive interaction* implied; aversive exchanges (such as the chase-and-dodge interaction described later) as well as positive ones (such as facial mirroring) are bidirectionally regulated.

We use the term self-regulation to denote the capacity of the partners to regulate their respective states. From birth onward, self-regulation refers to the management of arousal, the maintenance of alertness, the ability to dampen arousal in the face of overstimulation, and the capacity to inhibit behavioral expression. It includes variations in the readiness to respond and in the clarity of cues, such as how clearly a baby conveys hunger, sleepiness, or approach–avoidance (see Korner and Grobstein, 1976; Sander, 1977, 1995; Als and Brazelton, 1981; Gianino and Tronick, 1988). Self-touching, looking away, and restricting the range of facial expressiveness are examples of self-regulation strategies that dampen arousal. Across the life span, self-regulation is a critical component of the capacity to pay attention and engage with the environment. Sander (1977,

1995) suggested that, in adulthood, self-regulation includes access to, articulation of, regard for, and capacity to use inner states. Figure 3 illustrates self-regulation in the systems model.

By giving equal emphasis to self- and interactive regulation, we retain the traditional interest of psychoanalysis in the organization of the individual. At the same time, we emphasize that the organization of the individual is always in a "dialogue" with the dyad, infuencing and being influenced by the nature of the interactive regulation. Behavior is simultaneously communicative and self-regulatory. Shifts in influencing and being influenced by the partner are accompanied by simultaneous shifts in self-regulation, behavior, and arousal. Self-regulation in the adult includes (unconscious) fantasy, day dreaming, symbolic elaboration, and defenses.

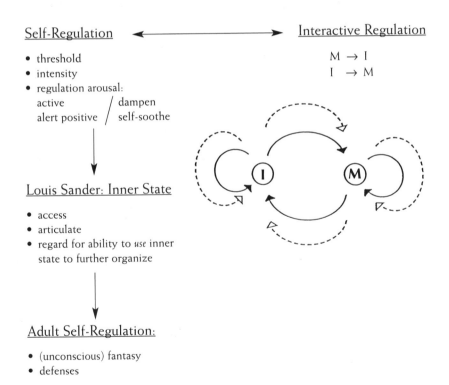

Self-Regulation ←——————————→ Interactive Regulation

- threshold
- intensity
- regulation arousal:
  active / dampen
  alert positive / self-soothe

M → I
I → M

Louis Sander: Inner State

- access
- articulate
- regard for ability to *use* inner state to further organize

Adult Self-Regulation:

- (unconscious) fantasy
- defenses

Figure 3. Self-Regulation in the Dyadic Systems Model.

Sander's Description of the Systems Model

The most general description of a systems model for infant research has been provided over the last two decades by Louis Sander (1977, 1985, 1995). He emphasizes the primacy of process over more static notions of structure. In systems thinking, a person is always embedded in an ongoing engagement with a context. The organization of the system refers to a principle of ordering that stabilizes the pattern of a large number of elements of both person and environment. This pattern recurs, but it also changes slightly with each engagement between the individual and the environment. Thus, an interactive system is always in process, with a dialectic between predictability and transformation.

A central theme of Sander's work is the description of self-regulation, interactive regulation, and their integration. Infants, like any other living system, must be capable of self-regulation and self-organization. This self-regulation process, however, is continually modifying and being modified by the nature of the interactive regulation (see also Fogel, 1992a, b). An infant's experience of "agency" is organized through the self-regulation process, but only insofar as the interactive regulation "grants" or facilitates this agency. In Sander's terms, agency is a "systems competence." Self-regulation accrues to awareness of inner experience (state, emotion, expectation) from the beginning of life. Thus we are simultaneously aware of inner exerience and of interactive context.

To illustrate, the study of disordered interactions in infancy previously tended to locate the source of difficulty in one partner or the other, for example, in infant temperament difficulties or in maternal intrusion or withdrawal. Instead, it is essential to disentangle the relative contributions of self *and* interactive regulation of *both* partners. By not privileging inner or relational processes, and by highlighting their co-construction, a systems view examines how dyadic process may organize and reorganize both self- and interactive regulation. Simultaneously, changes in self-regulation in either partner alter the interactive process. This point of view informs our discussions of therapeutic action throughout the chapters to follow.

Recent findings by Kaminer (1999) illustrate Sander's concept that infant agency is a systems competence. The nature of a mother's speech to her four-month-old infant, as well as the infant's gaze patterns, were coded from videotape, second by second. One of the maternal speech codes was "action/agency" defined as the mother's commenting on the infant's autonomous action, for instance, "Oh, you're wiggling" or "What are you looking at?" or "You're smiling now." Kaminer also asked the mothers to fill out a questionnaire designed by Blatt, D'Affliti, and Quinlan (1976, 1979) to tap vulnerability to depressive experiences around interpersonal loss (the DEQ dependency scale). Mothers who scored low on Blatt's scale, that is, who were less vulnerable to depressive experiences, tended to make action/agency comments while the infants were looking at them. Mothers who were high on Blatt's scale, that is, who were more vulnerable to depressive experiences, tended to make action/agency comments when the infants were not looking. We hypothesize that, in the former case, infants will eventually learn that their own agency is included within the mutual gaze engagement. In the latter case, infants may learn that their agency is noted by the mother only when they are visually "away" or more "separate." These more vulnerable mothers tended to frame their action/agency comments in terms of "Where are you looking?" and "You are not looking at me." These babies may learn that their agency occurs only when they are more separate, or somehow "against" the mother.

Sander's premier questions are: how does coherence of the system emerge from complexity? and how does the system grant the individual agency and identity? His answer uses Weiss's (1970) principle of "matched specificities," which maintains organization and wholeness in the system. This principle is "a sort of resonance between two systems attuned to each other by corresponding properties" (p. 162).

An example of matched specificities is the selective recognition of sound waves in tonal identification, or the selectivity of nerves in connecting with only certain types of peripheral tissue. An example from mother–infant research is the documentation that mother and infant, as well as stranger and infant, track each other's vocal rhythms. Furthermore, the tightness of the tracking (degree of predictability of one person's behavior from that of the other) differs according to the security of the infant's attachment (Jaffe et al., 2001). The principle of matched specificities is illustrated in the vocal rhythm study by the finding that only certain ranges of tightness of rhythmic coordination are optimal, in particular partner and site contexts, for particular developmental outcomes.

Sander (1977, 1985, 1995) has argued that matched specificities, shaped by the recurrence of patterns in the flow of engagement, generate expectancies in the infant. Coherence of organization is achieved in any living system through a process of adaptation or fitting together. The capacity for mutual adjustment must be present in each partner in order for them to fit together. It is just this concept that the infant research on vocal rhythm coordination illuminates.

The principle of matched specificities underlies Sander's concept of the "moment of meeting," further developed as a theory of therapeutic action by The Process of Change Study Group (see Lyons-Ruth, 1998; Sander, 1998; Stern et al., 1998; Tronick, 1998). Matched specificities between two systems attuned to each other yield awareness in each partner of the state of the other. In a moment of meeting, two states of consciousness are matched such that the way that one is known by oneself is matched by the way one is known by the other (Beebe, 1998). This match in the moment of meeting facilitates the development of agency and identity. In the moment of meeting, a mutual recognition occurs that changes the patient's ability to act as an agent in his own self-regulation.

Sander's work impels us to find new ways of thinking about "organization" in infancy and adulthood. He recommends that we shift our conventional view of psychological organization as the property of the individual to a view of psychological organization as the property of the mutually organized infant–caretaker system (Sander 1985, 1995).

We are extending Sander's thinking to the adult patient–analyst system. We view the adult patient's experience as the property of the mutually organized patient–analyst system. Nevertheless, as repeatedly emphasized by Sander and others, each individual brings a unique history to the interactive encounter. But this uniqueness can be fully understood only in the context of how that particular partner and that particular individual "co-create" their relatedness.

Infant Research Illustrates a Theory of Interaction for Psychoanalysis

The value of infant research for psychoanalysis is often derived from the ways in which this research can help an analyst and a patient imagine the patient's infancy (see, e.g., Kiersky and Beebe, 1994). Despite the importance of this use, however, we are primarily interested in using infant research in a different way, that is, to illustrate organizing principles of interactions relevant for psychoanalysis.

Psychoanalysis is currently seeking an expanded theory of interaction. Organizing principles of interaction can be discerned when mother and infant are viewed as a system. Despite the many differences between mother–infant and patient–analyst interaction, we propose that these principles can illuminate how interactions are organized at the nonverbal level in adult treatment. These organizing principles of interactions describe self- and interactive *process*, not dynamic content.

A theory of interaction for psychoanalysis must ultimately address the nonverbal or "implicit" (procedural/emotional), as well as the verbal or "explicit," dimension of the interaction. The nonverbal dimension is usually outside awareness, but it provides a continuous background of moment-by-moment mutual influence. The verbal system is usually in the foreground and more intermittent (speaking and listening). Simultaneously with the exchanges on the verbal level, patient and analyst are continually altering each other's timing, spatial organization, affect, and arousal, on a moment-to-moment basis. This is the fundamental nature of social behavior. Figure 4 illustrates the systems model in adult treatment. It shows that self- and interactive regulation occur in both the explicit and the implicit realms, roughly equivalent to the verbal narrative and nonverbal action sequences, respectively. The arrow between the explicit and implicit realms indicates that, ideally, each realm can be translated into the other. The broken arrow indicates that, in some communication difficulties, the two realms cannot be translated back and forth.

The nonverbal interactive process between two conversing adults using language is obviously more complex than that between mother and infant. Nevertheless, the organizing principles we offer can illuminate the nonverbal dimension of psychoanalysis. Furthermore, the ways in which the nonverbal dimension is organized affect such familiar dynamic issues as safety, efficacy, self-esteem, mutual recognition, intimacy, separation and reunion, boundaries, self-definition, and aloneness in the presence of the partner.

These organizing principles can be viewed in several ways. In our previous work (Lachmann and Beebe, 1992, 1996a, 1997) we suggested that the principles can be used to generate analogies (but not one-to-one correspondences) between mother–infant and adult communication. This remains a useful approach. More fundamentally, however, the organizing principles describe lifelong modes of regulating interactive processes at the procedural/emotional level of action sequences, as long as we continue to recognize that the addition of language makes the conceptualization of the process more complex. That is, the only "language" mother and infant have is the nonverbal process. Adults have two "languages," one verbal and the other nonverbal, each of which continuously bears upon the other.

Linking the Organization of Inner and Relational Processes

Internal processes and interactive processes are organized concurrently and affect each other. For infants and adults alike, face-to-face communication involves experiences of influencing and being influenced by the partner, as well as continual shifts in arousal and self-regulation behaviors. How is it possible to translate between inner experience and interactive behavior before language? Remarkably, infants are capable of coordinating their own inner state with the nature of the interaction. By examining how infants do this, perhaps we can learn something about how adults may do it.

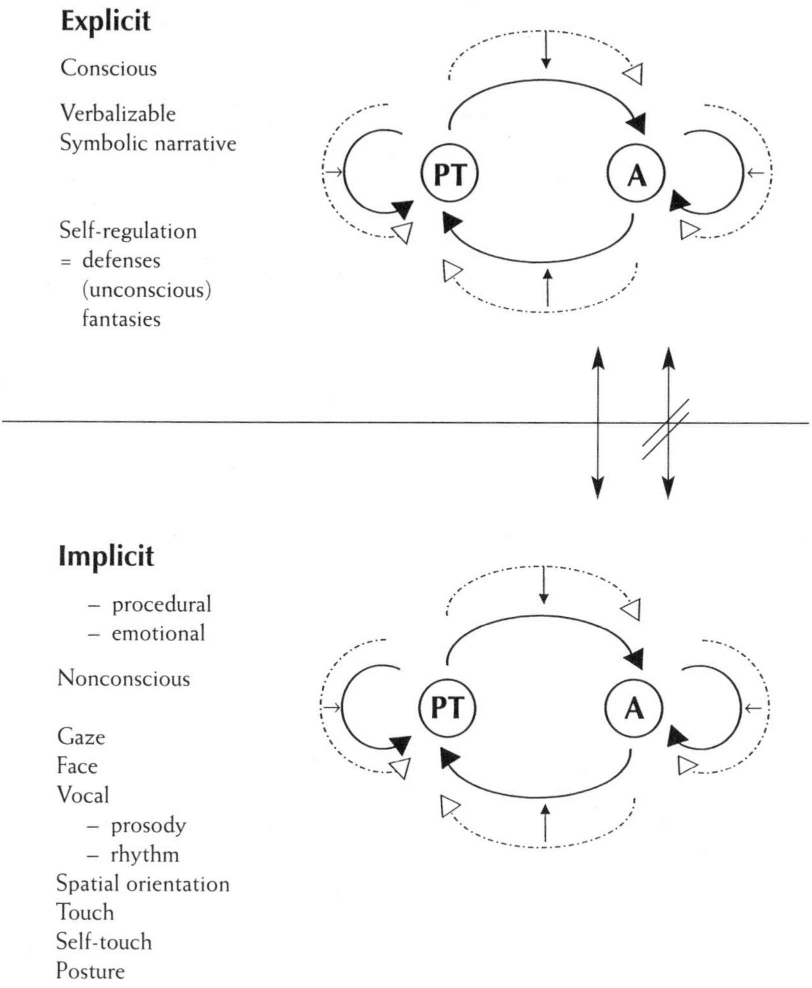

Explicit

Conscious

Verbalizable
Symbolic narrative

Self-regulation
= defenses
  (unconscious)
  fantasies

Implicit

  – procedural
  – emotional

Nonconscious

Gaze
Face
Vocal
  – prosody
  – rhythm
Spatial orientation
Touch
Self-touch
Posture

Figure 4. The Systems Model in Adult Treatment. Arrows indicate predictability ("coordination" or "influence") between partners. Dotted arrows represent the history of the pattern of predictability. The arrow between the explicit and implicit realms indicates that, when necessary, the implicit and explicit systems can be translated back and forth; the broken arrow between the two realms indicates that, in some difficulties of communication, this translation is disrupted.

Internal processes and relational processes are inextricably coordinated and are organized concurrently. Experiences of influencing and being influenced by the partner, as well as concomitant shifts in self-regulation behaviors and arousal, are inherent in the infant's, as well as the adult's, face-to-face communication and social-information processing. Across development, interactive regulation reorganizes inner as well as relational processes; reciprocally, changes in self-regulation in either partner alter the interactive process. This integration of self- and interactive regulation is one way of conceptualizing the organization of experience. Infant as well as adult research studies are reviewed to illustrate this position.

Cross-Modal Perception of Correspondences

Meltzoff (1985, 1990) has shown that infants as young as 42 minutes can imitate the facial expression of an adult model. Infants perceive the correspondence between what they *see* in the face of the model and what they *feel* proprioceptively in their faces. How can they do this? Through cross-modal matching. Detecting matches from the beginning of life, infants can translate between environmental information and inner proprioceptive information. They can bring their internal states and behaviors into a correspondence with the environment. Meltzoff argues that cross-modal matching provides a fundamental relatedness between self and other, between inner state and environment. He suggests that it provides the earliest experience of "like me." Cross-modal perception of correspondences is one mechanism for coordinating inner and relational states. Although Meltzoff's demonstation is in the modality of facial expression, this principle can be extended to other modalities, such as correspondences of timing.

Perception of Emotion in the Partner Creates a Resonant State in the Perceiver

There is considerable evidence that in adults certain regions of the two cerebral hemispheres are differentially lateralized for processing positive and negative emotional stimuli (Davidson and Fox, 1982). And, in studying infants, Davidson and Fox showed that, by 10 months, the brain is likewise lateralized for positive and negative affect. As an infant watched a video of a laughing actress, his brain showed the pattern of positive affect (EEG activation of the left frontal lobe). As an infant watched a video of a crying actress, his brain showed a pattern of negative affect (EEG activation of the right frontal lobe). Thus, *the mere perception of emotion in the partner creates a resonant emotional state in the perceiver.* Unlike the design of Meltzoff's (1990) study, these infants did not actually have to match the partners' behavior to be affected by the partners' facial expression. What an infant perceived on the face of the partner altered his internal state, and the infant could not escape the face of the partner. In this sense, internal state and interactive state are organized simultaneously. Schore (1996; see also Perry, 1996) has amassed extensive evidence showing that variations in the nature of maternal stimulation influence the developing organization of the infant's brain.

The link between the perception of facial expression and brain activation patterns in the perceiver provides a second mechanism through which the emotional state of the partner and the emotional state of the individual are coordinated. The Davidson and Fox (1982) research goes further than the Meltzoff (1990) study by documenting the concomitant reorganization of activation in the frontal lobes, thus further specifying the regulation of inner state. Both mechanisms (documented by Meltzoff and by Davidson and Fox) operate at the nonsymbolic, implicit level.

Elaborating on Davidson and Fox's work, Dawson (1992a, b) applied this method to the study of depressed mothers and their infants. She showed that by 10 months the emotional responsivity of infants of depressed mothers is already organized differently from that of normal infants. The same event that activates a positive affect behavior and EEG pattern in normal infants (mother playing peek-a-boo or mother returning after separation) elicits negative behavior and EEG pattern of activation in infants of depressed mothers. Again, interactive events and infant inner state are coordinated; but the infants of depressed mothers show a reversal of the usual organization.

Matching of Facial Expressions

Ekman, Levenson, and Friesen's (1983) study of adults found that a particular facial expression is associated with a particular pattern of physiological arousal. Matching the expression of the partner therefore produces a similar physiological state in the onlooker. Thus, a relational state and an internal state are simultaneously constructed. The Ekman work provides a third mechanism through which the emotional state of an individual can be transmitted to the partner, that is, specific matching of facial expressions. Like the Davidson and Fox (1982) work, it specifies the nature of the internal regulation of state at the physiological level. We have previously argued that, as two partners match each other's affective (as well as temporal) patterns, each recreates in himself a psychophysiological state similar to that of the partner, thus participating in the subjective state of the other (Beebe and Lachmann, 1988a, b).

Specific matching of facial expressions in adults has recently been empirically documented by Dimberg, Thunberg, and Elmehed (2000). Adult subjects were exposed to 30 milliseconds of happy, angry, and neutral target faces through a masking technique. The 30 milliseconds of the target face was "masked" by a five-second exposure to a neutral face before and after the target face, with the result that the subjects could not consciously perceive the target face. Simultaneously subjects were monitored for facial electromyographic activity by miniature electrodes. Despite the fact that exposure to happy and angry faces was not conscious, the subjects displayed distinct facial muscle reactions that corresponded to the happy and angry target faces. These results show that positive and negative emotional reactions alike can be evoked outside awareness, so that important aspects of face-to-face communication occur on a nonconscious level.

Inner Experience Is Organized in the Interactive Context

An important corollary of the mechanisms just described is that inner experience is organized in an interactive context. Sander (1977, 1983, 1985) has an extensive body of data demonstrating that, from the very beginning of life, inner experience is organized in the inter-active context. Infant management of state maintenance and state transitions (between sleep and wake) was studied in the first weeks of life, particularly the infant's achievement of day–night organization and an expectable pattern of the temporal organization of the 24-hour cycle. A complex interplay was documented between infant self-regulation and how mother and infant jointly negotiate the management of infant state transitions. Sander used this framework to propose that the capacity for inner experience exists from birth and consolidates around the experience of recurring states, which the infant comes to recognize. Inner experience begins in an expectable sequence of arousal, waking up, being fed, open spaces for play, and so on. This inner experience is getting organized, or remaining relatively more disorganized, in the interactive context, in which the regulation of state occurs. As an infant encounters both matches and mismatches of his expectancies of how the interactive regulation of state transitions will go, he becomes "aware" (at a presymbolic level) of his own states. The more regular the state periodicities, the more the infant can be aware of his states.

Sander (1983, 1985) argued that, as a function of the particular quality and success of the mutual regulation of states, the infant–care-taker system constructs a unique facilitation of, and constraint on, the infant's access to and awareness of his own states, his initiative to organize his own states, his regard for his states, and his ability to use his states in organizing his own behavior. These unique facilitations and constraints eventually contribute to the development of differences in (1) the person's ability to be aware, (2) what he is aware of, (3) how he uses it, and (4) how he feels about it. The potential pathology of the system is seen in an increasing inability on the part of the infant to be aware of his state, to be guided by that awareness, and to use his initiative to change his state—in essence, an increasing interference in the experience of agency with regard to his own states. Thus Sander's work provides another mechanism for the reciprocal coordination of inner and relational processes: the interactive regulation of the biorhythms of sleep–wake, activity, and feeding cycles.

Adult Data on the Co-Construction of Inner and
Relational Processes

The argument for the co-construction of inner and relational processes can be made with adult data as well. Adult facial behavior is simultaneously communicative and self-regulatory. Behavior, physiological arousal, and subjective state are all organized concurrently and are aspects of the same phenomenon (Tomkins, 1962, 1963; Izard, 1979; Ekman et al., 1983; Adelmann and Zajonc, 1989). All three are simultaneously organized in the interactive process. For example, there is now a substantial body of experimental adult data demonstrating that facial action is simultaneously communicative and self-regulatory, modulating physiological arousal and subjective experience. This research links facial action with internal state. It provides another body of data documenting that internal experience is organized hand-in-hand with interactive experience (see Adelmann and Zajonc, 1989; Laird, 1984; Winton, 1986; Winton, Putnam, and Krauss, 1984).

Tomkins (1962, 1963) considered the face to be central in expressing emotion both to others and to the self by way of feedback from the tongue and facial muscles, the sound of one's own voice, and changes in blood flow and temperature of the face (see Adelmann and Zajonc, 1989). Changes in facial action are associated with subjective changes, either intensifying or inhibiting the experience of the emotion (Adelmann and Zajonc, 1989; Izard, 1979; Ekman, Friesen, and Ancoli, 1980; Tomkins, 1962).

Ekman and his colleagues (1980) videotaped adult subjects while they watched films. The subjects' facial actions were coded. During a happy film, those subjects who showed greater positive facial action rated themselves as happier; during a negative film, subjects who showed more negative facial action reported more distress. Facial action can also influence subjective experience of emotion, even without awareness. In studies where spontaneous facial action was intensified without the subject's awareness, for example, by using reinforcement, canned laughter, or the presence of an observer, self-reported emotion increased correspondingly (Adelmann and Zajonc, 1989).

A dramatic example of spontaneous facial action intensified without the subject's awareness comes from a study by Heller and Haynal (1997). Fifty-nine patients who had attempted suicide in the previous three days were given an initial interview by the same psychiatrist. Two split-screen videotape cameras recorded the faces of both doctor and patient. One year later, 10 of these 59 patients, the "reattempter" group, had made another suicide attempt. Two forms of analysis (blind to one-year outcomes) were used to try to predict which patients would reattempt suicide. The first was the psychiatrist's own predictions written immediately after the interview, and the second was an analysis of the nonverbal communication of doctor and patient. The written predictions correctly identified the reattempt risk in 29% of the patients. For the analysis of nonverbal communication, another 11 of the original 59 patients who did not make another suicide attempt were chosen as the "nonrecidivist" group for purposes of comparison. These two subgroups were compared using Ekman and Friesen's Facial Action Coding System to code any facial action every .2 second. The nonverbal analysis correctly classified 81% of the patients analyzed. Thus the nonverbal analysis was more powerful than the written predictions. Furthermore, the psychiatrist's facial behavior was more powerful in discriminating the two groups of patients than was the patient's facial behavior. With his patients who would later try another suicide attempt, the psychiatrist frowned more, showed more head-and-eye orientation, and showed more overall facial activation and increased speech.

The greater activation and negative expressiveness of the psychiatrist can be seen as both regulating his own inner state and communicating with his patient, both probably outside his awareness. Using Davidson and Fox's (1982) work, we can imagine that the psychiatrist's perception of suicidal despair in a future reattempter patient created a resonant emotional state in the psychiatrist, which contributed to his nonverbal behavior. Using Meltzoff's ideas, it is not far fetched to imagine that the psychiatrist brought his internal state and behavior into a correspondence with his future reattempter patients, providing a fundamental relatedness between himself and his patient. Using Ekman's work, we can imagine that the psychiatrist specifically matched some of the future reattempter patients' frowning expressions, therefore producing in himself a physiological state similar to that of the patient. However, since the nonverbal behavior of the patients themselves did not discriminate the two groups of patients, the differential emotional pattern evoked in the psychiatrist by the future reattempter patients was not based primarily on a simple matching of expressions, but rather on something more evoked in the psychiatrist.

Dyadic Expansion of Consciousness

The mutual regulation model and a "dyadic expansion of consciousness" view of therapeutic action has been proposed by Tronick (1989, 1996, 1998; Gianino and Tronick, 1988), who has made a major contribution in conceptualizing the integration of self- and interactive regulation processes. For example, he considers that the maintenance of adequate internal regulation (homeostasis), such as the regulation of an infant's core body temperature, is a dyadic achievement. It is a joint product of exogenous and interactive processes. And each must come to know the state of the other if the regulation is to succeed (Tronick, 1996).

Tronick (1996) has suggested that, in the process of mutual regulation, each partner (mother and infant, or therapist and patient) affects the other's "state of consciousness" (state of brain organization). As each affects the other's self-regulation, each partner's inner organization is expanded into a more coherent, as well as a more complex, state: "each individual is a self-organizing system that creates its own states of consciousness—states of brain organization—which can be expanded into more coherent and complex states in collaboration with another self-organizing system" (p. 9). In this process, each partner's state of consciousness expands to incorporate elements of consciousness of the other in a new and more coherent form. Since both partners are affected by this process, there is a dyadic expansion of consciousness into a more coherently organized and complex state of dyadic consciousness (p. 13). Tronick suggests that this process describes a view of therapeutic action: both analyst and patient create and transform unique dyadic states of consciousness through mutual and self-regulation.

Summary

The various ways in which inner state and interactive process are linked are offered as organizing principles of the integration of self- and interactive regulation. Although much of the research we reviewed is based on interactions with infants, we contend that these principles are equally relevant to adults. This research documents a number of general principles for a theory of interaction at the non-verbal level:

(1) In a systems view, self- and interactive regulation are simul-taneous, complementary, and optimally in dynamic balance (see Figure 1). Thus the individual can be fully described only in relation to the dyad.

(2) Across the life span, each partner participates in a moment-by-moment reciprocal influence process at the nonverbal level, usually out of awareness (Jaffe and Feldstein, 1970; Langs, Badalamenti, and Thompson, 1996; Capella, 1991; Cohn and Tronick, 1988; Crown, 1991; Warner, 1988a, b; Jaffe et al., 2001).

(3) Each dyadic system constructs a unique facilitation of, and constraint on, the individual's access to, awareness of, regard for, and ability to use, his own states (see Figure 3) (Sander, 1977, 1985).

(4) Through cross-modal matching, we can link the behavior we see in the partner to our own inner proprioception, con-stituting a fundamental relatedness between self and other from the beginning of life (Meltzoff, 1990; Meltzoff and Gopnick, 1993).

(5) The mere perception of positive or negative emotion in the partner creates a resonant emotional state in the perceiver, reorganizing the frontal lobe of the brain (Davidson and Fox, 1982; Schore, 1994).

(6) Since a person's facial expression is associated with a par-ticular physiological pattern, matching the expression of the partner creates in the onlooker a similar physiological state (Ekman et al., 1983).

(7) In the reciprocal influence process, each affects the other's "state of consciousness" (state of brain organization)

(Tronick, 1996), especially in states of prolonged matching (Schore, 1994).

(8) Behavior, arousal, and subjective awareness are all simultaneously organized in the interactive process (Ekman et al., 1983; Izard, 1979; Adelmann and Zajonc, 1989).

These principles illustrate an integration of behavior, physiological arousal, proprioception, brain activation, and subjective awareness. Many others could be defined (see Schore, 1994; Perry, 1996). They suggest the multiple levels at which self- and interactive regulation interface. These organizing principles of regulation describe self- and interactive *process*, not dynamic content. They can apply to the verbal as well as nonverbal levels, and they affect such familiar psychoanalytic dynamic issues as, for example, safety, efficacy, self-esteem, separation and reunion, boundaries, self-definition, intimacy, aloneness in the presence of the partner, and mutual recognition. Observing and owning this process enriches our range and flexibility as analysts. Attention to this self and interactive interface is critical to restoring, expanding, and, in some cases, creating access to inner experience as well as interpersonal engagement.

3

INTERACTIVE REORGANIZATION
OF SELF-REGULATION

The Case of Karen

Empirical infant research can expand our understanding of therapeutic action in adult treatment. Our primary concern, however, is not dynamic content or reconstructions of early development, but rather organizing principles of interactions. In presenting the case of Karen, we build on our systems view that self- and interactive regulation are simultaneous, complementary, and optimally in dynamic balance. For Karen, the system was out of balance, drastically tilted toward self-regulation. Sander's (1977, 1995) view that inner experience is organized in the interactive context provided a guide for the treatment. By analogy to Sander, the patient–analyst system can construct a unique facilitation of, or constraint on, the patient's access to and awareness of inner states and the patient's experience of agency with regard to inner states. We use the case of Karen to illustrate both the origins and the transformations of her psychopathology. Chronically mismatched interactive regulations led her to premature, drastic self-regulations. We trace the interactive reorganization of self-regulation as the primary theme of therapeutic action.

The model of development derived from infant research cannot, of course, be directly translated into the adult psychoanalytic situation. In adults, the capacity for symbolization and the subjective elaboration of experience in the form of fantasies, wishes, and defenses, further modify the organization and representation of interactive and self-regulation patterns. What makes this model appealing for adult treatment, however, is that it makes no assumptions about the dynamic content of adult experience. It focuses entirely on the process of interactive regulation.

The ability to respond and be socially engaged depends not only on the nature of the partner's input, and on one's own responsivity, but also on the regulation of the internal state of both participants (Beebe and Lachmann, 1994). The word state is used broadly to refer to affect, arousal, and the symbolic elaboration of state. From infancy onward, people differ in the crucial capacity to modulate arousal, shift state, and tolerate and use stimulation to organize behavior in predictable ways (Korner and Grobstein, 1976; Als and Brazelton, 1981).

Specific failures in self-regulation affect the quality of interactive regulation. For example, infants with specific self-regulatory difficulties may place undue burdens on the responsivity of their partners. Whether derived from variations in individual endowment or failures in interactive regulation, difficulties in self-regulation affect the quality of engagement.

Likewise, specific failures in interactive regulation may compromise self-regulation. For example, as in the case discussed in this chapter, affect regulation (Socarides and Stolorow, 1984/85), anxiety, tension, and aloneness (Adler and Buie, 1979) may then be relegated to solitary measures, without a sense of support. Expectations of being abandoned when one is vulnerable may be organized. Rather than a growing self-reliance and self-sufficiency, aversions, anxieties about relationships, or self-protective depersonalization may ensue.

Our integration is designed not to supplant dynamic formulations but, rather, to provide the analyst with a more differentiated view of the regulation of interactions and the organization of experience that goes beyond interpretation. We are not proposing a new technique, nor arguing for decreased attention to dynamic issues in treatment. Instead, we are reversing the figure–ground perspective customarily used in describing analytic treatment. We are placing the mutually regulated nonverbal exchanges into the foreground. Dynamic conceptualizations are in the background.

Many well-established psychoanalytic concepts already cover some of the same terrain as self- and interactive regulation. For example, ongoing regulations have been subsumed within discussions of patterns of transference and countertransference, the "holding environment" (Winnicott, 1965), and the "background of safety" (Sandler, 1987). The nonverbal interactions on which we focus have been included among noninterpretive analytic behaviors (for example, Freud, 1909; Ferenczi, 1930; Lindon, 1994). These interventions have been made when words were considered to be inadequate to retain a therapeutic connection with certain patients. We hold, however, that nonverbal interactions, like noninterpretive actions, do constitute interpretive activity, although they are not packaged in the customary form. Their intent is to provide a primary contribution to the patient's expectation of being understood.

Although the self- and interactive regulation of nonverbal exchanges is relevant to all treatments, attention to this dimension becomes particularly critical in contacting "difficult-to-reach" patients for whom the essential cues go far beyond the usual verbal exchange.

The treatment of Karen emphasizes the analyst's and the patient's interactions of affect, mood, arousal, and rhythm. We track interactions at the microlevel of rhythm matching, modulation of vocal contour, pausing, postural matching, and gaze patterns. We describe the ways in which these interactions powerfully affected the joint construction of the psychoanalytic relationship. Alterations in the self-regulatory ranges of both patient and analyst ensued.

The Case of Karen

Karen (treated by Frank Lachmann) began psychoanalytic therapy after her first suicide attempt. When her then-boyfriend flirted with another woman, she took all the pills in her medicine cabinet. Like an automaton, she watched her actions "from a bird's eye view from a corner of the room." This detached, depersonalized state felt to her as though she were "behind a pane of glass." In one of these states, toward the end of her second year of therapy, Karen made a second, similar suicide attempt.

Karen was seen on a three-session-per-week basis for eight years. When she began therapy, she was 27 years old. Her life had been declining since her graduation from high school. At that time her parents literally dragged her from her room to deposit her at an out-of-town college. She succeeded in remaining there for four years and excelled in some of her courses but at the same time barely passed others. After graduation, she gained admission to a drama school in England and studied there for a year.

Upon her return to the United States Karen continued to study acting and attempted to find work as an actress. She suffered from a severe sleep disturbance. Unable to sleep during the night, she tended to fall asleep in the early morning hours. When awake, she could not mobilize herself. She thus missed many auditions, missed callbacks when she did have a successful audition, and failed to appear for acting jobs when she did get hired. In addition, at times Karen would become aware that she had lost several hours and would find herself in a different part of town, with no memory of how she got there.

Karen found it difficult to speak to me. She felt she had nothing to say and began sessions by asking, somewhat mechanically, "What shall we talk about?" Initially, I responded by summarizing previous sessions, for example, "Last time we spoke about how messy and dingy your apartment is." She might then speak about an apparently unrelated topic, for example, encounters with various acquaintances. I would then label these experiences as leaving her with feelings of abandonment, disappointment, a sense of exploitation, or regret about her withdrawn manner. I did not comment on the lack of continuity from session to session.

Privately, I came to understand Karen's opening question as an attempt to orient herself and to determine whether or not a connection could be established with me. I believed that waiting for her to begin, or throwing her question back, would have failed to recognize her tentative attempt to reach out to me. Overtly, Karen hardly acknowledged my presence, although her opening question, "What shall we talk about?" did contain a "we."

Gradually, I came to appreciate that Karen dreaded conversing with me. She anticipated that she would have difficult feelings that she would have to regulate on her own. This expectation suggests an imbalance between self- and interactive regulation in her development. By analogy to the work of Tronick (1989) on depressed mothers and their infants, in the context of chronic interactive misregulation, a preoccupation with self-regulation and the management of negative affect on one's own can develop. For Karen, despite her preoccupation with self-regulation, her self-regulatory efforts were severely impaired. Her sleep disturbance, listless state, and lack of "desire" and dissociated episodes were evidence of this impaired regulation of affect and arousal.

What self-regulatory range did Karen bring to treatment? A narrow range of tolerable affect, arousal, and engagement; an immobile face; a tendency to "space out;" and massive efforts to dampen down her reactivity to all stimulation. In sessions she looked out of my office window as she sat in her chair with her coat on. When she did look at me, it was with a sideways glance. Interactions with Karen were dominated by her withdrawal.

Slowly Karen began to reveal her experiences in her family. From the age of five on, she had been awakened during the night by her parents' fights. She could hear their shouts through the walls of her bedroom. Her mother would accuse her father of staying out at night with other women, and her father would, at times, be physically abusive toward her mother. The fights terrified her, especially after her mother asked her who she would want to go with if she and her father separated. She remembered not wanting to go with either one. They never did separate.

Karen was born shortly after her parents' graduation from high school. Neither parent hid from Karen that their future plans had been scuttled by their marriage and her birth. In reaction, Karen began to pray at night. By the time she was seven, she had made a deal with God. If He would stop her parents from fighting, she would give up her life. From that time forward she was preoccupied with suicide and suffered from severe, persistent sleep disturbances.

In high school, Karen frequently cut classes because she could not tolerate the noise made by other students. Sometimes she would get as far as the classroom door, stand outside, but be unable to enter. She would then go home and spend the day studying alone. She did appear for examinations, on which she did very well. During afternoons and evenings she worked as a cashier at a local shopping mall. In fact, she worked continuously until the end of her high school years. Since then and until her treatment was well under way, she had not held a job.

By the age of 17, Karen had formed an intimate sustaining relationship with a fellow student, Brian. He was her best friend and confidant. When he unexpectedly died of a brain tumor, she was despondent. Her parents insisted that she get over her loss quickly. They could not understand that Karen had lost the one person to whom she felt close and whom she trusted. She retreated to her room, felt "without desires," and became increasingly aimless. This was not the first time she had experienced these states. At prior times they were more or less transient. At this point they crystalized as a recurring dominant state.

When Karen began therapy, 10 years later, these states were still prominant and affected the nature of our interaction. Though we sat facing each other, Karen looked away from me. Her face was immobile. Her voice had no contouring. Even when I spoke to her she did not look at me. Her self-constriction powerfully affected me. I felt reluctant to jar her precariously maintained presentation.

I responded to her constriction by partially constricting myself. I allowed myself to be influenced by her rhythm. I narrowed my own expansiveness to match more closely the limits imposed by her own narrow affective range. I did look at her continually, but I kept my voice even and soft. In my initial comments I remained within the limits of the concrete details that she offered. I thus altered the regulation of my own arousal, keeping it low and limiting my customary expansiveness. She was effective in communicating her distress, and I was able to respond by providing her with a range of stimulation that more closely matched the limited level of arousal she could tolerate. However, as I restricted my own expressiveness, at times I became fidgity and squirmy. She seemed oblivious to my moments of discomfort.

Gradually, her tolerance for affective arousal increased and I could become more expansive. She was able to talk about affectively more difficult material. Her voice remained soft but with more contouring. She spoke about social relationships and acting auditions, which raised the spectre of competition. But she felt that she had no right to live. She withdrew from these situations lest she draw attention to herself. Initially, these explorations had little effect on her life. Our dialogue, however, did increase the affective range that she could tolerate in the sessions.

During the first two years of the treatment, Karen moved from descriptions of her environment, that is, the inanimate world, to descriptions of interpersonal relationships and to explorations of her subjective states. At the same time, I also shifted from summaries of the previous sessions to elaborations of her feelings and reactions. Sometimes anticipating her formulaic opening, "What shall we talk about?" I began sessions by asking her how she was feeling. Sometimes, before she responded verbally, her right upper lip would twitch and constrict briefly or her leg would jiggle rapidly. I came to understand these signals as an indication that she was tense and had been feeling moody, depressed, or without energy since our last meeting. We focused on her specific reactions and tried to find a context for them. I detailed nuances of feelings and moods, such as annoyance, rebuff, eagerness, enthusiasm, and disappointment. I told her that it seemed to me that she experienced many emotions as though they were annoying intrusions. After some time, I was able to add descriptions of Karen as "considering," "hoping," "planning," or "expecting." That is, I distinguished among categories of affect and time and acknowledged her authorship of her experience. I kept apace with Karen's gradually more personalized communications. Nevertheless, the extent of her visible discomfort waxed and waned. However, she did appear more comfortable about accessing, revealing, and understanding her subjective life in both its reactive and in its proactive aspects.

Although I was not unaware of restricting and monitoring my responses to Karen, I was not following a premeditated plan of non-verbal treatment. Qualities of nonverbal communication, such as vocal rhythm, pitch, contour, and the level of arousal, are usually out of awareness, but we are able to bring them into focused attention. It was mostly in retrospect that I became aware of the salient role played by these nonverbal, mutually regulated interactions and their effect on Karen's and my self-regulation. I assumed that, through these interactions, Karen felt some sense of validation leading to the tentative engagement of a selfobject tie.

To enable Karen to maintain the fragile developing selfobject tie, I did not make explicit the possibility that Karen was refinding aspects of her experience with Brian in the therapeutic relationship. To do so could have increased her self-consciousness and her propensity toward overstimulating anxiety. She would have needed to protect herself against a repetition of another attachment and loss-abandonment sequence.

Instead, I recognized Karen's affective reactions as well as her dread of retraumatization in her current relationships. We translated her associations, symptoms, nightmares, enactments, and hallucinations into more direct statements about herself and her experience. We discussed the vagueness that characterized much of her life as indicating what she was afraid to perceive, feel, believe, wish, imagine, or remember. My comments were directed toward recognizing her attempts at self-definition. In this way, her prior, almost exclusive reliance on drastic self-regulation through withdrawal, depersonalization, and derealization began to shift. Her sense of agency increased. For example, as her dread of retraumatization in new situations diminished, she showed a wider variation of facial expressions. Occasionally, she smiled. Furthermore, she registered for some classes, attended, and participated.

In the course of the first two years of treatment, Karen recalled her parents' fights and was increasingly able to describe other painful events. Until we explored them, these memories had been retained as unconnected experiences. They correlated with Karen's sense of fragmentation. In making connections among these memories, her feelings, and their current relevance, I continually depicted Karen as living and having lived a life with temporal, affective, and cognitive dimensions. I described the events to her, with some slightly increased affective elaborations. Increasingly, she could tolerate my amplification of her affect.

These memories spanned the fifth to eighth years of her life. In the earliest event we pieced together, Karen was required to mail a letter for her mother at the post office. Karen recalled feeling abject terror at having to walk past some derelicts to mail the letter.

Karen recalled that she could not leave her mother's side. Nor could she explain to her mother why she was so afraid. Her mother encouraged her to mail the letter by telling her how big and grown up she was. We came to understand that walking alone past the derelicts meant to Karen that she would be showing her mother that she was "growing up." She would then be telling her mother that she was able to fend for herself. I said that her fear of revealing her "growth" grew out of her belief, based on the fights she had overheard, that her mother wanted to "dump" her and, in fact, could not wait to do so. Showing independence would result in imminent loss of support. Karen responded with silent tears. This was unusual since she rarely responded to such reconstructions directly. It was at times like this that new recollections emerged.

Another memory concerned a visit to a department store where Karen had one of her first asthmatic attacks. She tried to tell her mother that she could barely breathe. She could not keep up with her as they rushed from one department to another. Her mother told her that the shopping was important and Karen should not complain so much. Karen recalled the department store visit as we were exploring how she neglected her health, teeth, skin, and allergies. I commented that through her body and frequent upper respiratory illnesses, her complaints were given voice. There she retained an eloquent record of her feelings. The twitch of her upper lip and her foot jiggles also constituted such a silent record of her moods and feelings.

Karen had come to consider her physical state as unimportant. She could now imagine that she must have felt hurt by her mother's dismissive and neglectful behavior. She had been anxious about her breathing difficulty but, most of all, fearful of evoking her mother's disapproval by complaining. Her solution in the department store had been to redouble her efforts to stay close to her mother, attempt to dampen her own arousal, and hope that the ordeal would soon be over.

A third memory involved Karen's sleep difficulty, which continued even after the parental fights ceased. To cure her sleep difficulty she had been confined to her room. While exploring this symptom, Karen reported that she currently had been feeling a sudden urge to travel to Iceland. She then recalled that she had attempted to deal with her sleep problem by putting herself to sleep in an empty bathtub. There she could fall asleep because "it was quiet." But, most important, the "whiteness" and the hardness of the tub felt so good. It afforded her a sense of security and protection. When her parents discovered her, however, she was sent to her room immediately after supper so that she could try to get to sleep early.

Obediently, Karen remained in her room. She watched the outside world from her window. She felt excluded and frustrated and began to draw on the walls of her room. These creative, exploratory, assertive efforts were quickly punished. She was given a bottle of cleaning fluid and told to undo the damage. Later, however, she was presented with a paint set, but she felt too resentful toward her parents to use it. The paint box was never opened. Some years later, in a similar vein, she was given a chemistry set because she had shown some interest and ability in her science classes. Aside from presenting her with the paints and chemicals, though, no one in her family took any interest in her. No one inquired about the two sets. Neither was ever used. Karen acknowledged that she would have liked to use the paint and the chemistry sets but could not bring herself to do so.

Karen clung to her room until she was dragged by her parents to college. Her room was her refuge, and she felt protected in it, even though alone. Her banishment and "voluntary confinement"

to her room paralleled my sense of her inaccessibility in the therapeutic relationship. I made this connection with the expectation
that Karen's inaccesibility could be explained and thereby diminished more directly. She thereupon dreamt of a "barren countryside." In association, she recalled hallucinatory experiences. When
she was confined to her room and would look out of her window,
she sometimes saw cars go by without drivers. We discussed the
"barren countryside" dream, a self-state dream, as conveying her
sense of barrenness. We connected it to the "aimlessness" depicted
in her hallucination. I told her that she depicted herself as living in
a world in which no one was at the wheel. Perhaps she longed for
someone in her family to take an interest in her and assume some
control. I also inquired whether she might be feeling this way currently in her treatment. Such heavy-handed transference queries
never yielded much. On further reflection, however, I felt that my
expectations of her exceeded a level of functioning that she could
tolerate. Through her dream and her recollection of the hallucinations, she was reminding me of her still-depleted state, her barrenness. She was letting me know that I should not rush ahead of her
(as her mother had in the department store) and lose sight of the
severity of her difficulties. Her dread of being dumped at the first
signs of "growth" still prevailed.

The three memories of being at the post office, in the department store, and confined to her room constitute a series of model
scenes (Lachmann and Lichtenberg, 1992). Each one shaped seg-
ments of our interactions, though the "confinement" theme dominated the others.

The model scene of standing in her room and looking out at life
through her window gathered together a number of prior salient issues
and shaped subsequent experience. In her room, she was protected
from the injurious expectation of her family and the "noise," and potential exploitativeness, of her peers. In her room, she did not need to
fear that she might "blow others away" or become an object of envy.
She also avoided the danger of feeling helpless, frustrated, and out of
control. Through her continuous self-sacrifice, she maintained a firm
grip on her parents' tie to her and her claim on them.

The mother–daughter relationship, encapsulated by the model scenes, depicted patterns of mutual regulation that tilted Karen toward solitary self-regulation. At first she attempted to regulate heightened, painful affect states, such as her terror at the post office and in the department store, by trying to elicit her mother's participation. She pleaded with her mother at the post office and clung to her in the department store. Feeling ignored, she expected that independent steps would lead to abandonment. Therefore, heroic efforts at self-regulation were undertaken. In essence, drastic self-regulation attempts substituted for a balanced integration between self- and mutual regulation (Tronick, 1989).

By the time Karen was confined to her room, she had come to tolerate her aloneness and restrict her activity. Her efforts to engage her family had all but ceased. Her physical symptoms and her hallucinations increased her withdrawal. She felt ineffective in engaging her parents and confined herself to altering and influencing her physical and subjective states. Drawing on her walls served as a desperate signal for attention. But her refusal to touch the paint and the chemistry sets suggested that her withdrawal contained a significant degree of self-sacrifice and defiance. Karen could not risk putting herself in the position of expecting recognition from her parents and being disappointed. To avoid this danger, she kept her creative and intellectual interests to herself. She lived out her grim, unconscious belief (Weiss and Sampson, 1986) that she had "no right to a life" (Modell, 1984). Her suicidal preoccupation, her neglect of her physical well-being, her propensity to disregard physical illness, her social withdrawal and minimum functioning in life, her retreat from attention much as she desired it, all converged in her conviction that her parents' life (and hence the world) would have been better off had she not been born.

Her relationship with Brian in late adolescence was a notable exception to these convictions. Through her relationship with him, Karen had retained some hope for a reciprocal connection and sensual and sexual responsivity. A significant sector of her life had evidently been left relatively intact and revived in this relationship. However, overall her development remained constricted.

Karen developed physical symptoms in lieu of accusations and complaints, withdrew from people, and found solace in the bathtub. As a solution, the bathtub differed from the others in that she created her own protected environment. Her further confinement to her room became an enforced exclusion from her family. Yet it provided some protection against the overstimulating parental quarrels and her parents' obliviousness to her needs.

During the treatment, the self-protective aspects of Karen's bathtub experience reappeared, symbolically transformed as a visit to Iceland. In Iceland, she wrote poetry and made new friends. Karen began to acknowledge the talents that were unrecognized by her family. Her creativity had remained sequestered in her private world with considerable ambivalence. For example, she studied acting but did not perform.

Convinced that she had been a burden to her parents and the source of their difficulties, Karen considered her solitary confinement to be justified. In refusing to make use of the resources that her parents gave her, she found a self-defeating but nevertheless modest triumph. Within the confines of her imagination, creative elaborations of her experience continued in silence and in private. These could be accessed in the course of her treatment and became the imagery of her poetry.

Karen had written poems at various times in her life. During her second year of treatment she turned to writing poetry in a more determined way. A poem she brought to a session was dedicated to the memory of Brian. In it she depicted her loneliness and her alienation from her family. She ended with a plea to Brian, "Run after me but never let me go."

To "use" therapy, for which her parents paid, meant to Karen that she had to surrender her defiance and to capitulate to them. She had not used the paint box, the chemistry set, or the acting classes. Why surrender now? It became clear then, why, during the first two years of treatment, she continued to indicate that she had made no progress and that she was as depressed as ever. On the basis of Karen's failure to work and earn money, her parents echoed her feeling that she had not made any progress in therapy. I asked

Karen what would happen if her parents were to stop their financial support of her. She said, "I would probably be dead now." It was as though Karen were giving her parents another chance to decide, do you want me to live or not? Since the financial support included payment for her treatment, I also understood her remark to allude to her need for therapy and its importance to her.

During the first two years of treatment, Karen usually came to the sessions encased in the room in which she was isolated by herself and her family. She either stayed in her room literally, by not coming to sessions, or figuratively through her communicative difficulties. Often sessions felt to me as though we were meeting for the first time. She never made any reference to what had gone on in a previous session, so I did. She did appear to be moved by some of my affect-laden descriptions of her experience. When she was moved, tears would roll down her cheeks. Usually, she could not say why she was crying.

In these first years of treatment, Karen missed at least one of her three weekly appointments and arrived late for the other two. Missing sessions or arriving late increased her sense of failure. When I gently inquired about this pattern, she told me that it was an achievement that she could get herself to the sessions as often as she did. During this time Karen also had two abortions, to which she reacted with increased depression. Although we had discussed her difficulties with a boyfriend who kept coming in and out of her life, she did not mention the abortions until the last minute.

Toward the end of the second year of treatment, Karen made the second suicide attempt. During the first two years I had referred Karen to a psychopharmacologist, but she did not take the medication with any regularity. Fortunately, the unused medication was not at hand. Instead she used whatever was in her medicine cabinet. Following this attempt, I met with Karen and her parents twice. The parents could not grasp the severity of Karen's difficulties. Her mother stated, "We all get rather blue sometimes." I felt that Karen was still a high suicide risk.

After this suicide attempt, waiting to see whether or not Karen would arrive for her appointments became very anxiety arousing for me. I felt that, without some more active intervention on my part, her depersonalized state and the suicidal potential would continue. I needed more reliable and intensive contact with her. I needed to feel less worried and to feel that I had a chance of reaching her.

Thus, at the beginning of her third year of treatment, I decided to telephone Karen about two hours before every appointment. I reminded her of the time of our meeting and told her that I looked forward to seeing her. Within about three or four months, Karen no longer missed sessions.

Karen had engaged me sufficiently that I began to feel desperate. When I had decided to call her, I was not conscious of her plea in the poem, "Run after me but never let me go." However, I was evidently responding to it. In retrospect, my enactment exactly matched the presymbolic quality of many of Karen's communications. We may ask if her longstanding, continuously reinforced conviction that she was fundamentally unwanted would have budged in the face of verbal interventions and explanations alone. Could attuned understanding have better facilitated the therapeutic process? Were my calls an extension of empathic immersion in her subjectivity? Or was I requiring Karen to connect with me on my terms and at her expense?

Though valid, these questions imply that my self-regulation and my role in the interactive regulation could have been reduced or eliminated. Although a dramatic departure from customary analytic work, the telephone calls emerged out of a context in which my capacity to tolerate anxiety had reached a limit. Furthermore, my enactment concretely made the interpretation to Karen: You are wanted. In retrospect, it is clear that this enactment was a critical part of the regulatory process and therapeutic action in this case.

Despite Karen's detachment, her responsivity to some of my comments did evoke an intense engagement on my part. Her dramatic response to my calls by coming regularly to sessions indicated how profoundly she could be influenced by me. Moreover, her response exactly matched what I needed to feel, so that the treatment, and she, had a chance. In the earlier stages of the therapy, her sense of efficacy had been promoted as I restricted and dampened my natural responsivity. Now my sense of efficacy was promoted as she expanded her responsivity and reorganized her relationship to me and the treatment. Thus a complex and intricately matched mutual regulation took place.

By the end of the third year, the gradually firming selfobject tie made suicide less likely and diminished her depression. She had to admit that she had not felt so well in many years. She even volunteered that she did not think she could ever make another suicide attempt.

During the first year of my calls, if she were still asleep, her answering machine would pick up and I would leave a message. As Karen became less depressed and felt more energetic, she often left her house before my call. She would then come to the sessions without a reminder and would receive my message only upon arriving home in the evening. On several occasions I asked how she felt about my telephone calls. She told me that it was "OK" for me to call. I understood her "OK" as her only way of saying that she wanted the calls. She could not acknowledge that she needed them. In her "OK" she gave me permission to call, as if also reassuring me that I was not intruding. In this response it is apparent that Karen was still quite detached and protected herself in the privacy of her room.

By the beginning of the fourth year of treatment, Karen appeared more alive and accessible. The gradual establishment of a relatively reliable selfobject tie shifted Karen's self-regulatory capacities toward greater tolerance for affect and arousal. Although she remained rather constricted, she gained increasing access to her own experience and to her own history. Past and current impressions gained expression in her writing.

In this fourth year Karen wanted to talk to her mother about the recent death of an acquaintance. It was an event that bore certain similarities to the death of Brian. Her mother suggested that they meet to talk about this death at a bar that had music. Karen then telephoned me. She had felt guilty about her actions at the last meeting with this acquaintance, and she was now also disappointed and furious with her mother for fending her off. Thus, in spite of her continuing state of detachment, she was able to use our tie to restore herself in this crisis.

In her fifth year of treatment, Karen's interest and talent as a writer enabled her to enroll in a graduate program, attend classes, and submit assignments. After her visit to Iceland, she succeeded in having some poetry published. Though she still sought relationships with unstable, irresponsible, charismatic men, she was no longer so compliant and dependent. She practiced "safe sex."

Karen's conviction that she would cause fewer problems for her family by shutting herself away remained a dominant theme. In fact, it received continual confirmation when she visited her parents. They did not seem to be aware of her widening range of affect and ability. They told her not to come into the living room when they were entertaining friends because her depressing and uncommunicative manner put a pall on the company.

After five years of therapy, Karen emerged as an adventuresome, foolhardy, overly trusting, resourceful, funny, and still somewhat self-sabotaging person. In her own succinct way, she summarized her gain in her treatment: "I used to not be able to talk to people. Now I can talk to people."

Karen terminated treatment after eight years when she obtained a job as a reporter outside of New York. She would call me once or twice a year to let me know how she was doing. Five years after termination, she continues to be productive and self-suppporting.

Discussion

Karen's lifelong experiences of rebuff led to a premature reliance on drastic and restricting self-regulatory measures, such as avoidance, depersonalization, derealization, and dampening of her own affect. Designed to avoid retraumatization, these measures only partially protected her. She maintained a precarious balance between self-expression and self-annihilation.

In Karen's development, sounds had become shattering noises obstructing emotional contact. Vision had become a remote sense. She felt as though she were looking at herself and her experiences from a distance. Breathing, sleeping, and spatial orientation were impaired. Sensual-affective experiences were overarousing and emerged as physical symptoms and disruptive imagery, such as hallucinations and nightmares. Unable to regulate affect states on her own, she avoided emotionally arousing, and thus potentially disruptive, experiences.

The relationship with Brian revived Karen's expectations of being affectively validated and part of a dyad. It rekindled her expectation that she could trust her feelings, that she could be included in someone's internal life, and that she could form a bond. We assume that the tie to Brian reengaged an earlier, precarious selfobject tie to her parents. With the death of Brian, Karen was traumatized (Lachmann and Beebe, 1997). Not only did she lose the only person to whom she felt connected, but her parents also failed to validate her profound devastation. Thus selfobject ties were irreparably disrupted.

The treatment of Karen illustrates the role of interactive and self-regulation in the therapeutic establishment of the selfobject tie. Karen's feelings were labeled, differentiated, and affirmed. Her fears of retraumatization were investigated and, over the course of the treatment, disconfirmed. As she had with Brian, she feared that attachment would lead to loss. Furthermore, her restricted self-regulatory range had interfered with her ability to tolerate the excitement and hope generated by the expectation of being accepted, understood, and included in a bond. These difficulties pervaded her friendships, classes, work possibilities, and her treatment.

Karen's immobile face, flat voice, sitting with her coat on, not looking, and having nothing to say required extraordinary measures. To reach her, the therapist had to restrict the range of affect and activity so that Karen's level of arousal remained tolerable to her. Speaking in a soft and even voice, and slowing the rhythm, increased Karen's tolerance for arousal. With a voice and face that were more alive, she began to talk about her life. The therapist was able to expand the level of his own arousal and address her fears. In turn, Karen was less withdrawn. Fragments of her history emerged, from which three model scenes could be constructed. This increasing coherence led to Karen's ability to report a dream and a hallucinatory association of "cars without drivers." Her inaccessibility and her world where no one was at the wheel could then be interpreted.

Although Karen was able to acknowledge that she would be dead without this therapy, her two abortions, extensive depersonalizations, a second suicide attempt, frequent latenesses, and continually missed appointments led the therapist to make the dramatic intervention of telephoning her before every appointment. That Karen was able to respond equally dramatically by coming regularly enabled the therapist to feel that he could continue to work with her. The treatment had evidently mobilized a remarkable resilience in Karen. She was able to experience her own influence on the therapist's activity, and she could experience her therapist's influencing her level of arousal. For both, self-regulation was altered through these reciprocal mutual regulations. Thus, extensive work on Karen's depersonalized state and efforts to reregulate both of us set the stage sufficiently well that the telephone calls could make a dramatic impact.

We have focused on the nonverbal dimension to illustrate the contribution of self- and interactive regulation to therapeutic action. When the treatment began, solitary self-regulation was Karen's main method of survival and it was failing. The treatment attempted to open up her self-regulation so that it could be included in a dialogue. Instead of viewing analyst and patient as two isolated entities, each sending the other discrete communications, we have illustrated a view of the treatment relationship as a system. This theory of interaction specifies how each person is affected both by his own behavior (self-regulation) and by the behavior of the partner (interactive regulation) on a continuous, moment-by-moment basis.

We have illustrated how our dyadic systems view can refine our approach to the process of psychoanalytic treatment. Rather than emphasizing dynamic content, we have placed into the foreground nonverbal interactions at the level of rhythm matching, modulation of vocal contour, pausing, postural matching, and gaze regulation. This nonverbal system of self- and interactive regulation is an essential dimension of therapeutic action.

Turning to the origins of this system in the first year of life, the next chapter reviews the infant's early capacities that define the presymbolic basis for emerging self- and object representations. In the chapter following that, we review patterns of early interactive regulation during face-to-face play. We use this research to argue that the very interactive process itself is represented in presymbolic form by the infant. In subsequent chapters, as we consider the relevance of this research for adult treatment, our intention is not the reconstruction of the adult patient's infancy, but, rather, the formulation of organizing principles of interactions in infancy that illuminate the patient–analyst interaction.

4

EARLY CAPACITIES AND
PRESYMBOLIC REPRESENTATION

Contemporary research has provided us with a view of the infant as an astonishingly competent creature. From the very first hours of life, the infant is engaged in highly complex interpersonal interactions. How the infant does this, and what kinds of interaction patterns are set up, inform us about the human capacity for relatedness. In this chapter we focus on how the infant comes to represent interactions during the presymbolic period. In particular, we review the infant's perceptual and cognitive abilities that lead to early expectations about how interactions proceed. This research is used to describe the presymbolic basis for emerging self- and object representations. It addresses the most fundamental ways in which the mind is initially organized. This knowledge, in turn, is of use to us when we address adults in treatment.

Self- and object representations are addressed here in terms of their *presymbolic* origins. We use Piaget's (1937) timetable in placing the emergence of symbolic thought at the end of the first year, undergoing major reorganization at 16 to 18 months, and consolidating in the third year. *Symbol formation* is briefly defined by the capacity to imitate an object that is not physically present and to refer to an object in a way that is not defined by its physical features, that is, through a conventional (linguistic) symbol (Piaget,

1954; Werner and Kaplan, 1963). But prior to symbol formation, a complex presymbolic representational capacity can be documented.

In this chapter, the evidence for a presymbolic representational capacity is presented. At the end of this chapter, we argue that these capacities, documented under experimental laboratory conditions, are actually used by infants to represent ongoing interactions. In chapter 5, this presymbolic representational capacity is related to patterns of interactive regulation during face-to-face social play. Thus, two different infant literatures, on presymbolic representation and on the regulation of face-to-face play, are related to the psychoanalytic theory of self- and object representations.

Interaction patterns are defined as the characteristic ways in which mother and infant influence each other as the interaction unfolds. These patterns include both how the infant regulates his or her own arousal (self-regulation) and interactive regulation. Interaction patterns are organized through the dimensions of time, space, affect, and arousal. The infant comes to recognize, expect, and remember these recurrent patterns. As they recur, they become generalized and begin to organize the infant's experience. What will be represented, at the presymbolic level, is the dynamic interactive process itself, the reciprocal interplay, as each partner influences the other from moment to moment. These are interactive or dyadic representations. It is the infant's experience of the dyad that is represented.

Although self and object are richly conceptualized in psychoanalysis, the dyad is not. The concepts of self and object, as individual, discrete, static entities, do not capture the dynamic nature of the relatedness generated by the dyad (see Modell, 1984, 1992). We therefore need a theory of the dyad as a system within which the relationship of self to object can be conceptualized. A number of philosophers have shown remarkable agreement in describing how interactions are organized dyadically: Mead (1934), Lashley (1951), Habermas (1979), and Bruner (1977), respectively, refer to a system of mutuality, a system of reciprocal relationships, mutual recognition, and a shared set of rules (see also Tronick, 1980). The research we describe here actually documents in detail how such a dyadic process works.

As we suggested in chapter 2, the organization of behavior in infancy should be viewed primarily as the property of the mother–infant system rather than as the property of the individual (see Weiss, 1973; Sander, 1977, 1983, 1985). It is the dyad, rather than the individual, that is the unit of organization. Nevertheless, the individuals are the components of the system. Thus the system is defined by both self-regulation and interactive-regulation processes (see also Hofer, 1987).

The argument that early interactions organize experience is based on the position that continuity in development is at the level of generalized relationship patterns (Zeanah et al., 1989). Continuity is not based on a linear model of development (see Reese and Overton, 1970). Instead we use a transformational model in which there are continuous transformations and restructurings. As Sameroff (Sameroff, 1983; Sameroff and Chandler, 1976) has argued, development is in a constant state of active reorganization. Furthermore, as Sameroff has argued, it is not possible to predict from the child alone or from the environment alone. Prediction is possible only from the transactions *between* the child and the environment, and their regular restructurings. We assume that there will be many transformations and restructurings of relationship patterns after the first year.

The Presymbolic Representation of Interaction Patterns

How does an interaction pattern get represented? On what capacities is a presymbolic representational capacity based? In the last decade, research on infant perception and memory has radically changed our concepts of representation. Whereas in the past, representational and symbolic capacities were traditionally equated, researchers have now documented experimentally that some kind of rudimentary representational capacity, not yet symbolic, appears in the second month of life. This research demands a different way of thinking about representation. In this view, symbol formation occurs as a later development in a system that already possesses a rudimentary representational capacity.

We now turn to a description of the evidence for this presymbolic representational capacity in the early months of life. We will suggest that, prior to the development of symbolic capacities, the infant is able to represent expected, characteristic interaction patterns, including their distinctive temporal, spatial, affective, and associated arousal features. Toward the end of the first year, representations of expected interaction patterns are abstracted into generalized prototypes. These generalized prototypes become the basis for later symbolic forms of self- and object representations. The dynamic, mutually regulated interplay between infant and caretaker creates a wide variety of potential patterns of interaction from which prototypes are abstracted (see Beebe and Stern, 1977; Stern, 1977, 1985).

Underlying the work on presymbolic representation is an information-processing model of motivation. The infant brings primary endogenous activity and his or her own intrinsic motivation to process and order information. Play, curiosity, and exploration are as decisive as the need to reduce hunger, pain, or fatigue. The nature of the information itself—its novelty, complexity, match, incongruity, or surprise—provides an intrinsic motivation for behavior (Piaget, 1954; Hunt, 1965; Berlyne, 1966). Emde (1988, p. 20) quotes Haith (1980), who suggests that "the infant is biologically prepared to engage in visual activity in order to stimulate its own brain" and is "self-motivated to detect regularity, to generate expectancies, and to act on these expectancies."

Discrimination Between Mother and Stranger

Babies are primed to respond to people. In the first 15 hours an infant can distinguish its mother's voice and prefer it to a stranger's voice (DeCasper and Fifer, 1980), prefer its mother's smell to a stranger's smell (MacFarlane, 1975), and prefer its mother's face to a stranger's face (Field et al., 1982). "Preference" in these studies refers to a statistically significant bias in pattern of response.

Learning in Utero

Learning occurs in utero. DeCasper and Spence (1986) studied pregnant women during the last trimester. These women read a Dr. Seuss book, *The Cat in the Hat,* aloud to their fetuses, accumulating 15 hours of reading. At birth the babies preferred a tape recording of the mother reading the story heard in utero to hearing her read another Dr. Seuss story, *The King, the Mice, and the Men.* Infants exposed to their mothers' voices over the course of the pregnancy are able at birth to distinguish slight differences in rhythmicity, intonation, frequency variation, and phonetic components of speech (DeCasper and Fifer, 1980).

Auditory Discrimination of "Self"

Martin and Clark (1982) demonstrated that in the first day of life a neonate recognizes his or her own vocalizations and discriminates between them and those of other infants. When a calm baby hears a tape recording of his or her own cry, the infant vocalizes less, whereas the infant vocalizes more when hearing the cry of another infant; a crying baby hearing his or her own cry cries less, whereas the baby cries more when he or she hears the cry of another infant. This work has been interpreted as evidence for an auditory specification of "self" from birth (Butterworth, 1990) in the sense that, at a presymbolic level, the infant discriminates between his or her own sounds and those of the environment and that there is no original perceptual confusion between organism and environment. (For a further discussion of the discrimination between self and environment, see Bahrick and Watson, 1985; Stern, 1985.)

Contingency Perception and the Creation of Expectancies

A series of experiments by DeCasper and Carstens (1980) showed that an infant's attention, memory, and very capacity to learn are affected by whether or not the environment provides contingent and expectable stimulation. First, an infant's baseline sucking rhythm was assessed. Then the infant was taught that, by lengthening or shortening the pauses between his sucks, he could turn on music. The music's playing was contingent on the infant's alteration of his or her sucking rhythm. The only way an infant could possibly learn to do this is with the ability to time the duration of these pauses.

In another phase of this experiment the researchers played a dirty trick on the infants. After the infants had learned to lengthen or shorten their pauses, the music was stopped. The infants fussed, whimpered, and grimaced—and some of them stopped sucking altogether. They had learned to expect a certain contingency between their own behavior and the environment's response, and the violation of this expectancy produced negative affect.

Haith, Hazan, and Goodman (1988) present evidence that three- to four-month-old infants develop visual expectations rapidly and tend to organize their behavior on the basis of these expectations. One of the infant's eyes was videotaped as he watched a series of slides of checkerboards, bull's eyes, and schematic faces. Two series were shown, one regularly alternating to the left and right of visual center and the other appearing randomly in time and in left or right spatial position. The infants detected the spatiotemporal rule that governed the appearance of the regularly alternating series, developed expectations for the impending event in the series, and used these expectations for adaptive action. They manifested this detection through anticipatory eye movements and enhanced reaction times to the slide onsets.

Haith and colleagues concluded that

> as early as 3.5 months of age, the baby can create an action-based perceptual model of the situation he or she confronts, can generate short-term expectations from this model, and can support action. . . . This modeling, expectation, and action sequence serves to maintain continuity in an ever-changing perceptual world . . . infants are motivated to detect regularities in dynamic events and to develop expectations partly in order to bring their behavior under self-control . . . these findings suggest a natural motivation in babies at a very early age to control their own perceptual activity [p. 477].

In summary, infants detect contingencies between what they do and what the environment does immediately following their actions. This contingency facilitates the development of a sense of agency or effectance. Infants develop expectancies about when events will occur and, as in the sucking experiment, about whether the environment will respond. Infants can use this ability to develop expectancies about how social interactions will go (see Beebe and Stern, 1977; Stern, 1985; Watson, 1985; Beebe and Lachmann, 1988). These expectancies are crucial links to the organization of early representations.

Memory

Infants have extraordinary memory capacities. The Rovee-Collier group at Rutgers used a paradigm in which a ribbon was tied to a baby's ankle and connected to a mobile; the baby learned that if he kicked his feet, the mobile would move. Infants as young as two months could remember in detail exactly what objects were in the mobile, and could detect changes after a 24-hour delay (Fagen et al., 1984; Hayne et al., 1986; Greco et al., 1986).

If infants as young as two to three months can encode and remember the specific details of the mobile for 24 hours, this finding challenges the conventional view of infant memory: that not until approximately 8 to 12 months can an infant remember an earlier experience and compare it with a discrepant event in the immediate perceptual field (see Kagan, 1978, 1979; Mast et al., 1980, Hayne et al., 1986). Hayne and colleagues (1986) and Mast and colleagues (1980) argue that infants as young as three months can maintain a fairly detailed representation of the mobile and that the representation can influence an infant's behavior for 24 hours.

Memory and Affect

A remarkable experiment from this group (Singer and Fagen, 1992) shows that a two-month-old infant's affect at the time of learning influences its memory. Using the same paradigm, the researchers first taught babies to kick in order to move a 10-item mobile. When a two-item mobile was substituted, half the babies cried. One week later, the infants who had cried did not remember the mobile well enough to kick to get it moving. The infants who did not cry, however, remembered for up to three weeks that if they kicked, they moved the mobile. For the infants who cried, the intense negative affect at the moment of learning seemed to interfere with memory.

The Rovee-Collier group also gave these babies a "reminder cue": they simply showed the infants the mobile and moved it, but not contingently. Those babies who had cried and did not remember the mobile three weeks later, did remember it once they were given the reminder cue. The researchers concluded that the problem for these babies was not the storage of memory but its retrieval. The heightened negative affect at the moment of learning interfered with access to the memory. Memories are viewed by these researchers as permanent. Instead of asking what is remembered, they are asking under what conditions retrieval is possible, and what conditions interfere with retrieval (Singer and Fagen, 1992). This point of view fits recent neurophysiological evidence reviewed by Hadley (1983, 1989), which suggests that everything is stored and that the question of interest is the conditions of retrieval. This point of view also fits Bloom's (1993) position that language acquistion proceeds optimally under "cool" rather than "hot" affect conditions.

Singer and Fagen (1992) concluded that a young infant's memory is more elaborate than we previously believed. An infant's own emotional state is part of its memory. This work points to an interactive view of the organization of memory, which sees the nature of the organism's state as interacting with the organism's capacity to remember the environment. Thus affect may powerfully influence the nature of early memory development. This research is relevant to questions of amnesia, dissociation, and memories of trauma. Events occurring under conditions of heightened negative affect may be stored but not easily retrieved, unless the retrieval cues are very specific (see chapter 7 for a discussion of the organizing impact of heightened affect).

The Perception of Time, Space, Affect, and Arousal

Time, space, affect, and arousal are salient features of the infant's perception. They are the dimensions through which social interactions are represented by the infant.

Time. Infants are born with the capacity to perceive time (Lewkowicz, 1989). They can estimate durations of seconds and fractions of seconds. At two months, infants distinguish differences in duration of 25 milliseconds (Jusczyk, 1985). Infants time their own behavior as well as environmental stimuli (DeCasper and Fifer, 1980). Infants have a remarkable capacity to perceive temporal sequences, to detect contingencies, and to develop expectancies of when events will occur (Lewis and Goldberg, 1969; Allen et al., 1977; Finkelstein and Ramey, 1977). Our study of the interpersonal timing of mother–infant vocal dialogue (described later) rests on the perceptual ability of the infant to time the duration of his or her own and the partner's behavior.

Space. Infants have remarkable spatial perception from birth. Neonatal auditory-visual coordination permits the localization of a sound in visual space. In response to a stimulus looming into the infant's face on a collision course, the infant will duck the head and put his or her hands up in a defensive reflex (Bower, Broughton, and Moore, 1970).

Experimental studies of posture and balance in two-month-old infants seated in a room where the walls slowly approached or receded. The infants compensated for a nonexistent loss of balance with postural and head movements. The optic flow pattern has prestructured proprioceptive information about the relationship of the infant's own motion to the environment (Gibson, 1966; Butterworth, 1990).

Mandler (1988, 1991) reviewed the experimental evidence demonstrating that three- to four-month-old infants understand that objects are permanent, continue to exist when hidden, and are solid—that is, two objects cannot inhabit the same space. Three-month-old infants distinguish between objects that engage in "biological" motion and those which do not. In these experiments the infants distinguished between two cartoons of moving dots, one conveying human movement patterns and the other conveying mechanical movement. At four months, the infants recognized the spatial trajectories of objects and their causal relations. They categorized differences in primitive agency, discriminating between the trajectory of an object moving on its own and one in which one object causes the other to move.

Mandler argues that infants form image-schemes of the trajectories of objects and their interactions in space. She suggests that an infant's prelinguistic understanding of objects and events includes a simplified spatial structure of objects, their animate or inanimate category, and their trajectories in space, both caused and uncaused. As we describe later in the illustration of a derailed interaction (chase and dodge), this capacity to form schemes of the trajectories of objects and their interactions in space is the perceptual underpinning of our finding of complex and rapid approach–avoidance spatial patterns.

Facial Affect. Infant expression and perception of facial affect are also remarkably sophisticated. At seven months in utero, facial innervation is almost fully myelinated (Oster, 1978). At birth, infants make nearly all the facial-muscle movements of adults, although the full display of expressions is not available until infants are three to four months old. The presence at six months of the basic emotions of interest, joy, disgust, surprise, distress, sadness, and anger has been demonstrated in infants cross-culturally (Izard, 1979; Ekman, 1983).

An infant's perception of the partner's facial affect is sufficiently accurate that the emotional state of the partner is of fundamental importance to the infant's own emotional state (Tronick, 1989). Neonates discriminate among surprise, fear, and sadness expressions in an adult model; they express this discrimination through corresponding expressions of their own. The correspondence is sufficiently good that an observer can guess which facial expression of a model the infant is looking at (Meltzoff and Moore, 1977; Field et al., 1982). Infants look longer at an adult's joy face than at an anger face. If the mother displays an anger face, the infant does too (Field et al., 1982; Malatesta et al., 1989).

By ten months, infants actively seek out affective information from the partner to help them to interpret the environment. In the visual cliff experiment (Sorce and Emde, 1981; Klinnert et al., 1986) infants were tempted to cross a glass table by an interesting object at the other end, although it looked as if the children would fall off a "cliff." If the mother displayed a fear face, the child would not cross; if the mother displayed a smile face, the child would cross the visual cliff.

Davidson and Fox (1982) have shown, by patterns of EEG activation, that by 10 months, the brain is lateralized for positive and negative affect. If an infant is shown a videotape of a smiling-laughing actress, the pattern of EEG activation is one of positive affect;

if the infant is shown a distressed, crying actress, the pattern of EEG activation is one of negative affect. The infant cannot escape the emotion of the partner as reflected on the partner's face.

Vocal Affect. Affect is also perceived by infants through such features as melodic contour and pitch. In a series of cross-cultural studies, Fernald (1985; Fernald and Kuhl, 1987) showed that infants in the first six months of life discriminate "positive" (rising pitch) from "negative" (falling pitch) contours, orienting toward the positive and orienting away from the negative. Stern (1985) had similar findings.

Arousal. Gardner and Karmel (1984) showed that level of arousal affects information processing in neonates. If neonates are in a state of low arousal (swaddled and fed), they look longer as the temporal frequency of flashing lights increases. In a state of high arousal (unswaddled, unfed), they look less as the frequency increases. Thus infants seek to maintain an optimal level of arousal (see also Hadley, 1989). Self-regulatory arousal processes interact with the infant's processing of the environment.

Field (1981) has shown that, during a face-to-face social interaction, infants use a brief visual disengagement from the mother to regulate their level of arousal as measured by heart rate. Five seconds before the infant looks away, heart rate shoots up from baseline, indicating a "protective" response, or decreased information-processing. Five seconds after the infant looks away, heart rate returns to baseline, indicating a "facilitative" response, or increased information processing. Shortly thereafter the infant returns to looking at the mother. Field and colleagues (1988) have also shown that, by six months, infants of depressed mothers have elevated heart rates and cortisol levels. These infants seem to be in a heightened arousal distress state. These studies indicate that level of infant arousal varies systematically with social interactive conditions and information processing.

Feature Detection and Schema Formation

Babies detect features of stimulation—for example, color, brightness, shape, and pattern—and specific features of speech. Infants detect similarities and differences between patterns (Fantz, Fagan, and Miranda, 1975; Bornstein, 1979, 1985; Eimas, 1985; Kuhl, 1985; Mehler and Fox, 1995). At three months, after seeing an event only twice, infants can determine whether it is likely to recur, generating rules that govern their expectances (Fagen et al., 1984). These rules are based on their determination that a pattern is the same or different. At five months, infants recognize a photograph of a face after a two-week delay (Cohen and Gelber, 1975). Infants watch a stimulus, create models of distinctive features of the stimulus, store these models, and compare a later version of the stimulus with the model (Fagen, 1974; Cohen and Gelber, 1975; Bornstein, 1979, 1985; Meltzoff, 1985). We assume that the same kinds of models or schemas that the baby generates for inanimate stimulation will be generated for the human partner as well.

This process of schema or model formation is so fundamental that it is possible to predict verbal intelligence at two to five years from an infant's capacity for schema formation at three to five months (Bornstein, 1985). Presumably the infant's ability to form schemas emerges from an interaction between innate endowment and environmental receptivity. In Bornstein's experiment, infants were given auditory and visual stimuli over and over. When they stopped attending to stimuli, they were said to have habituated, habituation being an index of schema formation. When infants were shown a new stimulus, they looked more at the novel than at the familiar, indicating that they recognized what was new and could compare it with their memory of the familiar. An infant's speed of habituation—that is, how rapidly he or she constructs a schema of the stimulus—predicts verbal intelligence at ages two to five. The ability to form a schema is an index of a primitive capacity to categorize and create representations, and it predicts developmental outcomes. Bornstein suggests that this representational capacity provides an underlying process through which certain continuities in development can be perceived.

Cross-Modal Perception

Infants also have remarkable cross-modal perception. They can translate a rhythm expressed in light flashes into a rhythm expressed in auditory beeps (Lewkowicz and Turkewitz, 1980). In a frequently cited experiment (Meltzoff and Borton, 1979), two small rubber balls were used, identical except that one had small nubs protruding from it. The infant was blindfolded and one of the balls placed in the infant's mouth. When the blindfold was removed and the infant was shown the two balls, he preferred to look at the one he had had in his mouth. He was translating information from his tongue, that is, whether the ball was nubbed or smooth, into visual information. Cross-modal perception allows the infant to abstract a pattern from different modalities and thus promotes a constancy of the object at a perceptual level (Bornstein, 1985).

Presymbolic Categorization

Finally, a variety of presymbolic categorization processes are now well documented (Strauss, 1979; Bornstein, 1985; Younger and Cohen, 1985; Mandler, 1988, 1991; Stern, 1985; Younger and Gottlieb, 1988). Categorization is inferred when an infant can treat discriminable entities as similar. A category is formed as the infant perceives regularities and forms an average, or "prototype," from these regularities. Category formation facilitates perception, memory, and information processing by reducing variation and supplying organizing principles (Bornstein, 1985). The capacity to abstract what is common among perceptually discriminable entities, and to generalize on the basis of that abstraction, also makes possible a rudimentary form of representation. The ability to categorize in a very rudimentary way provides the beginning of a framework for language and symbol formation. Shields and Rovee-Collier (1992) suggest that infant categorization "is ubiquitous across ages and should not be regarded as an emergent, higher-order cognitive ability. Rather, it appears to be a natural by-product of the normal, ongoing process of memory encoding and retrieval" (p. 257).

It is helpful to differentiate three levels of category formation (Bornstein, 1985). At the sensory level, the common attribute of the category is some concrete sensorimotor feature such as shape, size, or color. At the conceptual level, the common attribute of the category is more abstract, such as a spatial relationship or gender, but nevertheless remains tied to concrete sensory-motor information. By six months, for example, infants classify faces by gender (Lewis and Brooks, 1975). At the linguistic level, the common feature of the category is the symbol, and here a far greater level of abstraction may obtain, such as truth or beauty. Only the first two levels of category formation occur in the first year.

The evidence for categorization forms the basis of Stern's (1985) concept of the RIG (Representation of an Interaction Generalized). This category allows the baby to generalize on the basis of some perceptual or conceptual feature of the interaction. Stern's argument, and our own, is that expectancies about how interactions typically proceed are summarized into categories toward the end of the infant's first year.

Expectancies about how interactions proceed can be seen as organized by three salient principles. The most basic principle is that expectancies are organized by how interactions typically proceed, which we term "ongoing regulations." In chapter 7 we add "disruption and repair" and "heightened affective moments" as further principles that also organize expectancies about interactions.

Presymbolic Representation

Thus a remarkable set of presymbolic representational capacities exists in an infant's first year. The infant perceives features, can translate cross-modally, can detect whether or not the partner is acting contingently, and can tell whether behavior patterns are similar or different. The infant develops expectancies of these patterns, remembers them, and categorizes them. These expectations are organized through time, space, affect, and arousal. This is the equipment the baby uses to develop presymbolic representations of characteristic interactions.

Toward the end of the first year, the infant's representations of expected interactions are abstracted into generalized prototypes, which become the basis for the infant's symbolic forms of self- and object representations. Following Piaget (1937), experiences of the first year will be radically transformed with the onset of symbolic thought, which begins at approximately 9 to 12 months, undergoes major reorganization at 16 to 18 months, and is constituted by approximately 36 months. By using symbols, the child can refer to an object in a way that is "arbitrary," that is, not defined by its physical features. The child is now capable of imitating a model that is not physically present. With the ability to symbolize relationships between objects, the child can perceive himself as an objective entity (Kagen, 1979; McCall, 1979; Sroufe, 1979a). This stage is the culmination of the process of constructing self- and object representations in the first three years of life. This process continues in significant ways throughout life.

Bucci (1985), in her dual-code theory of representation, argues that there are two parallel systems of representation, verbal and nonverbal, and that both develop symbolic capacities. In the verbal mode of representation, we store information in linguistic form; in the nonverbal mode, we store information through such perceptual modes as image, sound, and smell. An architect or an artist, for example, may have a highly elaborated nonverbal symbolic representational capacity. We assume that the representations the infant is organizing will become symbolic primarily through the nonverbal representation system. We do not necessarily assume that they will ever be translated into the verbal representation system. In fact, Bucci suggests that one task of adult psychoanalysis is translation between the verbal and nonverbal representation systems. We concur with Zelnick and Buchholz (1990) and Modell (1992) that these early interaction structures at the presymbolic level will later constitute largely unconscious organizing structures or memory structures in the child or adult. Our use of the term unconscious is similar to that of Stolorow's (Atwood and Stolorow, 1984; Stolorow and Atwood, 1992) "prereflective" rather than "dynamic" unconscious.

Evidence for Presymbolic Organization of Social Interactions in the First Year

How do we know that the infant capacities investigated under experimental laboratory conditions are actually used by infants in their ongoing social interactions? The experimental perception literature and the naturalistic social interaction literature remain divided in infant research. To some degree this is a necessary state of affairs, because the very control of variables that makes possible the experimental study of perception would destroy the phenomena observed in the naturalistic study of interaction. It therefore remains largely a *hypothesis* that the perceptual capacities demonstrated in the laboratory also operate in the natural social interaction. Nevertheless, it is an excellent hypothesis, for two reasons. First, social stimuli are far more salient, redundant, and capable of generating meaningful, consistent, and contingent feedback than are variables manipulated in the laboratory. Therefore social stimuli should elicit the use of the infant's most *advanced* perceptual capacities. Brazelton and colleagues (1975) and Tronick (1982) have made just this point in describing the face-to-face situation. Second, various kinds of evidence that speak to this hypothesis have begun to accrue.

There is now both experimental and naturalistic evidence that the kinds of perceptual capacity demonstrated in the laboratory setting are operative in the social setting as well. The sources of this evidence include: (1) organized behavior patterns, which can be shown to repeat from session to session, across multiple sessions around one point in time, and across home and lab settings; (2) infants of depressed mothers, who generalize the aberrant pattern of interaction with the mother to a nondepressed unfamiliar adult; (3) the pattern of EEG activation in infants of depressed mothers, which is different from that of normals; (4) on the basis of Tronick's and colleagues' (1978) still-face paradigm, in which the mother becomes still-faced, infants expect a normally responsive partner, remember the still-face manipulation, and their method of coping with the still-face violation predicts the security of their attachments; (5) longitudinal evidence that (a) at one and two years infants can remember an unusual single event that occurred at six months; (b) interaction patterns in an infant's first six months of life predict social and cognitive outcomes at years one and two; and (c) case histories from child and adult treatments detail the effects of events in the first year of life that are registered, organize subsequent experience, and powerfully shape later symbolic and bodily experiences.

Evidence that organized patterns of behavior repeat comes from Stern (1974; Stern et al., 1975) and Zelner (1982), who showed session-to-session consistency for six mother–infant pairs filmed up to a dozen times across a one-month period. Weinberg (1991) also showed session-to-session stability from six to six-and-a-half months in measurements of infant facial affects, looking patterns, and gestures.

Field et al. (1988) showed that by six months infants of depressed mothers show "depressed" behavior with a nondepressed, optimally attuned novel female adult. One possible understanding of these results is that the aberrant pattern with the depressed mother, including massive protest and disengagement, is sufficiently organized that the infant expects similar interactions with the stranger and thus behaves similarly.

Dawson (1992a, b) has shown that by 10 months infants' brains reflect maternal depression, and from the work of Davidson and Fox (1982) we know that the left and right frontal lobes are specialized for positive and negative affect respectively. In Dawson's data, the same event that activates a positive-affect behavior and EEG pattern in normal infants (mother playing peek-a-boo) elicits negative behavior and EEG pattern of activation in infants of depressed mothers. The reverse is also true. Thus by ten months the emotional responsivity of infants of depressed mothers is already organized differently from that of normal infants.

In Tronick's (Tronick et al., 1978) still-face paradigm, following two minutes of naturalistic play, mothers were instructed to face their infants for two minutes without moving their face or vocalizing. Smiling and cooing, the infants made repeated efforts to greet their mothers, showed surprise expressions when she failed to respond; and cycled through disengagement and repeated efforts to elicit a response. Murray (1991; Murray and Trevarthen, 1985) has shown a similar pattern of infant attempts to elicit a maternal response, and similar distressed disengagement, in the "violation of contingency" experiment. In this experiment, an infant was shown a videotape of his mother responding to him in an interaction that had taken place *several minutes earlier*, so that the video mother was not at all contingently responsive to his present behavior. These experiments demonstrate infants' expectation of a contingently responsive partner and their distress when this expectation is violated.

Tronick (1989) has shown that the effects of the still-face experiment persist for several minutes after the mother's resumption of
normal play. The infant shows a negative mood and avoids looking
at the mother. Tronick concludes: "This finding suggests that even
three-month-old infants are not simply under the control of the
immediate stimulus situation, but that events have lasting effects,
e.g., are internally represented" (p. 114).

Cohn, Campbell, and Ross (1991) have shown that by six
months an infant's style of coping with the still-face situation has
become characteristic, or stable, and that it predicts the infant's
attachment status at one year. If by using positive behaviors such as
smiling and cooing the infant attempts to elicit a response from the
mother, the infant's attachment status is likely to be secure at one
year. The absence of such positive soliciting behavior predicts anxious attachment. Thus the stress of the still-face indexes the relationship history and provides a way of assessing the infant's "working
model" or "representation" of what he or she expects will work to
engage the mother. Positive soliciting demonstrates the infant's
expectation that his own positive behavior will succeed in engaging her.

Longitudinal evidence that memory of an unusual event at six
months (reaching in the dark for a rattle) persists in the second year
has been presented by Perris, Myers, and Clifton (1990). Jaffe and
colleagues (2001) have longitudinal evidence that patterns of
mother–infant vocal rhythm coordination at four months predict
attachment and cognition at one year. Longitudinal evidence that
social interactions in the first six months predict social and cognitive outcomes in the second and third years now constitutes a siz-
able literature (see, for example, Bakeman and Brown, 1977;
Ainsworth et al., 1978; Cohen and Beckwith, 1979; Martin, 1981;
Crockenberg, 1983; Lewis et al., 1984; Bretherton, 1985; Malatesta
et al., 1989; Isabella and Belsky, 1991; Lester and Seifer, 1990).

Finally, numerous case histories of child and adult treatments
document the continuing effects of events in the first year (Bernstein
and Blacher, 1967; Herzog, 1983; Casement, 1990). For example,
Casement describes an adult treatment case in which the patient

was preoccupied by having been severely burned at 11 months. This traumatic event was a major organizing theme in the adult analysis.

These sources of evidence provide a basis from which to infer that organization accrues across the first year. We define organization as relatively persistent patterns or classifications of information. These patterns are formed by the active process of constructing or reconstructing incoming information. The work on normal mother–infant pairs documenting the repetition of organized patterns of behavior, and the work on depressed mothers and their infants showing that disturbed interaction patterns generalize, yield data that satisfy the criteria for relatively persistent organized patterns. That there is a considerable degree of stability of interactive behavior by six months points to a strong early organizing process through which the infant's ways of relating are becoming stable and characteristic. The neurophysiological evidence that by 10 months the brains of infants of depressed mothers are organized differently from those of normals, and the various studies showing prediction of later outcomes from early interactions demonstrate that experience is being organized with discernibly differing consequences across the first year of life. On the basis of these sources of evidence, together with the work on early perceptual and cognitive capacities, we argue that early interaction patterns, when repetitive and characteristic, will organize evolving presymbolic representations over the first year. Nevertheless, we reiterate that these early interaction patterns will be subject to many transformations and reorganizations after the first year.

The Importance of Presymbolic Representation
for Psychoanalysis

Presymbolic representation has been seen in psychoanalysis chiefly as a "preamble" to symbolic representation. It was originally important as the putative beginning of primary processes, as contrasted to secondary processes. In more recent decades it was the putative source of autistic and symbiotic processes, or prototaxic distortions—longings and anxieties—difficult to translate into verbal and symbolic representation. But these formulations, whatever their clinical usefulness, distinguish this stage as a preamble to the ego or to the symbolic and verbal modes of processing. This way of thinking no longer obtains. In contrast, the early capacities reviewed in this chapter show that the infant begins life with an extraordinary organization. Through complex social and nonsocial interactions, as early as three to four months the infant rapidly generates a rich, discriminated set of experiences that come to be remembered and expected: presymbolically represented. Once we grasp these extraordinary early infant capacities, we see the first year, even the first half-year, as a period with its own inherent organization and importance, rather than as a preamble. This research is entirely consistent with, and greatly elaborates, Rapaport's (1960) claim that in early infancy the "ego" is already on board, attending to the organization of the environment, and learning the organization of the interactive process. In this sense, the bedrock of the person is not a chaotic "id" but an ongoing capacity for self-organization in the context of the interactive field. Although transformed in various ways, these same capacities continue to operate across the life span, and in the consulting room, usually out of awareness. They may be detected in the form of unconscious memories, enactments, or patterns of nonverbal interaction.

In the next chapter we go on to describe patterns of interactive regulation during face-to-face social play in the early months of life. Using the experimental research presented in this chapter, we argue that patterns of interactive regulation do become represented by the infant in a presymbolic format. This integration of the perceptual and cognitive capacities for presymbolic representation with the descriptions of early interaction patterns will lead to our view of the origins of self- and object representations.

5

PATTERNS OF EARLY INTERACTIVE REGULATION AND THE PRESYMBOLIC ORIGINS OF SELF- AND OBJECT REPRESENTATIONS

Chapter 4 was concerned with presymbolic representation. We surveyed research on the perceptual and cognitive capacities of the infant and how these capacities become organized in terms of expectancies, memories, and ultimately presymbolic representations of interaction patterns. In this chapter, addressing a different domain of infant research on face-to-face play, we describe the exact nature of the interaction patterns between mother and infant. A salient feature of this research is the very careful "microanalysis" of sequences of behaviors from videotape and film. This work allows us to see how astonishingly subtle, complex, and rapid these early patterns of relatedness are. Presymbolic representational capacities are used to "code" or schematize these interactive patterns, yielding initial presymbolic trajectories of self- and object representations. In the chapters that follow we will return to the clinical arena and spell out the implications of the data presented here.

At three to four months there is a flowering of the infant's social capacity. The infant's repertoire of interactive capacities is most clearly seen at this age during face-to-face play, where the only goals are mutual attention and delight (Brazelton, Koslowski, and Main, 1974; Stern, 1977). This situation elicits the infant's strongest communicative skill (Brazelton et al., 1975). Furthermore, the patterns of regulation of this face-to-face exchange in the first six months predict cognitive and social development at one year (Martin, 1981; Roe, McClure, and Roe, 1982; Belsky, Rovine, and Taylor, 1984; Malatesta et al., 1989; Feldman, 1997). It is this face-to-face play paradigm that is used in the empirical studies we describe here.

An infant's interactive capacity in face-to-face play is predicated on a visual system that is highly functional at birth and by approximately three months achieves adult maturational status (Cohen, DeLoache, and Strauss, 1979). The capability for sustained mutual visual regard is present by approximately the second month. It is a fundamental paradigm of communication that is central to the developing relationship between mother and infant (Stern, 1977) and continues throughout life (Robson, 1967). Moreover, as Stern (1971, 1977) documented, mothers tend to gaze steadily; it is the infant who "makes" and "breaks" the visual contact. Infants have control over looking, looking away, and closing the eyes, which allows the infant, by two to three months, a "subtle instant-by-instant regulation of social contact" (Stern, 1977, p. 502).

Normal mothers and infants at play were studied when the infants were three to four months old. They were seated face-to-face, with the infant in an infant seat, in an otherwise bare room. Videotape cameras were placed unobtrusively in the walls. Mothers were instructed to play with their infants as they would at home. Each mother and infant pair was then left alone to interact. Two cameras, one on each partner's face and torso, produced a split-screen view of the interaction. This research paradigm specifically examines only the purely social exchanges during periods of alert attention. Although most of the research concerns mothers and infants, sufficient research on fathers and infants suggests that our conclusions are generally applicable to fathers and infants as well (see, e.g., Lamb, 1981).

The Integration of Self- and Interactive Regulation in the Video Illustration of Baby Elliot

When viewing these videotaped split-screen interactions, we evaluate not only how mother and infant interact and affect each other (interactive regulation), but also how each regulates his or her own state of attention and arousal (self-regulation). It is critically important that interactive and self-regulation be viewed as a system. For example, the difficult temperament of a baby who cannot be easily soothed or aroused will affect the nature of the interactive regulation, and that baby will be a more difficult partner. Similarly, the nature of the interactive regulation can facilitate or interfere with self-regulatory capacity. When conceptualized as a system, self- and interactive regulation affect each other continuously (see Gianino and Tronick, 1988; Lichtenberg, 1989; Beebe and Lachmann, 1994).

The first interaction to be described shows a five-week-old infant, Elliott, who plays with three partners in succession. There is no timeout when the partners change, and each interaction lasts approximately two minutes. With each partner, the infant has a very different self-regulatory ability, and a very different interaction is generated by each dyad.

As the video starts, the mother is a little tentative, a little flat-faced, perhaps slightly depressed. Elliott is slightly fussy, not making eye contact. The mother has no vocal prattle or facial play; instead she jiggles Elliott in a rapid rhythm. Such a rapid rhythm is somewhat unusual and, to the observer, feels aversive. Elliott is distressed, and the mother has a very restricted repertoire with which to engage him. At five weeks, Elliott is having a normal range of self-regulatory difficulty in the face-to-face play situation. Eventually the mother hits upon the strategy of singing him "Happy Birthday," which facilitates his self-regulation. The moment she starts singing, the infant's eyes change from unfocused to alert and he makes eye contact. This is the first moment the mother has provided much structuring of her stimulation, and Elliott is very responsive to it. She seems, however, to have no other strategies and eventually sings "Happy Birthday" again. Now Elliot is less interested, and the mother cannot regain his engagement.

The second partner is a student who is being trained to play with babies. Her face is very animated, but she is not matching Elliott's affect. She has a wide, fully open smile and looks really happy, but the infant is not happy. Elliott looks sober, with slight frowns, so that this interaction does not work well either. The student then picks the infant up and provides a whole-body rhythm; she holds him a little more upright, which facilitates his self-regulation. There is a brief moment of mutual visual engagement, but the interaction then disintegrates and Elliott begins to cry.

I (Beebe), the last partner, begin by vocally matching the infant's cry rhythm. After a time, I slow it down and lower the volume, and Elliott calms right down with me (see Stern, 1985, for a similar description). It looks almost as if Elliott is hypnotized. He becomes alert and visually engaged. Then Elliott's arousal level goes too low, and he begins to look sleepy. It is now necessary to increase the stimulation. I provide more stimulation with my face but keep my vocal volume down. What is needed is a complex combination of soothing and arousing: The infant must be aroused enough not to go to sleep, but the stimulation must be slow enough not to over-stimulate him. At this point Elliott does almost go to sleep. I then change my strategy and begin a faster rhythm with my face, voice, and head—the volume remains low, but the pace picks up. Elliott remains visually engaged, and he becomes more alert, making small opening movements with his mouth.

This interaction illustrates the self-regulatory ability that the baby brings to such an interaction, the attunement of the partner, and the dyad's ability to make use of whatever abilities the infant brings. The infant's self-regulatory capacity and ability to engage in the interaction is very different with each of the three partners. The success of the interaction is an emergent dyadic phenomenon. There are similar considerations in adult treatment.

This interaction also illustrates Stern's (1983) concept of "state-transforming," that is, a transformation of the infant's state—in this case from fussy and overaroused to alert and ready to be engaged. Whether or not the pair can successfully and reliably achieve infant state transformations makes a crucial difference to the emerging organization of the infant's representations (see also Sander, 1977).

What is at stake at this early age is whether or not the infant develops an expectation that his or her arousal will stay within a comfortable range and whether or not the infant's arousal range will easily include sufficient alertness to engage with the partner. Whereas regulation of arousal and alertness is a salient issue for infants of Elliot's age in the first two months, this issue is in the background by four months, the age of the infants in the studies that follow.

The Statistical Analysis of Bidirectional Regulation

The studies to be discussed are based in time-series analysis (Gottman, 1981), a statistical strategy for assessing bidirectional regulation, that is, whether each partner's behavior affects that of the other. A theory of interactive behavior must take into account how the person is affected by his or her own behavior, which can be conceptualized as one aspect of self-regulation (Thomas and Martin, 1976). This dimension assesses the degree of predictability of each person's own behavior and in time-series analysis is termed autocorrelation. A theory of interactive behavior must also take into account how each person is affected by the partner's behavior, termed interactive regulation (Thomas and Martin, 1976). In the attempt to determine whether regulation is actually bidirectional, the usual correlational methods can show only that the two streams of behavior vary together, go up and down together, but not who affects whom. Two streams of behavior that look highly correlated may be similar only as an artifact of strong self-regulation in both people (Gottman and Ringland, 1981). For example, if both people have a very strong and similar rhythm, so that the tempo and beat of each is roughly the same, they will seem highly correlated whether or not they actually have anything to do with one another. Recent applications of time-series analysis circumvent this problem.

The analysis first determines the regularity and predictability of each partner's own behavior (autocorrelation). Autocorrelation is then "controlled for" in each partner, so that its influence is removed from the analysis. Through standard multiple regression techniques, the analysis asks, for example, if, over and above the predictability in the mother herself (autocorrelation), there is any further variation in her behavior that is predicted by the infant's behavior (crosscorrelation). The same analysis is performed for the infant. "Regulation" or "interactive contingency" is defined as the prediction of one partner's behavior from that of the other, across the entire behavioral stream; causality is not implied. Thus the time-series analysis provides separate assessments of the mother's affect on the infant (is the infant's behavior predictable from that of the mother?), and of the infant's affect on the mother (is the mother's behavior predictable from that of the infant?).

Time-series analysis requires that a series of behaviors be carefully recorded in sequence, in actual time. For example, imagine movements of the mouth, eyes, and head, which are the basis for the facial-mirroring analysis described next. These behaviors include mouth openings, eyebrow raises, shifts of head orientation, shifts in direction of gaze, smiles, frowns, grimaces, soberings, and so on. The record comprises two parallel sequences consisting of every mouth, eye, or head behavior of the mother and of the infant, timed in fractions of a second. These behaviors last approximately one-quarter to one-third of a second (Stern, 1971; Beebe and Stern, 1977; Beebe, 1982).

Facial Mirroring

Facial mirroring is eloquently described in the psychoanalytic literature, and infant research took the term from psychoanalysis. Winnicott (1967) has one of the most famous descriptions: "The precursor of the mirror is the mother's face. What does the infant see when he looks at his mother? He sees himself" (p. 131). This is the familiar concept that the mother reflects back, or matches, the infant's affect. Most of the psychoanalytic literature, and much infant research, also tends to conceptualize mirroring with a one-way-influence model in which it is the mother who does the reflecting.

Face-to-Face Engagement Scales. To study facial mirroring, Beebe and Gerstman (1980) developed an ordinal scale of degree of infant and mother facial-visual engagement. By three to four months, an extensive range of interpersonal affective display is present in the infant. By turning the videotapes into 16-mm film and viewing them in slow motion, fleeting and subtle interactions were revealed that often are not visible to the naked eye. Observations of infants sustaining or disrupting the face-to-face play encounter led to the development of an infant engagement scale describing the various ways

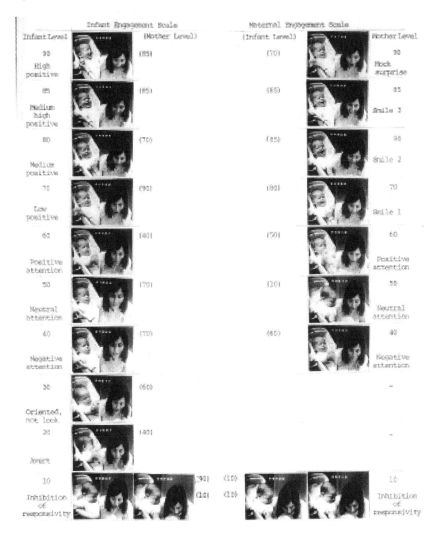

Figure 5. Photographic Illustrations of Infant and Maternal Engagement Scales. From Beebe and Gerstman (1980).

that infants combine their orientation to the mother, their visual attention to her, and subtle variations in their facial expressiveness (Beebe and Stern, 1977; Beebe and Gerstman, 1980). This scale was influenced by the concept that nuances of affective quality occur on a continuum of gradations, rather than only as discrete on-or-off categories (Marler, 1965; Tobach, 1970; Stern, 1981). Figure 5 illustrates two similar scales of increasing and decreasing affective engagement, one each for mother and infant. Although only the infant's scale is discussed in detail, the mother's scale operates in a similar fashion.

The scale is ordinalized by orientation, gaze, and facial expression. The scale shows to what extent the person is oriented toward the partner, whether the person is looking at the partner, and the person's facial expression. Consider first the upper half of the infant scale: at the neutral midpoint (50), the infant, oriented face-to-face with mother, visually engages her face, with neutral expressiveness. In the upward direction of increasing engagement, orientation and attention remain constant, and the scale is ordered by increasing fullness of display of mouth opening and mouth widening, which may be accompanied by thrusts of the head upward toward the mother and by positive vocalizations. At the highest level (90), termed the *gape smile*, the mouth is widened and opened to the utmost, with the head thrust forward, accompanied by prolonged visual regard—giving the impression of an exhilarating moment of delight (see Beebe, 1973).

The multidimensional nature of the infant's positive expressiveness, based on head movements and mouth opening and closing as well as increments in the smile display (mouth widening and narrowing), potentially provide the infant with a remarkable ability to communicate slight changes in intensity and quality of mood without necessarily changing orientation or visual regard (Beebe, 1973). The facial mirroring study described later primarily illustrates regulations in the upper half of the scale.

We now turn to the lower half of the infant scale, moving in the direction of decreasing engagement (or increasing compromises in engagement). Below the neutral midpoint (50), there is a loss of neutral expressiveness to "negative attention" (40), a constellation of oriented face-to-face, visually attentive to mother, but with a frown or grimace. The next level entails a loss of visual regard. although the infant remains oriented (30). This is followed by loss of face-to-face orientation as well and movement into "avert" (20), that is, head and gaze averted away from the mother. Finally, there is a loss of responsivity altogether, termed *inhibition of responsivity* (10), in that the infant maintains a limp, motionless headhang, regardless of mother's attempts at engagement. The derailment study described later primarily illustrates regulations in the lower half of the scale.

The facial-visual interactions of five mother–infant pairs when the infants were four months old were coded. Approximately four to five minutes of data per pair were analyzed (Kronen, 1982; Beebe and Kronen, 1988; Cohn and Beebe, 1990). Sections for analysis were chosen on the basis of the longest sustained period of infant gaze at mother. The 16mm film used contains 24 frames per second; the frames were numbered, and the onset and offset frame of each change of facial expression, gaze, and head orientation was identified (Stern, 1971; Beebe and Stern, 1977; Beebe and Gerstman, 1980; Kronen, 1982). We coded reliably to $1/12$ second. The duration of these behaviors is in the range of $1/4$ to $1/3$ to $1/2$ second (Stern, 1971, 1977; Beebe, 1982; Kronen, 1982). We used the engagement scales described earlier to index changes in intensity of affective engagement. The mothers changed engagement level once every $3/4$ second; the infants did so every $1\,1/4$ seconds. Time-series regression was used to evaluate facial contingencies.

Bidirectional Regulation of Facial Mirroring. In our study of facial mirroring using time-series analysis, we documented the existence of a robust bidirectional regulation process. Cohn and Tronick (1988) reported a similar finding. Thus, both mother and infant reflect each other's facial-visual changes. An example of a facial mirroring sequence is illustrated in Figure 6.

Does "Mirroring" Involve an Exact Match?

We asked what, precisely, is being matched and if the match is exact (as the mirror metaphor suggests). In fact, using our scale, we found a significant lack of exact matching. Instead, the partners are pri-

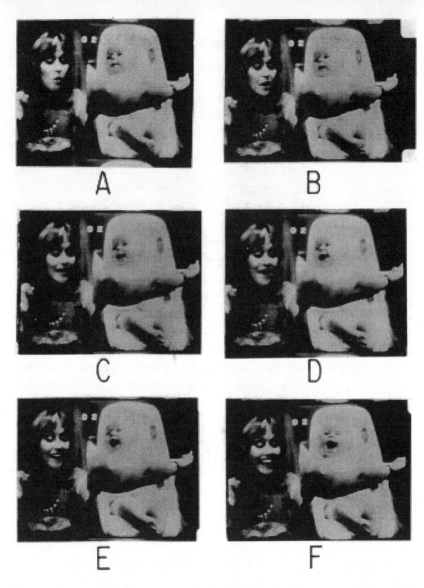

Figure 6. Photographic Illustrations of a "Facial Mirroring" Sequence. Mother and infant are seated face-to-face and are looking at each other. At point A, mother shows a "kiss-face," and infant's lips are partially drawn in, resulting in a tight, sober-faced expression. At point B, .54 seconds later, mother's mouth has widened into a slightly positive expression, and infant's face has relaxed with a hint of widening in the mouth, also a slightly positive expression. At point C, .79 seconds later, both mother and infant show a slight smile. At point D, .46 seconds later, both mother and infant further widen and open their smiles. Again, at point E, .46 seconds later, and F, .58 seconds later, both mother and infant further increase the smile display. Points E and F illustrate the infant's "gape-smile." At point F the infant has shifted the orientation of his head further to his left, and upward, which heightens the evocativeness of the gape-smile. Numbers at the top of the photographs indicate frames (24 frames = one second).

marily *moving in the same affective direction*, rising or falling together on the scale (Beebe and Kronen, 1988). Stern (1985) would call this "matching the gradient," and Werner (1948) would suggest that mother and infant are matching the "dynamic-vectorial quality" of behavior.

Rapidity of Facial Mirroring

We then asked how rapidly this facial mirroring happens (Cohn and Beebe, 1990; Beebe and Jaffe, 1992b). Stern (1971) proposed that mother and infant live in a split-second world where each partner responds to the other within fractions of a second. This hypothesis has not previously been readily testable because neither the appropriately fine-grained data nor the appropriate statistical methods were easily available.

To evaluate the rapidity of these bidirectional contingencies, Cohn and Beebe (1990) varied the sampling interval to see how fast it was necessary to sample in order to detect these facial contingencies. If, for example, we sampled the data once per second (the standard interval used in evaluating facial interactions coded from videotape), it would be impossible to find anything faster than one second. We used sampling intervals of one second, $1/2$, $1/4$, $1/6$, and $1/12$ second. We found no results when sampling at one second, the usual unit. Instead, the shortest sampling interval, $1/12$ second (which was also our limit of accuracy), was clearly the most powerful. For the mother, it picked up three times as many findings as did the next interval, $1/6$ second. For the infant, it picked up twice as many findings as did the $1/6$-second interval. Because our briefest event, both in duration and in onset-to-onset time, occupied four film frames ($4/24$ or $1/6$ second), the $1/12$-second sampling unit exactly satisfies the criterion of sampling data at least twice as fast as the fastest event to be studied.

At the $1/12$-second sampling interval, the findings are robustly bidirectional per dyad: the infant's behavior is predicted by the mother's and vice versa. Very fast sampling, therefore, seems to be necessary for the detection of this rapid facial-visual communication.

Our next question was, how fast does either partner respond to the other? We studied the contingency (coordination) structure of each dyad using the results of the $1/12$-second and $1/6$-second sampling intervals. We evaluated how many sampling intervals it is necessary to go back in order to detect coordination or interpersonal contingency. By counting how many intervals back the coordination remains significant, it is possible to determine how fast it is happening. Every infant and mother showed significant results at multiple intervals. In the evaluation of the fastest lag, three of the five infants responded within $1/3$ second. A fourth infant responded at $5/6$ second, and the fifth at $1 1/2$ seconds. Four of the five adults responded within $1/6$ second, and the fifth at $1 1/3$ seconds.

The findings in these five dyads are remarkably consistent both in the necessity of very frequent sampling to pick up the bidirectional effects and in the rapidity of response in both mother and infant. Bilateral contingency and rapid responsivity are probably general properties of the mother–infant communication system.

Facial Mirroring as the Creation of Anticipatory Facial-Visual Schemas

The mother is the faster partner, but both mother and infant participate in extremely rapid facial-visual exchanges. How can we explain the speed of these exchanges? We (Frank and Beatrice) suggest that this rapid responsivity cannot be based on stimulus-response, because it is too fast for visual reaction time. The time needed to receive and react to a single event is $1/3$ to $1/2$ second for an adult and $6/10$ to $8/10$ second for an infant (B. Karmel, personal communication, April 1992). Because the duration of the events we are discussing is approximately $1/4$ to $1/2$ second and the shortest lag times are $1/3$ and $1/6$ second for infant and mother respectively, many of the onset times are almost simultaneous. That is, before one partner's (extremely brief) behavior is completed, the other partner has already begun behaving.

These data fit Fogel's (1992a, b) continuous control model of co-regulated communication, in which each person's action is continuously modified by the simultaneously changing action of the partner. Haith's (1980; Haith et al., 1988) model of continuous visual anticipatory processing can help to explain this process. An infant at this age is capable of anticipatory processing of visual information, creating a continuous temporal and spatial prediction of a sequence. Thus the infant is responding to each behavior not only as a discrete event but also as an element of a predictable series.

This process has also been described by Stern (1977) as the creation of spatial-visual schemas that allow each partner to anticipate the sequence of the other person's actions in relation to his or her own. Explanation of these extremely rapid facial-visual responsivities leads to a conceptualization of the schemas that constitute these presymbolic representations and that eventually become the basis for more symbolic forms of self- and object representations.

Stern (1977) suggests that presymbolic representation can be defined as the expectancy of a temporal-spatial schema. He did a frame-by-frame analysis of a boxing match between Mohammed Ali and Al Mindenberger and found that 53% of Ali's jabs and 36% of Mindenberger's jabs were faster than visual reaction time (180 msec). He concludes that a punch is not the stimulus to which the response is a dodge or a block, that we must look beyond a stimulus and a response to larger sequences. Instead it is more reasonable to assume that a punch or a block is a hypothesis-generating or hypothesis-probing attempt by each person to understand and predict the other person's behavioral sequence in time and space. Stern argues that a successful punch means that one fighter was able to decode the other's sequence so that the other's next move was correctly anticipated in time and space. It is necessary to predict the opponent's move in order to have time to "get there" at the same time as the opponent is also moving. In more usual social situations, we are not trying to hide this information about our movements and we display our behavioral schemas very openly. We form temporal-spatial (and affective-arousal) schemas of another person's behavioral flow in relation to our own. Thus the presymbolic representation is a temporal-spatial-affective schema, a "miniplot" of the coordination of the two partners' behaviors (see Beebe and Stern, 1977; Stern, 1977, pp. 87–88).

Facial Mirroring and Self- and Object Representations

Time, space, affect, and arousal are all crucial in the organization of an interaction, but facial-visual affect carries unique information with an enormous degree of modulation and subtlety. How each partner's face attracts and responds to the other's is one of the foundations of intimacy throughout life. Facial mirroring is one of the interaction patterns that contribute to the presymbolic organization of self- and object representations. To the degree that facial mirroring interactions are positively correlated, so that the partners are changing in the same affective direction, the infant represents the expectation of matching and being matched (in affective direction). *What is represented is the split-second, moment-by-moment, contingent, dynamic, interactive process of matching and being matched.* The concomitant arousal pattern and mode of self-regulation are part of the representation. The infant represents the experience of seeing the mother's face continuously changing to become more similar to his or her own; the infant also represents the experience of his or her own face constantly changing to become more similar to the mother's face. These "matching" experiences contribute to feeling known, attuned to, on the same wave length. Each partner affects the other so as to match affective direction, and this matching provides each with a behavioral basis for entering into the other's feeling state.

Interpersonal Timing: Matching of Temporal Patterns

The analyses of facial mirroring in the previous section examined the "content" of mother and infant behavior, that is, the level and direction of affective engagement. But the *purely temporal* organization of these same behaviors can also be examined. Timing and rhythm alone, irrespective of the content of behavior, are powerful organizing principles of communication across the life span. Behavioral timing itself, regardless of its content or modality, conveys vital interpersonal messages about the relatedness between partners. Temporal patterns refer to such phenomena as rate, rhythm, pausing, reaction time, interruption, and turn-taking. The coordination of interpersonal timing refers to whether or not two parallel streams of behavior are correlated. Coordination of temporal patterns provides one crucial way in which social relatedness is organized. As we shall see, the coordination of interpersonal timing is essential to understanding infant presymbolic representations.

The process of relating to another person requires that each have more or less continuous feedback about the state of the other, and rhythms can provide this information (Byers, 1975) since each person always has a rhythm. Timing and rhythm are generally not in focal awareness or under deliberate control. Yet rhythms underlie all motor and vocal behavior (Lenneberg, 1967). Variations in rhythms thus provide continuous information about the state of the partner. Some rhythms we experience as "good" ("good vibes"), and some we experience as disturbing. One can assess the rhythm of one's partner only by reference to one's own rhythm. Therefore we are continuously assessing an interpersonal rhythm relationship (Byers, 1975).

The examination of mother–infant temporal patterns was first suggested by studies of adults. Asked to converse about a neutral topic, unacquainted adults were found to match the purely temporal rhythms of dialogue, irrespective of the content of the speech (Jaffe and Feldstein, 1970; Feldstein and Welkowitz, 1978; Feldstein, 1998). Of special relevance was the finding of a relationship between matching rhythms of dialogue, and empathy and affect. When the adult strangers matched rhythms, they liked each other more and perceived each other as warmer and more similar than they did when their rhythms did not match. Thus similarity in the temporal pattern of communicative behavior is associated with interpersonal attraction and empathy.

Conversely, a speaker who speaks very rapidly and barely pauses long enough for the partner to get a word in edgewise powerfully interferes with the exchange: the partner may become frustrated and "tune out." Subtle changes in timing, such as hesitation or interruption, also affect the listener's experience of the relatedness. In adult conversation we depend on the matching of temporal patterns to know that the other is "tuned in" and to take turns smoothly.

Timing is an excellent system to study in infants because they are born with the capacity to perceive time and to estimate durations of intervals lasting seconds and fractions of seconds (Lew-kowicz, 1989). An infant times his own behavior, as well as environmental stimuli (DeCasper and Fifer, 1980; Haith et al., 1988). Our study of the interpersonal timing of mother–infant interaction rests on this perceptual ability of infants to time the durations of their own and their partners' sounds and silences.

Microanalysis of film has revealed that mother and infant live in a split-second world where the behaviors last for less than half a second. Each partner responds to the other extremely rapidly, the time ranging from simultaneous to one-half sec (Stern, 1971, 1977; Beebe and Stern, 1977; Beebe, Stern, and Jaffe, 1979; Peery, 1980; Beebe, 1982; Kronen, 1982; Jaffe et al., 2001). This rapidity suggests that, at least for the mother, these split-second adjustments occur partially or fully out of conscious control.

A matching of rhythms similar to that of adult dialogues has been found in mother–infant vocal and facial-visual communication as early as three to four months. Through the use of time-series analysis, bidirectional regulation of various temporal patterns of behavior between mother and infant has been documented (Alson, 1982; Jasnow, 1983; Mays, 1984; Beebe et al., 1985; Jaffe et al., 2001). Each partner is extremely sensitive to the durations of the other's behavior, and each tracks and matches these durations on a moment-to-moment basis. In this interlocking temporal responsivity, the infant acquires a basic microstructure of "being with" another person.

Vocal Rhythm Coordination and the Prediction of Infant Attachment and Cognition

The most extensive study of interpersonal timing in infancy and its implications for infant development was conducted by Jaffe et al. (2001; see also Beebe et al., 2000). This study examined the vocal rhythms of mother–infant and stranger–infant face-to-face interactions, at home and in the laboratory, in 82 normal four-month-old babies. The strangers were female graduate students. At 12 months, the infants were assessed for attachment (Ainsworth Strange Situation Test) and cognition (Bayley Scales of Infant Development). Using time-series analysis, mother and infant, and stranger and infant were found to coordinate vocal rhythms, and degree of coordination at four months predicted attachment and cognition outcomes at 12 months. But the "meaning" of coordination was different as a function of partner, site, and particular outcome measure.

To study these mother–infant vocal dialogues, the face-to-face interaction was audiotaped, such that each voice was on a separate channel. Each infant interacted face-to-face with his mother and with a "stranger," at home and in the laboratory. An automated coding system sampled sound and silence at 250 msec. Using the rule that a partner gains the "turn" at the instant he or she vocalizes unilaterally, the *duration* of sounds and silences of each partner was then timed: "vocalizations"; "pauses" (where the same person resumed vocalizing); and "switching pauses" (where the turnholder pauses and the other partner begins, constituting a turn exchange). Since this coding system has no phonetic, syntactic, or semantic information, it captures the purely temporal aspects of dialogue and yields an interpersonal grammar of conversational exchange in the time domain, at any age.

Time-series regression revealed robust bidirectional coordination at four months. Both mother and infant, as well as stranger and infant, coordinated (or "tracked") the durations of each other's vocalizations, pauses, and switching pauses, and each partner's durations were predictable from those of the other. For example, as one partner's durations of vocalizations became longer, the other's became shorter, and vice versa. This correlation can be positive or negative. Thus mother–infant and stranger–infant interactions are coregulated at four months.

Since infants at four months participate in a similar bidirectional system with a stranger as with the mother, we suggest that the coordination of vocal timing taps a general social-perceptual ability, not restricted to the attachment figure. The robustness of these interpersonal temporal coordinations suggests that they are a biologically primed capacity, appearing early in infancy. They constitute one critical form of interpersonal monitoring and relatedness.

There is a turn-taking structure in the mother–infant and stranger–infant data that is strikingly similar to that of adult speech. Switching pauses mark the boundaries of the turn exchange.

Coordinating switching pauses means that each partner pauses for a similar duration before the other takes a turn. Switching-pause coordination is also a prominent feature of adult dialogue. The implication is that a turn-taking, or dialogic structure is already in evidence at four months and is being regulated in the same way as is seen in adult speech. Infants thus have this aspect of temporal coordination of language prior to speech onset (see Beebe et al., 1988).

These indices of temporal coordination of mother–infant and stranger–infant vocal dialogue at four months predicted infant attachment and cognition at one year. Thus these developmental outcomes are co-constructed as well. The equations where the infant was contingent on the adult and the equations where the adult was contingent on the infant were all powerful in predicting the 12-month outcomes, but in different ways for attachment and cognition.

There are three competing hypotheses in the literature about the meaning of interpersonal coordination. One suggests that high coordination and interpersonal coordination are optimal for communication (Chapple, 1970). A second suggests that high interpersonal coordination indexes pathological communication (Gottman, 1981). A third proposes that midrange coordination is optimal (Warner et al., 1987). The findings of the Jaffe et al. (2001) study suggest an even more complex picture in which all these hypotheses can be correct as a function of particular partner, site, and outcome measure.

A high degree of bidirectional coordination between mother and infant was a risk index for attachment, predicting an insecure form of attachment termed disorganized. Midrange scores of bidirectional coordination were optimal. High coordination in attachment can be interpreted as an attempt to cope with difficulty by making the interaction more predictable. Attachment was also predicted by the stranger–infant interaction: again midrange scores of bidirectional coordination predicted secure attachment. There were also unidirectional stranger–infant findings: high stranger coordination with infant (but not vice versa) predicted anxious-resistant attachment; low infant coordination with stranger (but not vice versa) predicted avoidant infant attachment.

In our measure of cognition (the Bayley test), however, a high degree of coordination between infant and stranger in the labora-tory predicted the most optimal Bayley scores. High coordination between infant and stranger was interpreted as an index of optimal information-processing. Response to novelty is central to intelli-gence at all ages, and a large body of research shows that higher infant response to novelty predicts better cognitive outcomes (Fagan, 1982; Berg and Sternberg, 1985). Thus the "meaning" of degree of vocal rhythm coordination is complex and completely dependent on context: where, with whom, for what developmental task.

In the prediction of attachment, very high coordination is seen as an index of vigilance, overmonitoring, or wariness. Very high coordination may be an adaptive attempt to counteract some dis-turbance in the interaction. In other studies, very high coordination was also found in disturbed marital pairs (Gottman, 1981). In a com-parison of friends, "enemies," and strangers among college students, Crown (1991) found the strangers to exhibit the highest coordina-tion. Mothers of premature infants showed higher coordination than did mothers of normal infants (Hitchcock, 1991). Malatesta et al. (1989) found that very high maternal facial coordination with infant facial changes predicted avoidant attachment in the infant, whereas low to midrange maternal facial coordination predicted secure attachment. (Infant coordination with mother was not examined.) Tobias (1995) found that mothers and infants alike were more coor-dinated in a group where the mothers had an insecure (preoccu-pied) attachment history than was a group where the mothers had a secure history. Very high coordination may index the need for structure or regulation in the interaction (Crown, 1992), since it provides a highly predictable, contingent sequence. Disordered sys-tems are highly structured and less flexible.

The Jaffe et al. (2001) study provides us with a "midrange model" for predicting secure attachment, since midrange values of coordi-nation were optimal. In this range mother and infant, or stranger and infant, significantly affected each other's patterns, but inter-personal constraint was not tightly coordinated. Midrange coordi-nation leaves more "space," more room for uncertainty, within the experience of correspondence and matching. Whereas very high or very low coordinators are "stuck" in (biased toward) one extreme in

the distribution of values, midrange coordinators more freely uti-
lize the range of values, preserving more fluidity in the capacity to
locate the partner's mean value. We speculate that the full range of
degrees of coordination, including the extremes, is probably necessary
for empathy, so long as mobility across the range is retained. In contrast, pathological relatedness may be indexed by a person's being
"stuck" at either extreme of very high or very low coordination of
vocal temporal patterns.

Thus, in the prediction of attachment, the concept of "matching"
and coordination must shift. Whereas the infancy literature has often
assumed that more matching, or more coordination, was "better" or
was an index of being more "related," this vocal rhythm study shows
that "more is not necessarily better" (see Cohn and Elmore, 1988).
Midrange coordination was optimal in the prediction of secure attachment, and either pole of excessive or insufficient coordination predicted insecure attachment.

The four-month stranger–infant interaction provided a unique
source of information in this study since it had eight times more power,
in percent of variance accounted for, to predict 12-month Bayley scores
than did the mother–infant interaction; and the capacity to predict
attachment was as great from the stranger–infant as from the
mother–infant interaction (although different types of information
were operative). The stranger–infant interaction can be viewed as a
developmental challenge that pulls for heightened infant performance.

The Balance Model of Self- and Interactive Regulation

The results of the Jaffe et al. (2001) study of vocal rhythm and
attachment were used to hypothesize a systems view of a balance
of self- and interactive regulation by Beebe and Jaffe (1999) and
Beebe and McCrorie (in press), illustrated in Figure 7. From the
point of view of interactive regulation, midrange coordination predicted secure attachment, whereas scores outside the midrange predicted insecure. From the point of view of self regulation, a similar
optimum midrange was hypothesized. The midrange balance model
posits that, in the midrange, interactive coordination is present but
not obligatory, and self-regulation is preserved but not excessive.

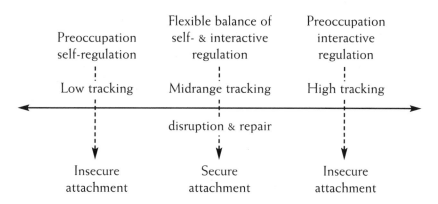

Figure 7. The Midrange Balance Model of Self- and Interactive Regulation.

Optimal social communication and development is hypothesized to occur with flexibility to move between self- and interactive regulation, yielding relatively optimal levels of infant attention, affect, and arousal. For each partner, operating outside the midrange may index an attempt to cope with a disturbance in the interaction (see also Malatesta et al., 1989; Roe et al., 1990). Excessive monitoring of the partner, at the expense of self-regulation, defines one pole of imbalance, "interactive vigilance"; preoccupation with self-regulation, at the expense of interactive sensitivity, defines the other pole of imbalance, withdrawal or inhibition. At each pole of imbalance we assume that the infant is struggling with nonoptimal levels of attention, arousal and affect (Jaffe et al., 2001; Beebe and McCrorie, 1996, in press).

Excessive self-regulation at the expense of interactive regulation (withdrawal) is illustrated by Tronick's (1989) description of the infants of women with some types of maternal depression. He documented that various failures in interactive regulation in these dyads, without repair, were followed by infants' preoccupation with self-comfort and self-regulation of distress states on their own (turning away, loss of postural control, oral self-comfort, self-clasping, and rocking), accompanied by lowered interactive contingencies. Excessive monitoring of the partner (vigilance, or high tracking) at the expense of self-regulation is suggested by the prediction of insecure anxious–resistant and disorganized attachment types from the highest degrees of vocal contingencies, with presumably compromised self-regulation (Jaffe et al., 2001; see also Sander, 1995).

Interpersonal Timing and Infant Presymbolic Representation

That these interpersonal timing patterns of vocal rhythm at four months powerfully predicted one-year outcomes, and that different degrees of coordination were linked both to optimal and to nonoptimal outcomes, suggest that the temporal coordination of the interaction is an important dimension in the organization of development, representations, and the child's experience of relatedness. The coordination of the timing of vocalizations, as each tracks and affects the durations of the other's behavior on a moment-to-moment basis, organizes one temporal dimension of representations. Coordination of vocal rhythm means that each partner's durations can be predicted from those of the partner, moment by moment. It involves both contingency and relative match of duration. This temporal coordination provides a crucial aspect of the relatedness that will be represented in these early representations. It constitutes a "temporal signature" of the interaction. Just as facial-mirroring exchanges provide each partner a way of entering into the other's affective state, temporal coordination provides each partner a way of entering into the temporal world and feeling state of the other.

Our central hypotheses are: (1) since coordinated interpersonal timing at four months predicts both attachment and cognition, the timing of interactive behavior constitutes a mediating variable underlying many constructs that appear disparate as conventionally measured; (2) timing coordination is an early communication system in infancy and a scaffolding for the subsequent development of social communication; (3) the temporal structure of language derives from the interpersonal coordination of the time patterns of prelinguistic vocal and kinesic communicative behavior; and (4) the patterning and *degree* of timing coordination constitute a dyadic adaptation that may either facilitate or disturb communication and development (Jaffe et al., 2001).

Implications of Affective and Temporal Matching for the Organization of Infant Experience

The Sharing of Subjective States

Translation of the findings of the regulation of interaction patterns into the language of experience always involves considerable inference and is difficult at best. Whereas psychoanalysis emphasizes how self and object are experienced, mother–infant interaction research measures what the two partners do. In making inferences from behavior to experience, it is assumed that, at this age (in the first six months), the infant's observed actions closely parallel his or her experience. In later development, action and experience can be increasingly dissociated and even potentially contradictory. But the infant cannot hide his distress, pleasure, or fatigue.

The various ways in which mother and infant coordinate with each other to "match" or coordinate the timing and affective direction of behavior provides each a behavioral basis for knowing and entering into the partner's perception, temporal world, and feeling state (see Beebe et al., 1985). We use the term matching here in its most general sense, holding in mind that an additional key dimension, the *degree* of match, is a critical consideration. It is a common notion that when people empathize with each other, their language and communicative behavior become more similar (see Feldstein and Welkowitz, 1978, for a review of this literature). The process of becoming related to another involves, in part, becoming more similar, presumably on the basis of an increasing ability to predict the other's behavior. The implication is that similarity or symmetry in behavior is associated with a similar congruence of feeling states. What is the mechanism of this congruence?

In a dyadic process we can identify three processes that link the feeling state of one person to another. The first occurs when subjective feeling states are expressed in behavior. In a social interaction, this expressive display is perceived by the partner, and there is a strong tendency to match the outward display in some way (in its timing, affect, direction, etc.). This matching is a second intermediate mode of transmission of a feeling state. The third way is that the very act of matching generates a central emotional state in the receiving partner who matches. This concept is based on the work of Ekman (1983), which we introduced in chapter 2, as well as that of Zajonc (1985).

Ekman (1983) taught professional actors and scientists who study the face an exact set of muscle movements (e.g., contracting a particular forehead muscle in conjunction with particular eye and cheek muscles) that resulted in a series of facial expressions. In a second task, he taught the subjects to relive various emotions. During each task, autonomic indices, such as heart rate, temperature, and skin resistance, were recorded. Simply producing the facial muscle action patterns resulted in more clearcut autonomic changes than actually reliving these emotions. Ekman concluded that contracting facial muscles elicits the associated autonomic activity. His study thus suggests that the physiological state of the receiving partner who matches is very similar to the physiological state of the sending partner.

This experiment sheds light on empathy, and particularly the question of how the feeling state of one person can be transmitted to another. Ekman suggested, for example, that the onlooker's contraction of the same facial muscles as he perceives on another's face enables the onlooker to feel the same autonomic sensations as the other person. Zajonc (1985) expressed a similar view: "If muscular movements of the face, by virtue of their effects on cerebral blood flow and on the release of particular neurotransmitters, are sufficient to induce changes in hedonic tone and result in changes of subjective states, then reproducing the expression of another may well produce in the onlooker a similar emotional state" (p. 19).

We suggest that Ekman's and Zajonc's ideas apply more generally to a large range of matching phenomena, including matching of affective direction and temporal pattern as well as specific facial expressions. While reproducing the spatial or temporal pattern of another person's emotional display one feels one's own face and body and an associated autonomic activity. This is a cross-modal transfer from the perception of an external image or temporal pattern to an internal proprioceptive experience. Such cross-modal transfer can be demonstrated in the first months of life (Meltzoff and Moore, 1977; Rose, 1979; Lewkowicz and Turkewitz, 1980; Spelke and Cortelyou, 1981). As we noted in chapter 2, Meltzoff suggested that correspondences of facial gestures provide the infant with the earliest experiences of "like me." Matching the spatial or temporal pattern of another person's display evokes a similar psychophysiological state in oneself. This process may account for the emotional efficacy (for empathy, bonding) of matching phenomena that are ubiquitous in social interactions. Although he had no data on the physiological correlates of matching, Byers (1975) made a similar argument for the matching of temporal patterns. He suggested that two interactants in synchrony are brought into the same state by virtue of their mutual entrainment. As mother and infant match each other's temporal and affective patterns, each recreates in herself a psychophysiological state similar to that of the partner, thus participating in the subjective state of the other.

These processes have specific relevance for the origins of empathy. For example, empathy, defined as "mental entering into the perception of another; motor mimicry" (*American College Dictionary*, 1962), relates a behavioral similarity, motor mimicry, to a subjective state. To behave in the same way or with the same temporal pattern is to enter into an aspect of the other's perception and provides a behavioral basis for knowing an important aspect of how the other feels. The findings of similar temporal patterns presented here suggest that, when mother and infant time the durations of their behaviors in a similar way and each coordinates with the other so as to match the timing, then this matching provides each partner an entrée into an aspect of the other's temporal world and feeling state.

Matching an affective direction can be interpreted in a similar way. Each partner experiences similarities between what his or her face feels like and what the partner's face looks like. The findings of bidirectional coordination as each matches and tracks the other's affective direction, on a moment-to-moment basis, again suggest that mother and infant have remarkable access to each other's feeling states. Following our more general application of Ekman's (1983) work, as each matches the pattern (spatial or temporal) of the partner's emotional display, the matching evokes in each a proprioceptive experience that corresponds to that of the partner.

We suggest that the expectation of being matched, as well as the expectation of matching and participating in the state of the other, is one aspect of the infant's presymbolic representation of self and object. The representation includes some prototype of the experience of what it is like to match and be matched, or not, on a moment-to-moment basis. That is, the presymbolic representation includes the dynamic interactive process itself, as well as an associated proprioceptive pattern.

These experiences in matching affect and interpersonal timing are coded in an implicit, procedural format and may contribute to an expectation in the older child or adult of being attuned, known, or "on the same wavelength," in all the ways previously defined. We infer an experience not only of "I reflect you," but also of "I change with you. We are going in the same direction. I experience myself as tracking you and being tracked by you." We use the Jaffe et al. (2001) study to refine this argument by emphasizing that it is matching or coordination in the midrange that specifically facilitates optimal attachment. The dimension of self-regulation must also be added to this argument, since every pattern of interactive regulation is associated with a particular pattern and experience of self-regulation.

Interaction Patterns of Derailment

Every mother at times undershoots, or overshoots, an optimal level of stimulation. An infant has a virtuoso range of behaviors to use in coping with or defending against intrusion. The following study (Beebe and Stern, 1977) illustrates part of this range: maternal overstimulation and infant withdrawal. The infant is four months old. The instructions to the mother were: play with your baby as you would at home.

The pattern of the interaction, as documented through statistically significant sequences, is as follows. As the mother "looms" into the baby's face, the baby's head moves back and away. The mother then "chases" by moving her head and body toward the baby. As she chases, the baby simultaneously moves his head still farther away. These sequences occur with split-second response, so that, even before the mother has completed her head movement toward the baby, he has already begun to move away. These are semisynchronized mutual adjustments. Once the baby has moved his head quite far away, the mother tends to pick him up. But, as she is picking him up, the baby reflexively moves his head to the center without looking at her. As she puts him down on her lap, his head has already moved away again. Thus the very effort the mother makes to reengage the baby in eye contact has already failed even before it is completed, and he has "escaped" her yet again.

This baby has "veto" power: he can totally prevent a visual encounter with the mother. Although this is an aversive interaction, its regulation is still bilateral: the mother's movement toward the baby's face is predictably followed by the baby's move away, and the baby's movements of head and body away from the mother are predictably followed by the mother's chase. We have called this interaction chase-and-dodge, but it could as well be called dodge-and-chase. The infant's withdrawal elicits the mother's intrusion, and the mother's intrusion influences the infant's withdrawal. An example of the "chase and dodge" sequence is illustrated in Figure 8.

Illustration: Transcript of Chase-and-Dodge Film

This sequence begins 42 seconds into the interaction. Just the moment before, the infant had oriented briefly toward the mother and glanced at her face. The mother met the infant's gaze with an expression of mock surprise and "loomed" forward and down toward his face. During the "loom" the infant moved his head back and away, breaking visual contact. Throughout the next $6\frac{1}{2}$ seconds, to be described, the infant is never visually engaged; nevertheless he remains acutely sensitive, through peripheral vision, to every maternal head and body movement. There are 24 frames per second. By reading the frame onsets of each partner along with the particular behaviors, it is possible to see the "split-second world" of extremely rapid responsivities between mother and infant.

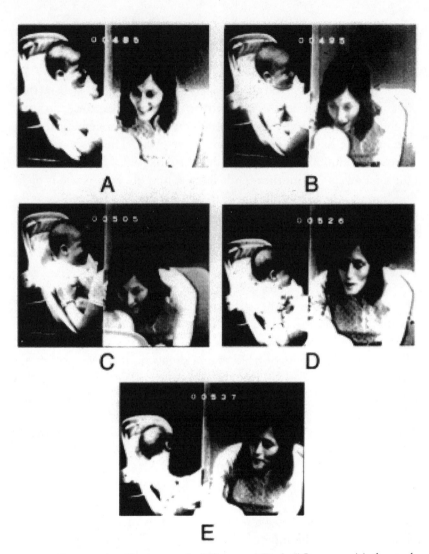

Figure 8. Photographic Illustration of a "Chase-and-Dodge" Sequence. Mother and infant are seated face-to-face. At point A, the infant is looking just slightly to the left of mother's face, and mother is smiling. At point B, .42 seconds later, mother "looms" in close to the infant's face, and she has a "mock surprise" expression. At point C, .42 seconds later, the infant has begun turning further away to his left, as mother completes the loom, with a smile. At point D, .87 seconds later, the infant moves still further away to his left, as mother begins to draw back, sobering. At point E, .46 seconds later, the infant completes a full 90° head turn away, while mother draws still further back, with a hint of a grimace. Numbers at the top of the photographs indicate frames (24 frames = one second).

112

Transcript

The mother picks the infant up slightly [frames 1035–1043]. She then follows with her head in the direction the infant has just moved in [frames 1071–1081] so that she is now face to face with the infant, who is oriented 30% from midline.

At $1/8$ second from the onset of mother's head-following movement, the infant arches [frames 1074–1082], moving his head up and back and both arms out and up, then [frames 1083–1089] turns his head farther away, to 45% from midline. Immediately [frames 1090–1104] the mother pushes the infant away from her and to her right, simultaneously sobering and looking very serious, gritting her teeth, and moving her head back.

The infant then [frames 1107–1113] turns his head through the midline with eyes shut, ending at 45% from midline on the other side; simultaneously the mother's face darkens, into a tight, sober expression. She now [frames 1119–1130] follows with her head in the direction of the infant's last head movement; then she lowers him slightly [frames 1131–1147], simultaneously moving her head down and forward, close to him. As she does so, he turns his head still farther away, to 60% from midline [frames 1142–1150]. Half a second later [frames 1164–1172] the infant again turns his head through the midline, eyes shut, and swings out to the other side to end up, eyes now open, oriented 30% from midline. The mother sobers, tight lipped [frames 1173–1183], as she moves back to an upright posture [frames 1173–1193] and grabs the infant's hands and begins to bounce him vigorously [frames 1185–1201].

Transcript Discussion

Examination of the onsets and offsets of these movements of the two partners reveals a semisynchronous system in which one partner frequently begins adjusting or "responding" before the other's action is complete. These data fit Fogel's (1992a, b, 1993a, b) "continuous control" model of co-regulated communication, in which each person's action is susceptible to modification by the continually changing action of the partner.

This baby stays sensitive to each maternal movement from moment to moment, even though in the direction of withdrawal. The interaction is a compromise between engagement and disengagement, because in some sense the baby is very engaged, highly responsive to every movement of the mother. The mother is also very engaged. Nevertheless, the quality of the engagement is never one of sustained mutual visual regard with positive affect: instead it has the quality of a chase and flight. Rather than the baby's tuning out, this interaction points to an aspect of early "coping" activity that might perhaps be best characterized as continuous responsivity and vigilance.

If this interaction were characteristic of the pair, the infant's experience would be organized by expectancies of misregulation without repair. What would be represented would be the delicately responsive interaction of mother chasing and infant dodging. A generalized spatial schematic of this sequence might be: As you move in, I move away; as I move away, you move in. The easy balance between moments of engagement and moments of disengagement would be disturbed. Too much of the energy of the interaction would be used to manage being away from, rather than being with, the partner. The later symbolic experience of the infant might be something like: When I stay close to you, I feel you are moving in on me; I feel overaroused and inundated. No matter where I move in relation to you I cannot get comfortable. I can neither engage nor disengage. Reciprocally for the mother, her verbalized experience might be something like: When I want to connect with you, I become aware of how much I need to be responded to. I feel you move away from me as I show my wish to engage. I cannot find a comfortable place in relation to you. I feel anxious and rejected.

Implications of Mutually Regulated Aversive Patterns for the Organization of Infant Experience

Bidirectional regulation may remain intact, and yet the pair may be misattuned in various ways: affect, arousal, timing, and so on. The chase-and-dodge interaction illustrates such a misattunement. Mother and infant continue a sensitive responsivity to each other.

"Relatedness," that is, bidirectional regulation, remains, since mother's chase behavior increases the probability of infant dodges, and vice versa. Rather, it is the quality of the relatedness that is compromised. Infant attention, affect, and arousal are not optimally regulated.

What makes this interaction atypical is that, although the infant's head aversion still has predictable effects on the mother's behavior, it is in the direction of increasing the intensity of maternal stimulation. In the normative pattern, when an infant looks and turns away, the mother temporarily decreases her stimulation (Brazelton et al., 1974; Donovan and Leavitt, 1978; Field, 1981; Langhorst and Fogel, 1982; Hirshfield and Beebe, 1987). The infant uses gaze aversion to reregulate his arousal. The infant's heart rate during play accelerates just before and decelerates just after a gaze aversion (Field, 1981). In this interaction, however, although the infant's own state of arousal decreases when he looks and turns away, the mother does not participate in the deescalation of arousal, in other words, in the infant's attainment of a calmer state. It appears that this mother has difficulty tolerating the infant's disengagement.

One could make various inferences about the infant's subjective experience in the chase-and-dodge interaction if this interaction proved to be typical of this particular pair. Normally, an infant experiences "efficacy": when events in the environment are contingent on his behavior, he experiences himself as the "producer" of these events (see DeCasper and Carstens, 1980). Because this mother's behavior is still contingent on the infant's behavior, this infant's experience of efficacy is to some degree intact. However, what this infant in the chase and dodge interaction can "produce" in his mother's behavior is not typical, because he "produces" escalating intensity of maternal stimulation. Thus, he may experience having to calm himself "by himself" and despite the mother's behavior. We speculate that the experience of efficacy itself is to some degree compromised because, although the infant's actions continue to produce effects, these effects are associated with negative affects and escalating arousal. The nature of the interactive regulation does not facilitate, and may actively interfere with, the infant's optimal regulation of his own arousal.

Typically, as the interaction proceeds, infant affect and arousal remain within an optimal range, and mutual gaze with positive affect is readily available (Stern, 1977, 1985). In an atypical interaction such as this one, predictability and bidirectional coordination remain, but nevertheless some aspect of the infant's behavior is not optimally regulated. Positive affect is dramatically interfered with, and the infant shows extreme postural aversion and withdrawal states. Expectancies of misregulation organize such an infant's experience. That is, the aversive stimulation is contingent on his behavior, and the infant will come to expect this kind of negative interaction. If this interaction pattern is characteristic of the pair, the infant chronically experiences extremes in certain affect and arousal states; these states have more or less of a tendency to dominate his experience, and the infant experiences less than optimal success in his extreme attempts to regulate these states. The interactive regulation pattern thus retains interrelatedness but does not succeed in the optimal regulation of infant attention, affect, and arousal.

We suggest that expectancies of such misregulation are stored as presymbolic representations. If they remain characteristic of the interaction, by the end of the first year they will be abstracted as prototypic. This composite prototype forms the basis for an emerging symbolic representation of self and object as misattuned.

Interaction Patterns and the Origins of Presymbolic Representation: Summary and Conclusions

A dyadic systems view of communication underlies our concept of the interactive organization of experience and representations. Mother and infant jointly construct a patterned sequence of movements and establish the "rules" for regulating these movements, through the dimensions of time, space, affect, and arousal. It is this interactive process, the expectation of a characteristic pattern of the dyadic sequence of movements, together with the self-regulatory consequences, that is represented in presymbolic form by the infant.

An early presymbolic representational ability is used to "schematize" those interaction patterns which are recurrent, expectable, and characteristic. In the early months, the infant perceives, orders, stores (and under certain conditions retrieves) information about regularities and features of the environment, as well as his social interactions. The infant is capable of comparing the nature of the interaction pattern at the moment with a model or representation of how the interaction typically goes and evaluating whether the two are similar or different. The infant is organizing a "representational world" in the first half of the first year, prior to the emergence of symbolic capacity.

What features of these characteristic, prototypic interactions will the infant find salient, retain, and use to generate a model of how the interaction typically unfolds? We suggest that time, space, affect, and arousal provide these features. In the dimension of time the infant will store the rate, rhythm, sequence, and contingency of the interaction. In the dimension of space he or she will represent patterns of approach-approach or approach-avoid. In the dimension of facial affect the infant will represent the way the faces move together, the pattern of moving in the same direction or not, and the positive and negative tones of the faces and voices. The infant will also store an associated arousal pattern, the relative ease of regulating this arousal pattern, and a proprioceptive experience of his or her movements.

The examples of interaction patterns we have given illustrate the dimensions of arousal, affect, space, and time in the early organization of experience: (1) state transforming, the expectation of being able to transform an arousal state, with the contribution of the partner; (2) facial mirroring, the expectation of matching and being matched in the direction of affective change; (3) interpersonal timing, the expectation of degree of vocal rhythm coordination; and (4) chase-and-dodge, the expectation of the misregulation and derailment of spatial-orientation patterns, without repair.

These qualitative differences in the recurrent configurations of self- and object representations, based on the early interaction patterns, then continue to organize, alter, and potentially limit subsequent experience (see Atwood and Stolorow, 1984; Main, Kaplan, and Cassidy, 1985). Main and her colleagues argued that these representations form a set of conscious and unconscious "rules" that guide appraisals of experience and behavior, thus permitting or limiting access to the kinds of information and memories available regarding attachment figures. Many authors suggest that, once organized, these representations may tend to resist reorganization, because they operate largely outside conscious awareness and because they tend to be actively self-perpetuating (Freud, 1938; Sullivan, 1953; Bowlby, 1980; Main et al., 1985; Sroufe and Fleeson, 1986).

We employ a continuous process model of representations, in which the infant represents the moment-to-moment dynamic interplay of his or her own actions in relation to the actions of the mother (caretaker). Thus, what is initially represented is not an object, but an object-relation: self-in-relation-to-object. These presymbolic representations of self and object are simultaneously constructed and are constructed *in relation to* each other. What is represented is an emergent dyadic phenomenon, the nature of the *inter-relatedness*, which cannot be described on the basis of either partner alone.

The inherently dyadic nature of these representations implies that both roles in an interaction are known to the person. This may explain why, in adult treatment, the patient knows both roles in the interaction intimately and in some cases may exchange them: for example, masochist–sadist, predator–prey, dodger–chaser, abandoner–abandoned. One side or the other may be disavowed, repressed, embroiled in conflict, ascribed to the partner, or sought at any price. Restoring access to the "missing" side may be necessary in the treatment (Winnicott, 1967; Ogden, 1989). Interaction patterns are a mutually organized and mutually understood code in which any role implies its reciprocal, and neither can be represented without the other. Thus there is no object representation that does not stand in relation to a self-representation, and vice versa.

This dynamic, process view of representations explicitly avoids a discrete, static, individualistic view. The examples of interaction patterns we have given illustrate in detail the basis for our position that all action and information in a face-to-face interaction is jointly constructed, that is, bidirectionally regulated. The research that we presented illustrates Fogel's (1992a, b, 1993a, b) concept of co-regulation by which all behavior simultaneously unfolds in one person while, at the same time, it is continuously modified by the changing behavior of the partner. In this continuous process model of communication (Fogel, 1992a, b, 1993a, b; Beebe et al., 1992) communicative information does not reside "in" either partner but is continuously constructed by both together.

We have presented evidence that there is a strong early organizing process in the first year. Ways of relating are becoming stable, characteristic, and predictable, and they have discernibly different consequences for adaptation and development. Nevertheless, we do not see representations as fixed. Our process model of representation leaves open the possibility of the transformation of representations as the dyad continues to negotiate patterns of relatedness. Thus, although self-in-relation-to-object representations take on their original patterning in the first year, they remain open to being updated. One definition of psychopathology is a relative restriction of this transformational quality, so that representations do indeed become increasingly static, fixed, or rigid (Field et al., 1988; Tronick, 1989; Fogel, 1992a, b, 1993a, b). Alternatively, psychopathology may entail a relatively progressive destabilization of patterns, such that representations increasingly lose their coherence. Healthy development may be characterized by an optimum degree of stability, balancing predictability and transformation.

6

CO-CONSTRUCTING INNER
AND RELATIONAL PROCESSES

*Self- and Interactive Regulation in Infant
Research and Adult Treatment*

Although the self and the object have been richly conceptualized in the history of psychoanalysis, the dyadic system has not. In contemporary psychoanalysis, theorists are struggling to articulate a theory of dyadic interaction. We do not argue that the issues being regulated in mother–infant interactions are necessarily similar to those of adult analytic dyads. Rather, infant research has defined principles of organization in dyadic systems. Although these organizing principles could be fruitfully applied to many forms of human exchange, we are here specifically interested in conceptualizing their application to adult treatment. Despite vast differences between the presymbolic and the symbolic mind, these organizing principles of nonverbal communication clarify the nature of the interactive process and its co-construction in both domains.

In this chapter we address the ways in which self- and interactive regulation fit together or exert an influence on each other. We argue that the dyadic interactive process reorganizes inner as well as relational processes in mother–infant and in analyst–patient interactions. Reciprocally, changes in self-regulation in either part-ner can alter the interactive process.

This chapter interweaves vignettes from infant research and adult treatment to illustrate the co-construction of self- and interactive regulation from four points of view: (1) dyadic access to self regu-lation, (2) special self-regulatory requirements for engagement, (3) hypervigilant forms of interactive regulation, and (4) orientational aversion. Many others could be identified. In each, we show that these forms of regulation can be found in both infant research and adult treatment.

Dyadic Access to Self-Regulation

In chapter 5 we described five-week-old Elliott, who played sequen-tially with three different partners: his mother, a stranger (a gradu-ate student), and Beatrice Beebe. Elliott was very different with each of the three partners; he displayed different patterns of engagement and fussiness, illustrating the dyadic organization of self-regulation. With different partners, an infant has a different access to his or her range of self-regulation capacities. The success, as well as distress, of an interaction is an emergent dyadic phenomenon.

We can conceptualize similar issues in adult treatment. What self-regulatory range does the patient bring, and what capability does this particular therapist and patient together generate to gain access to the patient's self-regulatory range and to expand it? With a different therapist, a particular patient may have access to a very different portion of his own self-regulatory range. Similarly, with different patients, therapists have different access to their own self-regulatory ranges.

The nature and range of a patient's self-regulation that is avail-able over the course of a treatment will depend on the quality of the interactive regulation and the styles of engagement and self-reg-ulation that both partners bring to the endeavor. Does the therapist envision the analytic task as matching and tracking the patient's attention and affect state ("joining"), stimulating and dampening the patient's affect and arousal ("altering"), or keeping a steady, relatively unvarying level of attention and affect ("neutrality")? How do patients respond to these different styles? And what of the patient's implicit (unconscious) interactive goals (making sure the therapist does not intrude; needing the therapist as a benign background; obtaining love and approval; attempting to find the therapist's own need for the patient, etc), and the therapist's response? In each pattern, interactive regulation and self-regulation will be different for each partner. These differences, and their implications for therapeutic action, are in dire need of study.

To this point we have illustrated these issues through the case of Karen, described in chapter 3. In this chapter we offer further clinical examples of patients who remained difficult to reach, where the interactive process itself often carried the brunt of the therapeutic leverage. Some of these interactive and self-regulatory patterns did not become accessible to intervention for long periods.

Dyadic Access to an Adult Patient's Self-Regulatory Range

This vignette is taken from the ninth year of the 13-year treatment of Paul (by Beebe). Initially seen three times per week (sitting up) for several years, Paul moved out of state, and the remaining treatment was conducted once a week thereafter. Paul was a severely schizoid man in his mid-30s. His father was a successful businessman who was emotionally abusive to his wife and children. The mother was depressed and alcoholic. The central nurturing figure for Paul had been the grandmother.

In the first seven years of treatment, Paul could barely participate beyond showing up for his appointments. He did not disclose major events in his life. Although he had severe difficulties with his long-standing live-in girlfriend, he could not discuss them.

In the seventh year of the treatment, around the time he was leaving his girlfriend, Paul gradually began to describe a recurrent sense of despair that he could not become more alive. Only after he had left his girlfriend did he reveal that he had been sexually abusive to her. He had been too ashamed to talk about his relationship with her because it would have meant discussing his fear that he could not love. He was afraid that, if he revealed to me how bad the relationship was, it might mean that they would have to split up, and he could not bear to contemplate that for many years. He told me that, in retrospect, if I had not continually "reached" for him in the early years of the analysis, while tolerating his disengagement, he would have been a "goner."

By the ninth year, the treatment had progressed dramatically. He finally really entered the treatment. For the first time, I felt I had an "ally." Paul was increasingly able to share and reflect on his experience. In this period, a major self-regulatory disturbance temporarily prevented further movement. I noticed a repetitive interaction across several different topics in which Paul's face was animated, involved, and smiling. However, he reported feeling nothing. At first I was so affected by the animation I saw in his face, and my own response to it, that I had difficulty believing that he experienced absolutely no feeling.

I investigated the possibility that Paul was too frightened to feel pleasurably involved with me. Further discussion revealed a more complex picture, however. He described an internal state of "steel doors clanging shut, becoming tightly sealed." I shifted my attention to an investigation of this tightly sealed inner state.

Pursuing evidence of a shutdown, from his associations I hit upon the idea of asking him to take his pulse. He counted out the beats, and it was about 40 per minute. Although he was somewhat athletic, he had nevertheless drastically dampened down his arousal, in an extreme self-regulatory measure, shutting himself down so that he would feel nothing. This self-regulatory strategy had evidently become "unhooked" from his animated facial responsiveness. He could participate in a seemingly normal related way. And yet anything that happened between us could not affect his internal state. He had interfered with his ability to experience our relationship on an affective-arousal level. Thus the mutual regulation was also profoundly disturbed by this extreme self-regulatory measure. Our increasing ability to describe this strategy gradually fostered the promotion of less extreme self-regulatory strategies and an enhanced ability for enlivened engagement with me.

Special Self-Regulatory Requirements for Engagement

Self Regulation and Infant Attachment

In the case of Elliott we illustrated normal self-regulatory difficulties in a five-week old. We now turn to a study that investigated the self-regulatory process in more detail, in four-month-old infants. We identified special self-regulatory requirements in those infants whose attachment in the Ainsworth separation paradigm at one year was classified as insecure-avoidant, as compared with secure (Koulomzin, 1993; Koulomzin et al., 1993). Eight infants were classified as insecure avoidant and 27 as secure at 12 months. Understanding that they are at four months *in the process of* becoming secure or insecure, we refer to these four-month infants as "secure" or "insecure."

On the basis of the work of Bowlby (1958, 1969) and Ainsworth and her colleagues (1978), current infant research tests attachment in the laboratory by separating mother and infant, and then evaluating their reunion. Secure infants are very upset at the separation but are easily comforted by the mother upon her return and can return to play. Insecure avoidant infants may seem unaffected by the separation, tend to avoid the mother at reunion, and remain involved with the toys. Although further insecure subtypes can be discriminated, in this study only secure and avoidant infants were examined.

Using videotape microanalysis of mother–infant face-to-face play at four months, we coded infant gaze, orientation, self-touch, and facial behavior second by second. In comparison with the secure infants, the avoidant infants at four months looked at their mothers less frequently. Only if engaging in tactile self-comfort, such as fingering or rubbing the body, clothing, or a strap, did the avoidant infants look at the mother as much as the secure ones did. Otherwise, without tactile self-comfort, the avoidant infants looked at their mothers half as frequently as the secure infants did.

The secure infants at four months tended to look at the mother while holding their heads in a stable *en face* orientation. The avoidant infants, however, could maintain this stable *en face* orientation while looking at mother only if they engaged in tactile self-comforting behavior. Otherwise the avoidant infants tended to look at the mother at a slight angle, as if "cocked for escape." Thus, tactile self-comfort appears to be a special self-regulatory requirement for mutual gaze and stable orientational engagement in four-month-old avoidant infants.

Facial affect is also relevant to an infant's capacity to maintain focused attention. The avoidant and secure infants did not differ when affect was neutral or negative. When affect was neutral, both the avoidant and the secure infants could maintain stable orientation and gaze. When affect was negative, both the avoidant and the secure infants exhibited a disruption of the attentional focus so that gaze at mother no longer constrained the head to stay *en face*. However, in the context of positive affect, the avoidant and the secure infants did differ. Positive affect disrupted attentional focus in the avoidant infants, such that looking at mother no longer constrained head movement to an *en face* orientation. Instead, when feeling positive affect, the avoidant infants were "cocked for escape," with their heads more likely to go into an upward, downward, or major avert orientation. In contrast, positive affect did not disrupt stable *en face* orientation or gaze at mother for secure infants.

This research demonstrates that internal state, regulated through self-touching, and relational state, regulated through mutual gaze and stable vis-à-vis orientation, are simultaneously co-constructed. In avoidant infants, a special self-regulation strategy plays a critical role in the capacity to sustain engagement.

Two-Year Follow-up: Subsequent Disturbance of Interactive Regulation

These same 35 infants were videotaped with their mothers in face-to-face play with toys at two years by Sarro (1993), Goldstein (1993), and Zicht (1993). For mothers and infants alike, vocalization, gaze, and manipulation were coded second by second to identify whether attention was on an object, the partner, or object-plus-partner.

The ability of toddlers to coordinate their attention to both a person and an object is a milestone of cognitive and social development. As the developmental heir to the early infant's face-to-face play, this ability is related to communicative competence and symbolically mediated conversation. Across the group, irrespective of attachment classification, robust bidirectional (mutual) regulation of attentional focus was demonstrated: there were as many findings of mothers influencing toddlers as the reverse. Over the group, toddlers were most responsive to their mothers in the modalities of vocalization and gaze, and mothers were most responsive in gaze.

In our examination of possible differences between the secure and insecure-avoidant groups, the secure and the avoidant toddlers and their mothers were similarly mutually responsive to each other's gaze behavior. However, whereas all the secure toddlers were responsive to mothers' vocal behavior, the avoidant toddlers manifested no responsivity in any modality to the mothers' vocal behavior. These are the same infants who, at four months, had to do self-regulatory self-touching in order to sustain visual engagement with mother. Thus, we can conclude that self-regulatory disturbance at four months predicts insecure attachment at one year and is followed by a disturbance in responsivity to mother's language at two years.

The insecure-avoidant toddler is thus unresponsive to the mother's vocal attentional focus, markedly altering the context for language acquisition. We suggest that, as a consequence, the insecure toddler's developing language will not be imbued with the same level of dyadically shared meaning (A. Harris, personal communication, April 10, 1993). In speculating about the transformational consequences we must ask, will this adult's experience of language, his associative web and his ability to track the language of the analyst be altered? Will this person's language be less object related? Will he have a lessened ability to use language within the dyadic context for relational purposes?

For her part, the mothers of the insecure-avoidant toddlers showed responsivity in twice as many of the gaze analyses as the mothers of the secure toddlers. For example, mothers of the avoidant toddlers were twice as likely to shift their gaze to match their infants' visual focus on an object, to sustain their gaze while both looked at an object, or to shift gaze into a mutual gaze encounter with the infant. Thus, mothers of the avoidant toddlers can be described as more vigilant in comparison with the mothers of the secure toddlers.

If mother and infant are viewed as a system, each can be seen as responding to the other. To what degree is the mother of an insecure toddler compensating for her toddler's lack of vocal responsivity by providing more gaze responsivity herself? And to what degree is the insecure toddler less responsive in reaction to the mother's higher levels of contingency? And to what degree is the avoidant toddler's absence of responsivity to the mother's vocal attentional focus a continuing index of disturbances already evident as early as four months?

We assume that all self-regulatory strategies are adaptive attempts to affect a compromise between the need to maintain engagement with the partner and the need to protect organismic integrity by keeping levels of arousal within tolerable ranges. Thus, an avoidant infant's self-touching is highly adaptive since this strategy enables the infant to look at the mother for as long as the secure infant does. It may also be costly, however, in deployment of energy and attention.

If not using a strategy of self-touching, the avoidant infant can use a strategy of cocking the head while looking at the mother. This latter strategy has the quality of simultaneously approaching and avoiding, whereas self-touching enables the infant to maintain *en face* engagement comparable to that of the secure infant.

The finding that positive affect disturbs the avoidant infant's ability to maintain a stable vis-à-vis orientation to the mother is fascinating. We assume that the heightened arousal of positive affect is difficult to manage. Again, there is a simultaneous activation of approach through positive affect and of withdrawal through the heads being "cocked for escape." As shown by Field (1981), looking away is a potent method of decreasing arousal.

Implications for Adult Treatment

Koulomzin and colleagues' (1993) finding that, during positive affect the head orientation of avoidant infants was no longer stable, may be relevant to adult treatment. For infant and adult patients alike, positive affect may be overarousing, indexing a self-regulatory difficulty. If the head is cocked, ready to avert, positive affect will be experienced differently by both partners. We suggest that the patient's own experience of positive affect will be problematic if his orientation is cocked for escape, probably associated with a different pattern of arousal than positive affect in a face-to-face orientation. We also suggest that the analyst's experience of the patient's positive affect will be altered by a head orientation that is slightly askew. The patient who is looking and feeling positive, but whose head is in a slightly averted orientation, may seem seem "ambivalent," "wary," or "flirtatiously coy."

Certain nonverbal patterns can be observed in the consulting room. They may be picked up by the analyst out of awareness and yet inform the analyst's verbal and nonverbal interventions. We would like to use the details of these nonverbal regulations to refine the analyst's ability to notice moment-by-moment self-regulatory attempts. These nonverbal patterns are rooted in adaptive efforts to effect a compromise between the need for engagement with the partner and the need to maintain one's own organismic integrity (arousal in a comfortable range). We are not interested in pathologizing these interactions nor necessarily drawing them into one interpretive system or another. When a patient comes with a history of disruption of engagement, these moment-to-moment shifts in self-regulatory strategies can inform both patient and analyst as to the kinds of compromises that have been and continue to be necessary.

These experiences are often very difficult to put into words. The patient may not be quite aware of them. The aspects of their history from which these behaviors are derived are also likely to be out of awareness. If the analyst can "read" the nonverbal communications, from the ongoing stream of behavior in both the patient and herself, they have the potential to alert her, often well before the verbal process can do so, to subtle difficulties in the engagement. Once the nonverbal communication is decoded, usually much investigation will be necessary to understand the history and meaning. Subtle nonverbal comunications are particularly powerful because they occur in the here-and-now of the interactive matrix. Thus they possess that special alive quality of something immediate for both.

We are also interested in the mother of the avoidant toddler. She is twice as responsive in her gaze behavior to her toddler as is the secure mother. As we have noted, it is impossible to know the degree to which the avoidant toddler's lack of responsivity to mother's vocalizations is (partially) a response to the mother's hypercontingency in gaze or, conversely, the degree to which the mother's hypercontingency in gaze is a compensatory vigilance in an effort to reach an avoidant child. From the latter point of view, this maternal strategy could be seen as playing to the avoidant infant's strength, since he remains as visually responsive as the secure infant. If so, the mother's hypervigilance in gaze might facilitate the interaction. However, it may also be intrusive, and these two possibilities cannot be distinguished in these particular data. Nevertheless, the avoidant toddler's lack of responsivity to mother's vocalization is an index of an interactive system that was already shown to be aberrant at four and twelve months.

By the time this toddler grows up and appears in our consulting room as an adult patient, the contributions of both partners are represented in an expectation of dyadic misregulation. To draw an analogy between the analyst and the hypervigilant mother of the avoidant toddler, compensatory vigilance is a common response to a patient who is difficult to engage. However, that very vigilance may itself disturb the interaction. It may be experienced by the patient as intrusive, shadowing, or suffocating. Other kinds of patients, however, may experience the analyst's compensatory vigilance as a lifeline: someone is looking, watching, noticing everything.

Special Self-Regulatory Requirements for Engagement in an Adult Patient

In the following adult treatment case, the issue of special self-regulatory requirements for engagement was a salient organizing principle of the treatment. The case illustrates the therapist's task of becoming aware of and decoding the nonverbal communication, through her own behavior and that of the patient, as well as the investigation of the history and meaning of the behavior.

Jennifer (treated by Beebe) is in her 15th year of treatment, the first half of which occurred on a five-times-weekly basis, and the second half two or three times weekly. In the first half of the treatment, Jennifer seldom appeared in person more than once a week for her sessions. The remaining sessions were held on the telephone. During this period Jennifer had a great deal of difficulty getting out of bed. In the first five years of the treatment, she was extremely suicidal.

Now Jennifer comes to sessions and she is no longer suicidal. She sits up but almost never looks at me. Her head is down, her curly hair partially covers her face, and she has nothing to say. She keeps her arousal inhibited, seldom moving or shifting. She keeps her coat by her side on the floor so that she can leave quickly at the end of the session.

Jennifer's mother was depressed and seldom got out of bed. In the course of the treatment, a model scene was constructed (Lichtenberg, Lachmann, and Fosshage, 1992). Jennifer was jubilant that her mother visited her in nursery school. One day she and her mother were in the school yard at the swing. As her mother pushed her higher, she felt that she was the "queen of the school." Suddenly, her mother abruptly departed, leaving Jennifer crestfallen. Jennifer resolved that she would rather be home with her mother and refused to return to nursery school.

A second model scene of abandonment also emerged. At home, the mother would frequently close off her "wing of the house," locking it with a movable wall. Jennifer would lie on the floor on her side of the wall for hours, often crying, but her mother never came. "I was so left alone, I wasn't sure if I was alive or not."

Unlike the Koulomzin et al. (1993) finding that it was the infant who broke the mutual gaze at the moment of heightened positive arousal, in Jennifer's history it was the mother who broke the contact at such a moment. The moment of heightened positive arousal thus became dangerous for Jennifer. At any moment, she could lose her partner and become crestfallen.

In the treatment Jennifer cannot look, keeps her head down, and must keep her arousal dampened lest she become excited, happy, and overaroused, anticipating at any moment that I will disrupt the contact. She does not trust me to "swing her." Parallel to the Koulomzin finding, Jennifer has developed special self-regulatory requirements in order to engage with her partner, that is, not looking and dampening her arousal. Only then is there a chance that she might talk.

Jennifer's behavior can be seen within the context of Tronick's (1989) model of the origins of psychopathology in infants of depressed mothers. He described interactions in which mothers were unable to monitor and respond to their infants' affect and arousal states. As these interactions failed to regulate the infants in an optimal range, the infants became increasingly preoccupied with self-regulation and the management of distress states on their own. The dampened arousal and gaze aversion in the treatment, as well as the child lying for hours on the floor in front of the wall, can be seen as Jennifer's preoccupation with an attempt to regulate her distress states on her own.

Our model of optimum development posits a balance between self- and interactive regulation, as described in chapter 5. In Tronick's (1989) study of depressed mothers the balance shifted toward excessive preoccupation with self-regulation of distress states. In disorganized-attachment infants and their mothers, in the vocal rhythm coordination study noted earlier (Jaffe et al., 2001), the balance shifted toward a preoccupation with interactive regulation, with a heightened level of monitoring the partner, and presumably with a sacrifice of access to inner state (Sander, 1985).

Jennifer seems to display difficulties on both sides of the imbalance between self- and interactive regulation. She describes herself as hypervigilant for rejection from the world. She reports that, whenever she has the attention of someone important to her, she feels happy but painfully overaroused and she cannot figure out what she, herself, feels or needs: "I'll lose the attention. Will I say something wrong? If only I could do it right this time, could I keep it? I almost want it to go away. It's good but it's too painful. It will become my fault when they do turn away from me. I feel so overstimulated. If I stay the victim and they are mean and I don't have the stage, it's easier. When I do have the stage, I lose myself. I talk too much or I interrupt."

Jennifer fears the possibility of having positive experiences that will destabilize her. Her vigilance leads her to focus only on cues of rejection. Rejection experiences do not lead to heightened arousal and excitement; thus they are "safe." As positive experiences occur, she does not process other social cues: when to talk and when to pause, or whose turn it is to speak; she describes herself as "interrupting or talking too much." We would describe her as very selectively hypervigilant. In this vignette she also reveals that, at the moment of hypervigilance for rejection, she loses access to her inner state and is unable to figure out what she needs.

Self-Regulatory Requirements for Engagement in the Analyst

Koulomzin and colleagues' (1993) data suggest that we pay more attention to the patient's self-regulatory movements. Instead of being judged as evasive, distracting, dissociative, or masturbatory, self-regulatory behaviors may actually facilitate the engagement. *Both* patient and analyst use these self-regulatory behaviors to stabilize the engagement. Patient and analyst are both alert to the other's state of comfort and minor fluctuations of this state. These behaviors, when subjected to analysis, can yield valuable clues to the state of each and the quality of the relatedness.

What are the self-regulatory, self-comforting behaviors that the analyst uses to sustain engagement? The analyst touches her hair, shifts her posture, wiggles her feet, rubs her hands together, blows her nose, coughs, yawns, and so on. In treating a traumatized patient, Dolores, I (Beatrice) had the opportunity to see myself in a videotaped therapy session. I discovered that I do a great deal of self-regulatory touching, much of it out of awareness. I did know that at times I rub my hands together, particularly when they hurt a little, but I did not realize how much I do it. I was also not aware that frequently I rub my thumb and forefinger together, very slightly. It is very unlikely that I would ever have become aware of this behavior without the aid of the videotape. Such behaviors may remain out of awareness of both patient and analyst but nevertheless are perceived at a subliminal level and operate as information to both.

In another session (not videotaped) Dolores (treated by Beebe) had a dissociated episode, and I could not make contact with her. During this time I became "squirmy," uncomfortable, shifting the pillow, moving around in my chair. My squirminess forced me to acknowledge to myself my degree of distress in the face of my inability to reach her. In turn, Dolores was able to notice and talk about her effect on me. In discussing this episode later on, Dolores reported that my squirminess had made it harder for her to "come back" and find a way to "rest" in me as she usually did. However, she also told me that my squirminess had made her more aware that I existed and in that sense did help her to come back to me.

In another episode in the treatment of Dolores, when I felt her to be inaccessible I began to rub my feet together. I recognized it as a gesture that I had used throughout my childhood to put myself to sleep at night. My behavior illustrates the usual and inadvertent self-regulatory requirements of the analyst and the impact of interferences in interactive regulation on the analyst's self-regulation. I commented to Dolores that I noticed that I had been rubbing my feet together. Dolores was then able to come forward and make the observation that it happened just when she was refusing a comforting interpretation that I was giving her, so I comforted myself. I very much appreciated her observation. A very intimate moment followed in which we both felt closer, and she expressed regret at having been so inaccessible.

These self-regulatory behaviors of patient and analyst, such as subtle head and gaze aversions and postural orientations, add valuable additional information to the treatment, when they are recognized and acknowledged and their place in the ongoing interaction is understood. They can provide critical information about the state of relatedness between the two partners and can disclose various difficulties in regulating the engagement.

Whereas the Koulomzin et al. (1993) data addressed self-regulation processes in infants, there is also adult work that bears on the self-regulation process in analysts. Freedman and his colleagues (1978) have been studying nonverbal self-regulation strategies and the role of self-touch in attentional focus for two decades. They argue that movements of the body can promote or retard listening in an interchange. They distinguish between self-focused body movements that reflect information filtering and decoding and object-focused movements that participate in the process of symbolic representation. Freedman emphasizes that nonverbal behavior in the adult is closely tied to verbal behavior: "The movements are a precondition for verbalization, and constitute the preverbal activities necessary for the attainment of full symbolic representation" (p. 173).

Freedman argues that self-focused body movements are a key aspect of the listening process. He considers various forms of self-focused body movements (scratching, grooming, rubbing) to be a compensatory response to some interference in the focusing of attention. These movements implement a change in state that facilitates more optimal information processing.

Freedman describes the listening process as composed of the oscillating demands of receptivity and engagement with the partner (receiving information) and the capacity to disengage from the partner sufficiently to "refocus." Refocusing is the ability to restructure information in terms of a preexisting frame of reference. During reflective refocusing, the listener may be more open to associations and memories. Freedman's group analyzed 142 listening sequences from 20 female college students who participated in a conflict-resolution discussion of a moral dilemma, each with another student. Their data suggest that bilateral continuous self-touching before the onset of the partner's verbalization seemed to enhance the listener's capacity to absorb the partner's message. On the other hand, a "contrasting" movement (motor discharge) at the point of the listener's transition from silence to verbalization seemed to create a body-state facilitating sufficient disengagement to allow refocusing.

Although this work is not specifically on therapists and patients, it has great relevance for the analyst's own self-regulatory processes and the necessity for considerable flexibility. It calls attention to different functions of self-touch behavior, which facilitate different aspects of the listening process. We would add that specific variations in the interactive regulation process will affect the analyst's use of these self-regulation strategies in the listening process. For example, we speculate that in the face of a patient's extreme affect-states, such as intense rage, or extreme deadness, the analyst may use these self-regulation processes more extensively and more out of awareness. Reciprocally, the specific variations in the analyst's use of these self-regulation strategies will affect the nature of the interactive process. For example, some patients are very distracted or derailed by the analyst's shifts in posture, head orientation, or gaze.

Hypervigilant Forms of Interactive Regulation:
A Case Illustration

In the Jaffe et al. (2001) study of vocal rhythm described in the previous chapter, the most problematic attachment outcomes ("disorganized") at one year were predicted from those mothers and four-month infants who showed the highest degree of rhythm coordination. The other end of the range, very low degree of rhythm coordination, also predicted insecure attachment (avoidant). Midrange degree of coordination predicted secure infants. Where coordination was very low, the two partners were acting more relatively independently of each other, construed as withdrawal or inhibition of interpersonal monitoring. Midrange degree of coordination was hypothesized to leave more "space," more room for uncertainty, initiative, and flexibility within the experience of correspondence (coordination). A high degree of coordination increases the predictability of the interaction. High degree of predictability was construed as a coping strategy elicited by challenge, novelty, or threat. In other data (Crown, 1991), adults who were strangers showed higher coordination than adults did who were acquainted.

The treatment of a hypervigilant patient by Shumsky (1996) illustrates the interaction pattern of high coordination in adult treatment. Shumsky's patient, Sandra, carefully monitored her analyst's subtle nuances of verbal and nonverbal communication. The analyst felt that she was not nearly as skillful as Sandra in attending to subtle communications. Unaware of Sandra's hypervigilance, the analyst kept listening, assuming that she would be able to make sense of Sandra's communications. But the more she listened, the more confusing, vague, and tangential Sandra became. The more the analyst attempted to clarify, to make sense out of what Sandra was saying, the more Sandra intensified her efforts to "set things right." The more Sandra retraced the same territory to adjust, reverse, or amplify, which later came to be called "spinning," the more the analyst, in parallel fashion, would "spin," or disengage to curtail the dizziness. If the analyst commented on the spin, Sandra would feel ashamed and spin some more.

Over time Sandra and her analyst came to understand that any hint of the analyst's anxious "not knowing" meant to Sandra that the analyst was "collapsing at the wheel." Sandra would then frantically take over. Sandra registered every tiny shift in the analyst's face, posture, breathing, or energy level. Sandra felt that she had to do something to restore the analyst's equanimity. On the basis of her childhood, Sandra felt that she was "too much," that she might overwhelm her analyst, as she had reduced her mother to tears and pleading apologies. In various ways the analyst had to show that she was not overwhelmed and undone by being with Sandra and that she could tolerate Sandra's torrential outpourings; that she was in control of the car.

Sandra's hypervigilant attention to every subtle nonverbal shift in the analyst, and the interactive pattern of spinning that both Sandra and her analyst participated in, show a strong similarity to the very high coordination of vocal rhythms between infant and mother documented in the disorganized attachment types by Jaffe et al. (2001). Jaffe et al. also refer to this type of coordination as hypervigilant. The task for the therapist is to appreciate the level of distress embodied in such a pattern. Shumsky's case demonstrates the possibility that, once the function of the pattern is understood, it can shift.

Orientational Aversion

In face-to-face interactions, we are tremendously affected by slight orientational aversions that indicate alterations and disturbances in the engagement process. This is a pervasive aspect of the face-to-face adult treatment situation. We briefly review here some infant data, an adult experiment, adult videotaped psychotherapy data, and an adult treatment vignette.

Research Case Studies of Infant Orientational Aversion

Severe orientational aversion illustrates infant self-regulatory efforts in the context of disturbances of interactive regulation. In Stern's (1971) study of one mother playing simultaneously with her two three-month-old twins, head and gaze behaviors were coded frame-by-frame from 16mm film (one frame = $1/24$ second). Whenever the mother oriented and looked toward one twin (Mark), this infant likewise oriented and looked toward her, and vice versa: either partner could start this process, and the other would reciprocate. However, with the other twin, Fred, the opposite pattern unfolded. Whenever the mother moved toward Fred, Fred would orient and look away; likewise, whenever Fred moved toward mother, mother would orient away toward the other twin. With Mark, the interaction structure was one of mutual approach-approach and withdrawal-withdrawal. With Fred, the interaction structure was one of mutual approach-withdrawal.

Stern first described in this case the extreme 90° aversions of Fred as he moved his head away until his chin was parallel with his shoulder. Extreme orientational and postural "cut-off" acts have been described by ethologists in both animal and child behavior (Blurton-Jones, 1972; McGrew, 1972; Chance and Larsen, 1996). Degree of orientation toward or away from the partner provides a powerful signal along a range of readiness to engage, tendencies toward disengagement, and relative severity of disengagement.

The "chase and dodge" interaction (Beebe and Stern, 1977), described in detail in chapter 5, revealed a similar pattern of maternal approach-infant withdrawal. This infant not only performed extreme 90° head aversions, but also pulled his hand from the mother's grasp, oriented his body away from her as she pulled him toward her, and increasingly resorted to losing postural tonus and going completely limp. This infant essentially had "veto power" over the mother's attempts to engage him visually. Although it was an aversive interaction, it was still highly bilaterally regulated; the mother's movement of her body and head toward the infant (looming) "influenced" the infant to move away, influence being defined as predictable sequences. And the infant's movements of the head and body away from the mother "influenced" the mother to chase. These sequences occurred with split-second responsivities, so that, for example, before the mother had even completed her head movement toward the infant, the infant had already begun to move away. In this pair, the infant's orientation into 90° aversion resulted in the infant's loss of peripheral visual monitoring of the mother's movements. This loss further disturbed the possibility of mutual regulation, since the infant sacrificed the realm of visual negotiation.

Research on Orientation in Adults

The power of head orientation and direction of gaze can be seen in an experiment by Frey et al. (1983) (cited in Fogel, 1993a), who asked viewers to rate the famous painting *Mona Lisa* with a list of adjectives. When the first group of subjects viewed the original painting, in which the famous lady's head and gaze are oriented toward the viewer, she was described as dreamy, friendly, sensitive, involved, honest, and inviting. A second group of subjects looked at an altered version of the painting in which her head and gaze were oriented slightly to the left, away from the viewer. These subjects were unaware that the painting had been altered. In this altered version, the lady was described by the subjects as proud, tense, unsympathetic, cold, and detached. This list of adjectives is strikingly similar to common descriptions of the narcissistic personality. Interestingly, the first list could describe an ideal therapist.

Videotape Analysis of Adult Psychotherapy

Trout and Rosenfeld (1980) have described that during psychotherapy sessions (sitting up), a report of higher rapport by patients and therapists alike is associated with a higher incidence of leaning the upper bodies toward each other and holding the limbs in mirror image postures. Thus rapport may be disturbed if either partner is involved in any degree of orientational aversion.

Davis and Hadiks (1990) coded videotapes of face-to-face psychotherapy sessions between a female patient and a male therapist. They coded orientational/position states (varying from full away to full face-to-face orientation). They also coded verbalization for level of experiential involvement. They found that the therapist's intensity and complexity of gestures increased as his verbalized affective immediacy and interpretive complexity increased. With higher levels of verbal involvement, the therapist also increasingly oriented toward the patient. Similarly, as the patient shifted from superficial discussion to actively exploring her internal reactions, her bodily position became more accessible, open, and oriented toward the therapist.

Davis and Hadiks concluded that orientation and bodily position are indices of subtle fluctuations in defensiveness and rapport and level of emotional involvement between the partners. The researchers also note that, while these subtle movement patterns are not likely to be experienced consciously by either partner, they are "read" by both, are an essential basis of the therapist's clinical intuition, and are a critical part of the therapy process. Thus, establishing rapport in therapy is highly associated with orientational engagement.

Vignette of Orientational Aversion in Adult Treatment: Elisa

Elisa (treated by Beebe) sat with her head 45° off midline, her gaze down, her chin tucked under onto her chest, her face in a grimace. When she glanced up at me from that position, her head was always oriented down and to the side; she never directly faced me. She seldom made eye contact. The fleeting moments when she looked up from underneath conveyed to me a feeling of much sadness, remoteness, and pain. She was inconsolable, and she despaired that I could help her. In my own feeling of isolation, at times I took notes.

In the third year of the treatment, this orientational and facial behavior began to recede strikingly when a selfobject tie began to consolidate. As she gradually became more capable of engaging with me, I stopped taking notes. Elisa was very struck by this shift in me, and she, in turn, shifted her orientation, beginning to sit in a more vis-a-vis posture, and making more eye contact. This shift in Elisa enabled me to be more spontaneous. The selfobject tie consolidated on both sides, and we both came forward. The nonverbal behavior itself was never interpreted, but it had been a powerful source of information about the severity of the disturbance in engagement, and it had affected my own capacity to respond to her.

Conclusion: Toward a Procedural Theory of Interaction

Psychoanalysis is currently seeking an expanded theory of interaction. We contend that this theory must ultimately address the nonverbal as well as the verbal dimensions of the interaction (see Bucci, 1985, 1997; Lyons-Ruth, 1998b; Pally, 1998, 2001; Stern et al., 1998). The nonverbal, procedural dimension is usually out of awareness, and it provides a continuous background of moment-by-moment mutual influence. The verbal system is usually in the foreground and is more intermittent (i.e., speaking versus listening). In parallel to the exchanges that occur on a verbal level, patient and analyst are continuously altering each other's timing, spatial organization, affect, and arousal on a moment-to-moment basis.

Moment-by-moment interactive regulation is a fundamental aspect of social behavior at the nonverbal level across the life span. Each partner has continuous rhythms of behavior on and off, and even the "off" moments of verbal or gestural "silence" are communicative (Jaffe and Feldstein, 1970). The rhythms of behavior of the two partners are always coordinated, in some way, usually out of awareness (Iberall and McCulloch, 1969; Chapple, 1970; Capella, 1991; Langs, Badalamenti, and Thompson, 1996; Warner, 1996).

In this chapter we have addressed the nonverbal, procedural dimension, using a theory of interaction that specifies how a person is affected by his own behavior (self-regulation) as well as by that of his partner (interactive regulation). Interactive regulation flows in both directions, on a moment-to-moment basis. Behavior is communicative, as well as self-regulatory, so that shifts in influencing and being influenced by the partner are accompanied by simultaneous shifts in self-regulatory behaviors and arousal. We have argued that this view of nonverbal interaction is as relevant to adult communication as it is to mother–infant communication. We return to this topic in the final chapter.

7

REPRESENTATION AND INTERNALIZATION IN INFANCY

Three Principles of Salience

In this chapter we return to one of the basic themes of the book: how the mind is organized in interaction. We revisit the subject of presymbolic representation in order to illuminate the origins of internalization. We suggest three organizing principles, three principles of salience, that determine the salience of events for the infant and organize what the infant expects from interactive encounters. These three principles are ongoing regulations, disruption and repair of ongoing regulations, and heightened affective moments. They further define the nature of self- and interactive regulation. They constitute hypotheses about how expectancies of social interactions become patterned and salient in the first year. In the next chapter we apply these principles of salience to an adult treatment case, showing how they can further specify modes of therapeutic action. These three principles give us additional ways of drawing analogies between adult treatment and infant research.

Of the three principles, the overarching one is ongoing regulations, based on the expected and characteristic ways in which an interaction unfolds. Disruption and repair captures a specific sequence broken out of the broad pattern. In heightened affective moments, one dramatic instance stands out in time. Thus the three principles provide a hierarchical definition of interaction patterns, temporally organized at three levels: the broad pattern, a sequence, and a moment. These three levels of organization should be seen as a nested series in which each level constitutes a context for the next.

Each of our three principles of salience provides a different perspective on the organization of representations and on the origins of internalization in the first year. Self- and object representations can be seen as based on early perceptual capacities; interaction patterns; and emerging capacities for category formation, abstraction, and, later, symbol formation. Interaction patterns are characteristic modes of interactive and self-regulation that the infant comes to recognize, remember, and expect. Whereas in previous chapters we used only the principle of ongoing regulations, we now conceptualize interaction patterns and representations as organized by all three principles.

This description of representations as organized by the three principles of salience can simultaneously illuminate the origins of internalization. Interactive regulation is a central concept both in the empirical infant literature and in discussions of internalization (Schafer, 1968). In our view, however, interactive regulations do not *become* inner regulations. Rather, interactive regulations have always been inner, in the sense that they always occur in tandem with self regulations. We suggest a view of internalization in the first year in which both partners jointly construct modes of regulation that include interactive as well as self regulations. The expectation and representation of the dyadic modes of regulation, as organized by the three principles of salience, constitute the inner organization.

Why Three Principles?

In considering the question of which principles determine the centrality of events for an infant, is it the infant's recognition of what is regular, predictable, and "invariant" in his interactions that becomes salient? Stern (1985) held this view in his discussion of the invariants of sequence, causality, affect, and memory. Similarly, we have also argued (Beebe and Lachmann, 1988a, b) that the predictable ongoing regulations in mother–infant interactions create expectancies that organize the infant's experience. Wilson and Malatesta (1989) also argued that repetitive interactive experiences influence what is subject to repetition in adult life—the principle we have called ongoing regulations.

Or is it the infant's recognition that something changes or disrupts his interactions or violates his expectancies, along with the subsequent effort to repair the disruption, that organizes his experience? Behrends and Blatt (1985), Horner (1985), Stechler and Kaplan (1980), and Tronick (1989; Gianino and Tronick, 1988) noted the formative impact of these interactions of disruption and repair. Kohut (1984), in the analyses of adults, emphasized this sequence in his discussion of structure formation through empathic ruptures and transmuting internalizations. We term this principle of salience "disruption and repair."

Or is it the power of heightened affective moments, both positive and negative, that colors and thus organizes experience? Demos (1983, 1984), Emde (1981), Socarides and Stolorow (1984/85), and especially Pine (1981, 1986), in his concept of "heightened moments," have put forth this point of view. This principle of salience is the one we are calling heightened affective moments. Wilson and Malatesta (1989) noted that it was still an unresolved empirical question whether chronicity of exposure, intensity of exposure, or an interaction of the two most contributes to later dispositions.

Rather than being viewed as operating separately, these principles need to be conceptualized together. For example, an ongoing pattern of regulation must first exist before a disruption can be perceived. The particular nature and sequence of disruption may itself become an expected interaction pattern. A heightened affective moment may function either as a disruption or as a repair. All three principles must be brought to bear on any particular interaction to explicate fully its organizing potential. The three principles constitute different angles of the camera. In a particular instance, however, one principle may be more compelling than the others. For heuristic purposes, we are pulling them apart; nonetheless, the three principles potentially interact.

Stern's (1985) theory of RIGs (Representations of Interactions Generalized) implicitly uses the principle of ongoing regulations to explain how RIGs are organized. That is, the RIG is based on a generalized abstraction of a typical sequence. In adding the principles of disruption and repair and of heightened affective moments, we define other critical aspects of interactions that organize experience. There may well be additional salient principles yet to be explicated that would broaden our understanding of how representations may be organized in the first year.

In addressing the question of which attributes of an infant's experience are dominant in the formation of representations, Stern (1988) argues that affect does not have a privileged role. He suggests that all attributes of experience (perceptual, cognitive, motoric, sensory, affective) organize representations and that any single one may play a central role for a particular event. We propose, instead, that there are privileged routes, salient organizing principles, that partake of, but cut across, Stern's wide range of factors. That is, perception, cognition, action, affect, and arousal are all organized by each of our three principles. While agreeing that affect is not necessarily the central organizer, we suggest that heightened affect *is* one salient route to internalization along with ongoing regulations and disruption and repair. Although affect is a component of all three principles, intense affect is a sufficiently unique dimension in the creation of expectancies to justify its consideration as a third principle of organization.

Affect and arousal are linked; nevertheless they are distinguishable. We reserve the term affect for facial display and vocal pattern (such as contour, pitch, and volume). We define arousal as the pattern of physiological indices, such as EEG, heart rate, and respiration. Nevertheless, in experience, a particular facial or vocal pattern is always associated with a particular arousal state (Ekman, 1983). Although numerous categorical approaches to affect (Izard, 1979; Tomkins, 1980; Malatesta et al., 1989) have been useful in studying infants, our approach lays equal emphasis on the gradient and display fluctuations within any particular affect category (Werner, 1948; Tobach, 1970; Beebe, 1973; Oster and Ekman, 1977; Stern, 1985). Affect is a component of all three principles.

Self- and Object Representations Are Rooted in Interaction Patterns

Interest in the formative role of interaction has a history within psychoanalysis, in which the representation of relationships has been an emphasis. Interactions with the object world have been viewed as constituting an inner regulation as well as an interactive regulation (see Behrends and Blatt, 1985, for a review; see also Hartmann, 1939; Jacobson, 1964; Schafer, 1968; Loewald, 1980; Spitz, 1983). Loewald (1960), discussing psychic structure formation, proposed that the internalization of the interactional processes of a person with his objects is an essential constitutive factor.

Other current conceptualizations view early experience as organized through dyadic interactions. The "dyadically forged mind" (Wilson and Malatesta, 1989), the "interpersonal self" (Kegan, 1982; Stern 1983, 1985, 1989), the "intersubjective matrix" (Stolorow et al., 1987; Benjamin, 1988), and the "relational mind" (Fast, 1988; Mitchell, 1988, 1993; Aron, 1996) all conceptualize self and object and their representations as rooted in relationship structures (see Zelnick and Bucholz, 1990 for a review). We emphasize that both self- and interactive regulation organize relationship patterns. This view is consonant with the work of Aron (1996), Demos (1983, 1984), Lichtenberg (1983, 1989), Sander (1977), Stern (1985), Stolorow et al., (1987), and Tronick (1989), among others. Thus, the influence of dyadic regulation is integrated with the critical contributions of self regulations.

We confine our discussion to representations of self and object. Historically the terms self- and object representations have conveyed encapsulated and atomistic images (Modell, 1984, 1992). In our view, representations result from interactions. We hold a dynamic process transformational model of representations in which a schema is constructed and transformed through the expected moment-to-moment interplay of the two partners. What is represented is the dynamic interactive process itself (Beebe and Stern, 1977; Stern, 1977, 1985; Beebe and Lachmann, 1988a, b; Beebe et al., 1992; Lachmann and Beebe, 1992).

Representations are more or less persistent, organized classifications of information about an expected interactive sequence. They are formed by the active process of constructing and reconstructing incoming information. Representations can be reorganized and transformed as incoming information is reinterpreted and reordered on the basis of past experience and current expectations. In this transformational model, development proceeds through a process of regular restructurings of the relations within and between a person and the environment (Reese and Overton, 1970; Sameroff and Chandler, 1976; Sameroff, 1983). Predictability in development is found not in the child, not in the environment, but, rather, in the transactions between the child and the environment and in their regular transformations (Sameroff and Chandler, 1976; Zeanah et al., 1989).

Basic to representation is the capacity to order and recognize patterns, to expect what is predictable and invariant, and to create categories of these invariants. The ability to categorize experiences provides the organizational framework for memory, language, and the symbolic function (Strauss, 1979; Bornstein, 1985; Stern, 1985; Younger and Cohen, 1985; Basch, 1988; Shields and Rovee-Collier, 1992). A category is formed as the infant perceives regularities and forms a summary or central tendency of the features that vary within the category. This ability develops between three and twelve months (Cohen and Gelber, 1975; Strauss, 1979; Sherman, 1985; Stern, 1985; Younger and Gotlieb, 1988; Shields and Rovee-Collier, 1992). For example, infants categorize colors (Bornstein, 1985), faces (Cohen, De Loache, and Strauss, 1979), and shapes (Ruff, 1980; Younger and Cohen, 1985). Shields and Rovee-Collier (1992) suggest that infant categorization "is ubiquitous across ages and should not be regarded as an emergent, higher order cognitive ability. Rather, it appears to be a natural by-product of the normal, ongoing process of memory encoding and retrieval" (p. 257).

A category is a representation of the common elements of a set of distinctive experiences that the infant discriminates (Strauss, 1979;

Sherman, 1985; Younger and Gottlieb, 1988). For an infant, this "representation" is presymbolic (see Meltzoff, 1985; Stern, 1985; Beebe and Lachmann, 1988b). In elaborating on this presymbolic representation, Mandler (1988) has argued that a primitive form of representational ability exists in the early months of life which links the infant's sensorimotor schemas to the later symbolic form of representation (see Werner and Kaplan, 1963).

We propose that over the course of the first year and beyond, the three principles constitute criteria by which interactions will be categorized and ultimately represented. In the same way that infants categorize faces, shapes, colors, and animals, they also form schemas or categories of interpersonal interactions (see Beebe and Stern, 1977; Stern, 1985; Beebe and Lachmann, 1988a, b).

After the first year, as representations become increasingly symbolic, following the principle of ongoing regulations, the eventual representation, if ever translated into verbal form, may be something like, "I can expect that things will usually go like this." Following the principle of disruption and repair, the representation may be, "This is what happens when things are off. I can expect that they will get fixed, and this is how we fix them." Following the principle of heightened affect, the representation may be "What a wonderful (terrible, awesome) moment." If these interactions are verbalized and labeled, this process may transform the original representions (Stern, 1985).

We assume that representations in the first year are encoded in a nonverbal, implicit mode of information, which may be motoric (procedural), imagistic, acoustic, or visceral. They may not necessarily be translated into linguistic form. Bucci (1985) suggests that verbal and nonverbal information have separate specialized systems for representation. Whereas verbal information is stored in linguistic form, nonverbal information is stored in perceptual channels through, for example, images, sounds, smells, touch, and temperature. Both systems are potentially accessible to consciousness. However, implicit processing, such as motoric or imagistic schemas, may under certain circumstances be inaccessible to attention or language, but may nevertheless continue to operate and affect how we act and feel. The nonverbal representational system begins in the first year of life, and the three principles of salience provide hypotheses about how such perceptual information will be organized.

The Principle of Ongoing Regulations

Ongoing regulations provides the most basic principle organizing representations. Authors from widely divergent vantage points implicitly use it to infer what organizes experience (for example, Loewald, 1971; Sander, 1977; Sandler and Sandler, 1978; Demos, 1984; Bretherton, 1985; Stern, 1985; Lichtenberg, 1989; Malatesta et al., 1989; Wilson and Malatesta, 1989).

The principle of ongoing regulations refers to those characteristic, predictable, and expected ways in which an interaction unfolds. A shared system of rules for the regulation of the actions of the two partners develops. In a well-ordered interaction, each partner's communicative behavior conforms to the other's expectations (Tronick, 1980).

The principle of ongoing regulations derives from a regulatory-systems perspective (Sander, 1977, 1983; Beebe et al., 1992). Organization is a property of the infant–caretaker system as well as a property of an individual. It is now well established that there are many such shared systems of rules for the regulation of joint action in the first year of life, well before language develops (see, e.g., Bakeman and Brown, 1977; Bruner, 1977, 1983; Stern, 1977, 1985; Field, 1981; Beebe et al., 1985; Cohn and Tronick, 1988; Tronick, 1989).

There is extensive experimental evidence that, from birth and even before, babies form expectations of predictable events (DeCasper and Carstens, 1980; DeCasper and Fifer, 1980; Fagen et al., 1984; DeCasper and Spence, 1986; Greco et al., 1986). Haith's research (Haith, Hazan, and Goodman, 1988; see also Emde, 1988) on visual activity in the early months suggests that infants are biologically prepared to detect regularity, generate expectancies, and act on these expectations.

That expectancies operate so pervasively, so early, accounts for the enormous influence they have in organizing experience (Fagen et al., 1989). Neurophysiological evidence also suggests that familiarity, repetition, and expectancy underly the most powerful organizing principle of neural functioning (Gazzaniga and LeDoux, 1978; Cormier, 1981; Hadley, 1983, 1989).

An infant's perception of ongoing regulations is thus based on his capacity to notice and predict what is repetitive and expectable in his environment and the critical ability to discern that the behavior produces consequences. The neonate detects "contingencies," predictable relationships between his own behavior and the environment's response to it (Papousek and Papousek, 1979; DeCasper and Carstens, 1980; DeCasper and Fifer, 1980; Watson, 1985). An infant develops an expectation of when events will occur and an expectation that his behavior produces consequences. Whether or not the environment provides contingent and expectable responses for the infant will affect his attention, memory, emotions, and the very ability to learn (DeCasper and Carstens, 1980). Reciprocally, the infant peceives predictable relations between environmental events and his own behavior. The infant develops an expectation that the environment affects him. Thus, both partners—infant and caretaker—develop exectations that each affects, and is affected by, the other in predictable ways.

The principle of ongoing regulations encompasses all characteristic patterns by which the two partners regulate their communicative behavior. "Successful" as well as "unsuccessful" patterns are embodied in this principle, which includes both self- and interactive regulation.

Ongoing Regulations: Interactive Regulation

The interactive regulation model is central to the principle of ongoing regulations. It has emerged over the past two decades in reaction to much previous work that focused on one-way influences in child development. The parent's influence on the child was primarily studied, to the relative exclusion of the child's influence on the parent (Bell, 1968; Lewis and Lee-Painter, 1974; Lewis and Rosenblum, 1974; Cappella, 1981; Gianino and Tronick, 1988). As recognition of infants' social capacities grew (Lewis and Rosenblum, 1974), however, interest in patterns of interactive regulation heightened. It came to be seen that, although each partner does not influence the other in equal measure or necessarily in like manner, both actively contribute to the regulation of the exchange. The mother obviously has greater range and flexibility in this process. By *mutual regulation*, we mean that each partner's behavioral stream can be predicted from the other's.

We (Beebe and Stern 1977; Beebe, 1985; Beebe and Lachmann, 1988a, b) have proposed a central role for early interaction patterns in the organization of infant experience. Consistent with the principle of ongoing regulations, interaction patterns are characteristic modes of mutual and self-regulation. The dynamic interplay between the actions (including perceptions, affects, and proprioceptions) of infant and of caretaker, as each influences the other, creates a variety of mutual regulatory patterns. The infant comes to recognize, remember, expect, generalize, and represent characteristic interaction patterns (Stern, 1985; Beebe and Lachmann, 1988b). In the following sections, interaction patterns are also defined by the principles of disruption and repair and heightened affective moments.

The study of the regulation of mother–infant interaction has been occupied to a considerable degree with detailing the various influences of each partner on the other's behavior. Patterns of interactive regulation have been variously termed synchronization (Stern, 1971, 1977), behavioral dialogue (Bakeman and Brown, 1977), protoconversation (Beebe et al., 1979, 1988), tracking (Kronen, 1982), accommodation (Jasnow and Feldstein, 1986), mutual dialogues (Tronick, 1980, 1982, 1989), reciprocal and compensatory mutual influence (Capella, 1981), and coordinated interpersonal timing (Beebe and Jaffe, 1992a, b; Beebe et al., 1985; Jaffe et al., 2001). Using diverse methods of coding and statistical procedures, researchers have demonstrated patterns of interactive regulation across such modalities as gaze, facial expression, vocalization, and spatial orientation (see Beebe et al., 1992, for a review). Although bidirectional influences are preponderant in the literature (see, e.g., Stern, 1971, 1977, 1985; Cohn and Tronick, 1988; Beebe and Jaffe, 1992a; Jaffe et al.,

2001), one-way influences, where one partner influences the other but without reciprocation, can also be found (e.g., Thomas and Martin, 1976; Gottman and Ringland, 1981; Zelner, 1982; Jaffe et al., 2001).

Using a definition of early presymbolic representation as the storage of distinctive features of information, we have proposed that the distinctive features of ongoing face-to-face regulations will be likewise represented (Beebe and Lachmann, 1988b). This proposal presumes that the patterns of regulation that have been demonstrated by researchers are also perceived as salient by infants. The distinctive features of these patterns can be described as the organization of the interaction along temporal, spatial, affective, and proprioceptive dimensions. For example, an infant will represent the temporal pattern, such as rate, rhythm, and serial order of both partners; the presence or absence of interpersonal contingencies and mutual influences; the pattern of the movement of the two partners in space such as approach-approach or approach-withdrawal; and the interactive regulation of facial affective patterns. The accompanying proprioceptive stimulation and pattern of arousal, and modes of regulating this stimulation, will also be represented. Thus, ongoing patterns of regulation as they are organized by time, space, affect, and arousal will organize the infant's experience and will be presymbolically represented.

Illustrations of Interactions Organized by Ongoing Regulations

We have described patterns of ongoing interactive regulation that illustrate qualitative differences in the expectancies of regulation that may be represented. One pattern, *facial mirroring*, illustrates moment-by-moment matching of affective direction, in which both partners may increase together, or decrease together, their degree of engagement and level of positive affect. We suggested that the infant will represent the expectation of being matched by, and being able to match, the affective direction of the partner. This matching provides each partner with a behavioral basis for knowing and entering into the other's changing feeling state.

A second pattern, *derailment*, also termed chase and dodge, illustrates the organization of the interaction primarily along the spatial dimension. In this interaction, the mother repeatedly attempts to engage the infant and the infant displays a virtuoso range of avoidance maneuvers. This interaction illustrates the possibility that a bidirectional regulation process may be intact, and yet the infant's attention, affect, and arousal are not optimally regulated. We suggested that, when such interactions are characteristic, they are represented as expectancies of misregulation.

A third pattern, *interpersonal timing*, describes the regulation of the mother–infant interaction along the temporal dimension and includes kinesic rhythm (Beebe et al., 1979), coactive and alternating vocal exchanges (Stern et al., 1975), vocal congruence (Beebe et al., 1988; Jasnow and Feldstein, 1986), and the interpersonal timing of vocal interaction (Beebe and Jaffe, 1992a; Jaffe et al., 2001). These studies document a remarkable temporal sensitivity on the part of both partners to the ongoing durations of their own and the partner's behavior. Each monitors and matches the durations of the other's behavior on a second-by-second basis.

Another group of studies documents effects into toddlerhood, predicted from interaction patterns in the early months of life. We refer to these studies as the *curvilinear prediction of attachment* described later. These effects are based on the attachment paradigm (Bowlby, 1969; Ainsworth et al., 1978; Sroufe, 1979a, b; Sroufe and Fleeson, 1986) that classifies toddlers as securely attached versus insecurely attached. Insecure attachment has three forms: avoidant, anxious-resistant, and disorganized. Following a brief separation from the mother in a laboratory setting, secure toddlers seek and maintain contact during reunion, are easily comforted, and can resume exploration of the environment. In contrast, insecure-avoidant toddlers avoid the mother; at the reunion, insecure-resistent toddlers both seek the mother and resist the contact, failing to be comforted. Insecure-disorganized toddlers show simultaneous approach and avoidance patterns during the reunion.

A number of studies (Belsky et al., 1984; Malatesta et al., 1989; Isabella and Belsky, 1991) now converge on a curvilinear relationship between maternal behavior in the first year and toddler attachment outcomes at ages one to two years. Infants who will later become securely attached have mothers who stimulate with a midlevel range of intensity, contingency, and reciprocity. Infants who will later become insecure-avoidant have mothers who are overstimulating, intrusive, high intensity, noncontingent, or overly contingent. Infants who will later become insecure-resistant have mothers who are underinvolved, detached, or inconsistent; who fail to respond; or who attempt to interact when the infant is not available.

A specific example of this group of studies is the work of Malatesta et al. (1989), who evaluated maternal contingent responsiveness in infants at two and a half, five, and seven and a half months, and toddler attachment outcome at two years. Maternal contingency was measured by a maternal facial expression change within one second of the onset of an infant facial expression change. Mothers who showed moderate levels of facial contingency to their infants had toddlers at two years who looked at them more and showed the most positive affect. Moderate levels of maternal facial contingency at seven and half months predicted secure attachment at age two, whereas high maternal contingency at seven and a half months predicted insecure-avoidant attachment at age two years. There were no insecure-resistant toddlers in the sample.

Whereas the foregoing studies focused exclusively on the nature of the mother's behavior, the study by Jaffe et al. (2001) predicted infant attachment at one year both from four-month infant contingent responsiveness to the mother and from maternal contingent responsiveness to the infant. Attachment outcomes in this study were also predicted by infant contingent response to stranger, and from stranger contingent response to infant. Using time series analysis, Jaffe and colleagues measured contingent responsiveness by the degree to which increases in the durations of one partner's vocalizations and pauses were systematically followed by increases (or decreases) in the duration of the other partner's vocal behavior. The finding was again curvilinear. Midrange values of infant and mother (and infant and stranger) contingent vocal responsiveness at four months predicted secure attachment at one year. Insecure infant attachment was predicted by contingencies at either extreme, high or low values.

This series of studies illustrates the principle that ongoing regulations of interactions organize infant experiences of relatedness over the first two years of life. Particular kinds of interactions are facilitative or disruptive of an infant's development. Evidence from different laboratories is converging on the powerful curvilinear finding that optimal interactions are midrange in intensity and contingency, both on the mother's part and on the infant's. Extremes of responsiveness at the high or low end, by either partner, predict compromised infant development.

Ongoing Regulations: Integration of Interactive and Self-Regulation

In the literature on the development of psychic structure and the self in infancy, some authors emphasize self-regulation as the key organizing principle (see, e.g., Emde, 1981; Stechler and Kaplan, 1980), other authors emphasize interactive regulation (see, e.g., Stern, 1971, 1977; Beebe and Lachmann, 1988a), and others emphasize an integration (see, e.g., Beebe et al., 1992; Sander, 1977; Demos, 1983; Gianino and Tronick, 1988; Lichtenberg, 1989). Sander's (1983, 1985) view that organization is an emergent property of the dyadic system, rather than solely of the individual, integrates the simultaneous influences of self- and interactive regulation. Because both processes are organized at birth and play a crucial role in the development of social relatedness from birth, we hold that they must be integrated in conceptualizing the development of representations.

The Brazelton (1973) Neonatal Assessment Scale is designed to evaluate infant self-regulation capacity in the context of graded degrees of support by the examiner (providing one's face, one's face and gentle vocalizing, adding touch, etc.). Thus, this scale evaluates an infant's capacity to participate in various forms of interactive regulation as a facilitation of self-regulation. For example, one dimension of the scale assesses the infant's capacity to dampen his state in response to aversive stimuli. At the same time it assesses how much help from the partner is required and can be used by the infant to stabilize his state after stress and to maintain engagement with the examiner.

The infant's capacity to respond and be socially engaged depends not only on the nature of the caretaker's stimulation and responsivity, and the nature of the infant's response to the specific stimulation, but also on the infant's regulation of his internal state of arousal. Babies differ from birth constitutionally and temperamentally in this crucial capacity to modulate their arousal, shift their state, and in general organize their behavior in predictable ways (Brazelton, 1973; Als and Brazelton, 1981). The importance of the initial intactness of the infant's capacity to tolerate and use stimulation alerts us to the enormous contribution of normal self-regulatory capacities that we usually take for granted. These capacities are a prerequisite for engaging with the environment (Resch, 1988).

Self-regulation has been demonstrated in the fetus (Brazelton, 1992). The fetus can change its state, dampen its arousal, and eventually put itself to sleep to cope with aversive stimulation. When the stimulation becomes more moderate, the fetus again changes its state and shows patterns of information processing. Thus, even a fetus can regulate its own level of arousal and responsivity as a function of the nature of the stimulation provided.

Although infants have the capacity to organize states, Sander (1977, 1983) has shown that this system is successfully established only by an adequate interactive regulation between infant and caretaker. In the normal caretaking environment, babies who room-in with their own mothers establish day–night differentiation within four to six days. Organizing states so that sleep occurs more at night and wakefulness more during the day is a crucial accomplishment of the infant in the first week of life. Maternal care is a mutually regulated process such that the mother is sensitive to the infant's cues of state change, and the infant is responsive to the mother's attempts to activate or dampen arousal.

Sander (1977), studying babies who were to be adopted, showed that the development of self-regulation is dependent on interactive regulation. For the first 10 days of life, these babies were placed in the normal hospital nursery with a set schedule and many nurses. Caregiving in this environment was not a mutually regulated process. During these ten days, the infants did not establish any day–night differentiation or stable sleep–wake patterns. For the second 10 days of life each baby was transferred to his or her own special nurse and caregiving was mutually regulated. Within 10 days, these babies all established day–night differentiation and stable sleep–wake cycles. The quality of interactive regulation affects the infant's internal regulation, sleep–wake cycle, and biorhythms. Only when adequate mutual regulation occurred did adequate self-regulation also occur. Although Sander did not specifically address the converse in his study, the intactness of an infant's self-regulation will affect the ease and quality of the interactive regulation as well. Sander's conclusions provide support for our position that ongoing regulation is based on an integration of self and interactive regulation.

In her studies of heart rate and looking patterns, Field (1981) also illustrated how self- and interactive regulation form an interdependent system. During face-to-face social play at two to six months, the infants in the study briefly looked away from mother and then quickly returned to look at her. Looking away provides an infant a major method of dosing the level of stimulation and regulating arousal (Brazelton et al., 1974; Stern, 1971, 1977). The infant's regulation of arousal is evaluated by examining heart-rate patterns. In the five seconds just before the infant looks away, his heart rate shoots up, indicative of a "protective" process in which information intake is decreased. In the five seconds just after the infant looks away, the heart rate shoots down again, indicative of a "receptive" process in which information intake is facilitated. The infant then looks back at the mother.

Field's study illustrated the infant's use of looking away to perform a self-regulation. At the same time, an interactive regulation process proceeds. If the mother can use the infant's gaze away to lower her level of stimulation while the infant is reregulating his arousal, and if the infant can likewise use the mother's lowering of stimulation so that he then looks back at her, adequate interactive regulation will be established. If, on the other hand, the mother "chases" the infant when he looks away and increases her level of stimulation, both self- and interactive regulation will be interfered with for the infant. If the mother "chases" and increases her stimulation, the infant will look away for a longer period and will withdraw more severely (Brazelton et al., 1974; Beebe and Stern, 1977; Stern, 1977; Hirschfeld and Beebe, 1986).

Optimal interactive regulation is also disturbed if the mother chases, since the infant is then deprived of the ability to influence the mother's behavior toward a more moderate range. If interactive regulation is optimal, the infant simultaneously can influence his own level of arousal and the mother's level of stimulation. The very same behaviors through which the infant regulates his arousal (e.g., looking away) function at the same time as interactive regulations. If the interactive regulation is optimal, the mother's lowering of her stimulation also influences the infant to return to face her more quickly.

Gianino and Tronick (1988) have made the integration of interactive and self-regulation central to their work. They have described the infant's repertoire of self-regulatory skills in detail. Their position is that self-regulation and interactive regulation occur at the same time. The same interactive repertoire with which the infant initates, maintains, and modifies well-regulated interactions and repairs, avoids, and terminates disrupted interactions simultaneously performs self-regulatory functions.

Tronick (1989) offers experimental evidence that the nature of interactive regulation is associated with the adaptiveness of the self-regulation. Infants were subjected to the stress of the "still-face" experiment, where the mother remained oriented and looking but became completely immobile and unresponsive. In those dyads where interactive regulation was going well, the infant's self-regulation capacity, as measured in the still-face situation, was more adaptive and vice versa. In the still-face experiment, those infants continued to signal the mother rather than turn to self-comforting, withdrawal, or disorganized scanning.

The integration of interactive and self-regulation has direct bearing on current conceptualizations of the development of representations as organized through the dyad. As we indicated in earlier chapters, the current concept that self and object and their representations are rooted in relationship patterns holds true only as long as relationship structures are broadly construed to include an integration of self- and interactive regulation. To posit the dyadic interaction alone as the source of psychic organization ignores the equally crucial contribution of the organism's own self-regulatory capacities.

The Principle of Disruption and Repair

In contrast to the principle of ongoing regulations, which emphasizes what is expectable in the interaction, within the principle of disruption and repair, interaction patterns are organized by violations of expectancy and ensuing efforts to resolve these breaches (Piaget, 1937; Klein, 1967; Stechler and Kaplan, 1980; Kohut, 1984; Behrends and Blatt, 1985; Horner, 1985; Tronick and Gianino, 1986; Gianino and Tronick, 1988; Tronick and Cohn, 1989).

Infants notice, and are powerfully affected by, the confirmation and violation of expectancies. The neonate has a remarkable capacity to detect contingencies between his behavior and environmental events and to develop expectancies of when these events will occur. DeCasper and Carstens (1980) have demonstrated that confirmation of an infant's expectancies is associated with positive affect and that violation of an infant's expectancies is associated with negative affect. Stern's (1985) work on affect attunement in 10-month-olds also provides evidence of infants' capacity to notice the disruption of an ongoing sequence and to notice if the disruption is repaired.

The concept of disruption has been used to cover phenomena of varying degrees of severity. The terms mismatch or violation of expectancy are less severe than the term disruption. In addition, various phenomena of normal development do not fit the definition of disruption as a violation of expectancy, but they nevertheless do elucidate the disruption and repair model. In particular, Tronick and Cohn's (1989) data on sequences of match/mismatch/rematch fit this category. Disruptions can be mild and expectable. We, therefore, propose the following distinctions.

We retain the metaphor of disruption and repair to refer to a broad array of phenomena from mild to severe. Whereas violation of expectancy occurs in many disruptions, we consider it too narrow a concept to cover the full range. We introduce the concept of *normative disjunctions* as a particular subtype of disruption to describe instances of nonmatch, or mismatch, which occur in normal interactions. They may or may not involve violations of expectancy, and they are relatively easily righted.

Not all violations of expectancy are experienced as disruptive. Slight variations on expected themes are necessary to prevent habituation. Mild violations of expectancy in the optimal range, such as the "I'm gonna getcha" game (Stern, 1982), are incorporated into playful exchanges and can produce positive excitement. We exclude these positive violations of expectancy from this discussion.

Three kinds of data illustrate the principle of disruption and repair. First, the consequences of actual experimental disruptions of the normal ongoing interactions come closest to operationalizing the concept of violations of expectancy. Second, in the study of normal interactions, disruptions are translated into the concept of mismatch of states of engagement, which we have termed normative disjunctions.

The study of clinically disturbed situations provides the third kind of data. While a survey of the literature on clinically disturbed interactions is beyond our scope, several studies can illustrate the organization of expectancies of misregulation. For example, depressed mothers are described as angry, poking, intrusive, and disengaged, and their infants as primarily protesting and disengaged (Cohn and Tronick, 1989a; Cohn et al., 1990; Field et al., 1990). These infants develop expectancies of interaction patterns characterized by chronic infant distress and protest, with maternal intrusion and withdrawal. Field et al. (1988) have shown that infants of depressed mothers show depressed behaviors even with nondepressed adults. Thus, an infant's expectancy of misregulation is "structured." It carries over into interactions with normally responsive new partners.

In this clinical example of depressed mothers and their infants, the definition of disruption as violation of expectancy must shift. These infants experience disruption in that their interactions are atypical, but we have no evidence that these disruptions actually violate infant expectations. It is more parsimonious to assume that chronic disruptions or misregulations come to be expected by the infant of a depressed mother. These expectancies are sufficiently organized to continue to hold in the presence of an optimally responsive new adult partner.

Within the interaction pattern of expected disruption, the infant also develops an associated self-regulatory style. Thus, the infant learns to expect chronic disruption and to expect certain consequences from self-regulatory efforts. What is being organized is both an expectable interactive misregulation and an associated self-regulatory style (E. Tronick, personal communication, May, 18, 1993).

Eventual longitudinal follow-up of such infants will enable us to describe the formation of representations where disruptions cannot be easily repaired. When there are unresolvable mismatches and disruptions without repair, which is characteristic of interactions of depressed mothers and their babies, the balance between self- and interactive regulation is disturbed. The infants become preoccupied with self-regulation and the management of negative affect (Tronick, 1989). As Tronick has argued, if self-regulation becomes the predominant goal, it sets the stage for psychopathology. In addition, the expectation of misregulation colors interactions with an unfamiliar adult, so that all interactions for such an infant are likely to be more negative (Field et al., 1988; Tronick, 1989). In this case, chronic disruption becomes the expectation of disruption and *non*-repair, and this expectation organizes new interactions.

Disruption and Repair: Disjunctions

The concept of disjunctions comes from research findings that mothers and infants do not necessarily match each other' states of engagement during normal successful play encounters For example, Kronen (1982) found that at four months, their infants and mothers significantly did not exactly match expression. Malatesta and Haviland (1983) found that only approximately 35% of mothers' contingent facial responses to infant facial changes were exact matches. Tronick and Cohn (1989) described mothers and infants at play at three, six, and nine months as continuously shifting back and forth between "matched" and "nonmatched" states; they spent approximately only one-third of their time in matched states.

In a state of nonmatch, a mother might be engaged in "social play," looking and smiling at her infant; but the infant might be in "social attend," looking at the mother with a neutral face without smiling (Tronick and Cohn, 1989). Such nonmatched states are prevalent in normal, successful interactions. They cannot be considered to be actual violations of what is expected. Thus we have termed them normative disjunctions. Likewise, matches are not considered a "repair," but a special state of coordination against a background of slight disjunctions. Matching constitutes too limited a model of the nature of facial-visual communication.

Tronick and Cohn's (1989) data on match and nonmatch are central to the disruption and repair metaphor. The researchers found that, when the two partners entered an unmatched state, within two seconds, 70% of the unmatched states returned to a match. Furthermore, an analysis of who influenced the interaction, that is, which partner was responsible for the repair, showed that mothers and infants both influenced the repair sequence (Cohn and Tronick, 1983; Tronick and Cohn, 1989). The repair of disruption is a mutually regulated achievement.

Disjunctions and the Organization of Representations

Mother–infant interactions can be described as continuously shifting back and forth between greater and lesser degrees of coordination, matches and disjunctions, with a flexibility to span the range. Data show that, when less coordinated states occur, there is a powerful tendency to right the interaction by returning to a more coordinated state within two seconds. Thus, repairing disjunctions is a pervasive interactive skill for infants. Tronick (1989; Tronick and Gianino, 1986) suggests that the experience of repair increases the infant's effectance, elaborates his coping capacity, and contributes to an expectation of being able to repair that he can bring to other partners. These capabilities suggest one definition of what is being organized in the infant's expectancies of interaction patterns of disjunction and righting.

The reparative function is a mutually regulated achievement. As usually described (Kohut, 1984; Stechler and Kaplan, 1980), it is the *infant's* efforts to resolve disruptions that contribute to psychic organization. We suggest that an interaction where the mother does not *also* contribute to the repair might interfere with the infant's experience of righting. The infant operates in a dyadic system to which both partners actively contribute.

Disjunctions and the ensuing search for righting following these disjunctions provide an important organizing principle. Although we include this principle within the metaphor of disruption and repair, it is different because it describes an ongoing characteristic process of regulating lesser and greater degrees of coordination. Disjunctions thus approach the ongoing regulations model as the resolution of minor mismatches becomes an expected sequence. The powerful tendency to search for coordination and righting following mismatch establishes the expectancy that nonmatches return to matches and thus constitutes an ongoing regulation. The expectancy is established that repair is possible (Tronick, 1989).

Experimental Studies of Disruption and Repair

Experimental disruptions of infant social expectancies have been studied by Tronick and his colleagues (Gianino and Tronick, 1988; Tronick, 1989; Weinberg, 1991). In the "still-face" experiment, the mother presented a completely still, unsmiling face to the infant (Tronick et al., 1978), a situation that can be seen as drastically violating the infant's expectations of a contingently responsive partner. It thus fits the usual definition of disruption as violation of expectancy. Recall that the infant first attempted to elicit the normal interaction by greeting the mother with smiles. As the mother continued to be nonresponsive, the infant repeated a sequence of looking at mother with animated face, then looking away. After a number of repetitions of this "eliciting" sequence and still no response from mother, the infant withdrew, head and body averted from mother, often slumping, losing postural tonus. The infant attempted to repair the violation of his expectation of a normally responsive partner. But when he could not, he withdrew, as if giving up.

The infant's performance in the still-face experiment has been compared to the mother's and infant's tendency to match, mismatch, and rapidly return to match in a normal interaction (Tronick and Gianino, 1986; Tronick, 1989; Tronick and Cohn, 1989). A coping scale for the still-face situation rates infants from most adaptive (attempts to continue signaling the mother, alternative focus on something other than mother, self-comforting behavior) to increasingly maladaptive (withdrawal through arching away, giving up postural/motor control, and generally disorganized state). At four to six months, infants who experience more repairs of nonmatch in the normal interaction are more likely to use the most adaptive coping behavior, namely signaling, in the still-face experiment. Furthermore, by six months, individual differences in this coping style stabilize, and the infant begins to rely on characteristic ways of coping. Finally, these differences predict developmental outcomes at one year. Infants who experience more repairs of nonmatch in the normal situation and who use more adaptive methods of coping in the still-face have more secure attachments to their mothers at one year (Tronick, 1989; Cohn, Campbell, and Ross, 1991).

Representations and the Reparative Function

These findings have implications for the organization of infant experience. In the face of the drastic violation of the expectation by a responsive partner, an infant will make repeated efforts to "repair" breaches and elicit expected responsiveness from her mother. This persistent effort to repair, demonstrated so early in development, gives the concept of repair a more firmly grounded developmental status. An infant of only two or three months will try to "repair" an unresponsive mother. Furthermore, the way disruptions and repairs are managed, both in the still-face experiment and the match–mismatch analysis of ongoing interactions, predicts the future quality of the infant's attachment to her mother. Experience is being organized with discernibly different consequences across the first year. These findings suggest that the reparative function is indeed a critical force in the organization of an infant's experience. The expectation of the possibility of repair facilitates the development of secure attachment.

Evidence for organization and representation can be inferred from these findings. When a mother resumes a normal interaction with her infant following the still-face, the infant continues a negative mood and looks less at mother. Tronick (1989) interprets this finding as evidence that the still-face episode continues to exert an effect on the infant and thus that a representation of the prior interaction has been organized: "This finding suggests that even three-month-old infants are not simply under the control of the immediate stimulus situation but that events have lasting effects, that is, they are internally represented" (p. 114). In addition, particular methods of coping with violations of expectancies become characteristic for the infant by six months. This finding attests to how quickly an infant's social capacities become organized in relatively enduring and characteristic ways.

A further source of evidence that expectancies become structured is the Field et al. (1988) study presented earlier, that infants of depressed mothers continue to be more negative in interactions with a nondepressed adult stranger. Already by six months the infant of a depressed mother has a more rigidly structured expectancy of relatedness. Whereas a normal six-month-old infant can engage positively with a stranger, the infant of a depressed mother brings the misregulated patterns that belong with the depressed mother to a new, potentially responsive partner. This infant seems to expect disruption without repair.

A final source of evidence that interactive behavior is being organized or structured in the first year comes from the work of Weinberg (1991). She examined the stability of behavior across two play sessions for 80 infants at six and six and a half months. Stability, or session-to-session consistency, can be construed as an index of the degree to which behavior is being organized: the degree to which there is a "way" of doing things that is relatively stable. A sequence of three episodes was videotaped for each dyad: face-to-face play, still-face, and resumption of face-to-face play. Infant inter-active behavior (infant looks at mother, looks at object, scans the room, signals to mother with vocalization and gesture) and infant affect (joy, interest, sadness, anger) were coded second-by-second. Robust session-to-session correlation was found. These session-to-session consistency findings corroborate session-to-session consis-tencies reported by Tronick (1989; Cohn and Tronick, 1989a) and Zelner (1982). That there is a considerable degree of stability of interactive behavior by six months points to a strong early organ-izing process.

Ongoing Regulations and Disruption and Repair:
An Integration of the Two Principles

The disruption and repair model has had a wide-ranging influence on psychoanalytic theories of internalization and structure forma-tion (Freud, 1917; Loewald, 1960, 1962; Klein, 1967; Tolpin, 1971; Kohut, 1984; Blatt and Behrends, 1987). Disruption, breach, loss, incompatibility, frustration, and disequilibrium are seen as nodal points around which new organization occurs. The new organiza-tion is variously conceptualized as a repair of the breach, as an inter-nalization of the lost object, or as a structuralization within the psyche of functions of the relationship that were disrupted.

Deprivation and frustration have generally been assumed to underlie the disruption and repair model of psychic structure for-mation. For example, Behrends and Blatt (1985) argue that it is the unavailability of the object that promotes internalization; with a fully available object there would be no motivation to convert the affective tie to an internal function. The most extreme version of this model posits that disruption is a necessary precondition for all psychological development, internalization, and structuralization (see, e.g., Meissner, 1981; Behrends and Blatt, 1985). In contrast, Loewald (cited in Behrends and Blatt, 1985) argued that, through intimacy or resonance, internalization can occur without disruption.

We suggest that there *is* an ongoing structuring process based on the creation of expectancies of characteristic interaction patterns. Disruption and disequilibrium and efforts to resolve these breaches of integration also undoubtedly generate powerful opportunities for psychic organization. However, disruption is not a *necessary* condition for such development. Expectancies of characteristic ongoing regulations are an equally powerful organizing dynamic.

In the ongoing regulations model, it is unnecessary to posit a deprivation motive. In fact, it is the very availability of the partner, the consistency and predictability of responsivity, that constitutes the organizing process. In our application of disruption and repair, we also do not assume a deprivation model of motivation. We assume an information-processing model in which the infant's perceptual capabilities insure an ability to seek out, perceive, and interact with social partners (Hunt, 1965; Berlyne, 1966; Ainsworth et al., 1978; Basch, 1988; Haith et al., 1988). The disruption and repair of expected interaction sequences will organize an infant's experience on the basis of her inherent ability to perceive confirmation and violation of expectations of ordered information.

We suggest that the two models, ongoing regulations and disruption and repair, organize different chunks of time and different aspects of experience. To the degree that ongoing regulations are in the optimal range, such as various midrange matching interactions, experience is organized by what is predictable, expectable, coherent, and coordinated. In this view, the goal of the system is optimal coordination. In contrast, the principle of disruption and repair points toward experience as organized by contrast, disjunction, and difference. The gap between what is expected and what is happening can also be repaired. In this view, the goal of the system is optimal or "normative" disjunction and repair. We consider these counterpoints to be simultaneously constituted.

The principle of disruption and repair organizes experiences of coping, effectance, righting, and hope (Tronick, 1989). Interactions are represented as reparable. The expectation develops that it is possible to maintain engagement with the partner in the face of strains and mismatches. In contrast, optimally cooordinated ongoing regulations organize experiences of coherence, predictability, fitting together with the partner, and being well related. The expectation develops that it is possible for the coordination to be sustained. We suggest that the firmer the expectation that coordination can be sustained, the better the infant will be able to tolerate and benefit from experiences of disruption and repair. Horner (1985) and Stechler and Kaplan (1980) have similarly proposed the integration of regularities and discrepancies in organizing the patterns of interaction.

The Principle of Heightened Affective Moments

Having discussed ongoing regulations and their disruption and repair as two basic principles of organization, we now turn to the third principle, heightened affective moments. According to this principle, interaction patterns are organized through heightened affective moments in which the infant experiences a powerful state transformation. Whereas affect is a component of the first two principles, we consider intense affect to be a sufficiently unique dimension in the ongoing creation of expectancies to justify its consideration as a third principle of organization.

Affect

Infants have innate patterns of facial, vocal, and bodily expressions of affect that are readily observable (Demos, 1984; Field et al., 1982; Malatesta et al., 1989; Oster, 1979; Oster and Ekman, 1977; Stern, 1977, 1985; Tomkins, 1980;). Izard (1979) has shown that newborns express interest, joy, distress, disgust, and surprise. Ekman and Oster (1979) have demonstrated that these affective patterns exist in various cultures, and they argue for their universality. Numerous studies show that a range of affect is regulated in complex and subtle ways in early interactive exchanges (see, e.g., Cohn and Beebe, 1990; Cohn and Tronick, 1988; Demos, 1984; Stern, 1977, 1985; Tronick, 1982).

Tomkins (1980) describes the amplifying function of affect: "affect either makes good things better or bad things worse . . . by adding a special analogic quality that is intensely rewarding or punishing" (p. 148). This amplifying function sets the stage for the power of heightened affect. Stern (1985) addresses heightened affect through his discussion of the importance of the "vitality" dimension of affect in the communication of emotion. Affects surge and fade, crescendo and diminuendo, varying according to intensity, degree of display and urgency, as well as by the nature of the category itself such as joy, distress, sadness, or anger (see also Werner, 1948).

We define a heightened affective moment in infancy as the full display of any facial or vocal pattern, such as a cry face or a fully opened "gape smile" (Beebe, 1973). The full expressive display of the face or voice will of necessity be accompanied by heightened bodily arousal (Ekman, 1983).

Heightened Moments

Pine (1981) described the power of affectively supercharged moments as an avenue to the accretion of psychic structure. These supercharged moments become central to the organization of an array of percepts and memories and are formative in their effect far out of proportion to their mere temporal duration. Pine gave as examples prototypic moments of merger, such as echoing, cooing voices of mother and infant in unison; the infant's falling asleep at the mother's breast; and moments of intense negative arousal in the absence of comfort or gratification.

Although the examples cited by Pine are heightened moments that tend to occur with some frequency in the ongoing daily rhythm of events, this concept also includes those heightened affective moments that are relatively rare and not part of everyday experience. Nevertheless, Pine noted that these heightened moments are organizing only if they capture the essence of similar though less intense moments. These affectively supercharged moments can thus be conceptualized as prototypes of a category of similar affective experiences. The organizing power of affectively supercharged moments thus derives from both the infant's capacity to categorize and expect similar experiences and from the impact of the heightened affect itself. When expectancies play a role in organizing affectively supercharged moments, an ongoing regulations model is already implicit within the model of heightened affective moments.

The Single Event

There is another type of affectively supercharged moment that can be conceptualized as a "one-shot" event rather than a prototype of a category of similar experiences. This description raises the issue of trauma. There is considerable controversy in theories of trauma over whether an adult's remembered traumatic event can be said to be based on a single event or is representative of a range of similar experiences.

It is difficult to assess whether the concept of one-shot trauma is a viable one in infancy. First, it is difficult to know whether an event indeed happened only once or whether it might not constitute the prototype of a series of similar events. Second, there is a dearth of research evidence addressing the question of whether or not a single event can organize infant experience. Nevertheless, there is some suggestion from neurophysiological data that certain single experiences can induce brain changes, particularly if those experiences possess certain qualities such as novelty (Spinelli and Jensen, 1979).

Some experimental work suggests that an infant's experience may indeed be organized by a single event. Gunther (cited in Stern, 1985) reported research on breast occlusion in neonates, where the infant momentarily could not breathe during feeding. Only one episode of breast occlusion influenced newborn behavior for several feedings afterward. It can be argued, however, that it may be the mother who was traumatized and that her continuing anxiety influenced the infant's feeding behavior.

It is also noteworthy that an experimentally induced singular event in six-month-olds, an event sufficiently unusual that it would not occur in the normal course of events, was remembered by these infants when they became one and two years old. In this study of memory (Perris, Meyers, and Clifton, 1990), infants reached to find an object that was making noise—a rattle. They reached first in the light and then in the dark. When these infants were retested as toddlers, they reached more frequently and were more successful in obtaining the rattle than was the control group, who did not reach without instruction. It is clear from this research that a single event from six months can be remembered a year and a half later. The organizing impact of this event, however, was not investigated. Therefore no conclusion can be drawn about whether or not it organized the infant's experience.

Further support comes from clinical work with adults in which a single traumatic event in infancy was organizing. Casement (1990) describes an adult treatment in which the patient was preoccupied by having been severely burned at 11 months. That singular traumatic event became a major organizing theme in the analysis. Bernstein and Blacher (1967) describe an adult treatment in which the patient remembered a traumatic physical sensation that he termed a "stick in the tushie," which was documented to have been a lumbar puncture at the age of six months.

Stern (1985) also discusses the possibility of a single event organizing the infant's behavior. In Stern's theory of RIGs, events that are similar are averaged and represented by a prototype, a central tendency of the category. The process of forming RIGs contains two sources of distortion. In the formation of prototypes, the averaging process itself may distort the event. These distortions err on the conservative side, so that more extreme examples of the category tend toward the central tendency. However, specific memories can also be a source of distortion, when one memory constitutes the category. One event then becomes more influential, since it is not averaged with many similar ones. Stern suggests that a specific memory provides a heightened affective influence as part of its power of distortion and therefore may be more potent than the averaged RIG. In this work Stern does not address the organizing potential of trauma per se.

Heightened Negative Moment

Experimental evidence suggests that heightened *negative* affective moments may not only organize memory, as Pine (1981) suggested, but may also interfere with memory (Fagen et al., 1985, 1989; Singer

and Fagen, 1992). Three- to four-month-old infants learned to produce movement in an overhead crib mobile containing 10 identical components. The infants were then switched to a mobile
containing only two components. Those infants who cried in
response to the switch in mobiles failed to show evidence of reten-
tion of learning one week later. However, the "forgetting" by the
crying infants was subsequently reversed by a brief reexposure to
the two-component mobile. Fagen et al. concluded that crying
affected a retrieval of the memory, but not its storage. The infants
who had cried needed the re-exposure to facilitate retrieval, but
they had not lost the memory. The infants' retrieval of the memory
of the training context was subject to modification and elaboration
by the intense affect of crying.

These experiments provide evidence for the concept that intense
affective experiences provide a unique dimension in the ongoing
creation of expectancies. Although affect is a central feature in all
three principles, these experiments further justify the inclusion of
heightened affect as a separate organizing principle. An infant's
retrieval of expectancies and memories can be altered by intense
affect. The infant's memory representation of events is more elaborate than previously believed and includes not only the details of
the learning cues but also his own emotional state (Fagen et al.,
1989; Singer and Fagen, 1992).

The Organizing Impact of Heightened Affective Moments

Our review took into consideration several dimensions: the singular moment, its storage, its heightened affective quality, and its
organizing impact. Neurophysiological evidence and the "reaching-
in-the dark" experiment simply illustrate infant capacity to store a
single event. The other studies expand the argument by providing
evidence that the singular event stored may include heightened
affect and may be organizing. Organizing impact can be inferred
from the breast occlusion experiment by the observation that the
infant's subsequent behavior was disrupted; from the "mobile" experiment by the observation that the infant's retrieval facility was
altered; from the adult treatment case from the observation that the

patient was preoccupied as an adult by the memories and bodily sensations of the burn. Although the infant data are suggestive and the adult treatment report is supportive, further evidence is necessary to evaluate the extent to which a single heightened event may organize infant and adult experiences.

We have argued that heightened affective moments potentially have an organizing impact. Now, addressing the nature of this impact, we propose that, at the moment of heightened affect, there is a state transformation. We use the term state broadly to include physiological arousal, affect, and cognition.

According to Sander (1983), states of alertness, arousal, activity, and sleep are socially negotiated, a product of interactive regulation. Sander suggested that the earliest experiences are organized through the infant's recognition of recurrent, predictable transitions of state, in particular interactive contexts. Thus, early state transformations are related to both self-regulation and the expectation that interactive regulation will facilitate or interfere with these transformations.

In the reaching-in-the-dark experiment (Perris et al., 1990), the moment of state transformation occurred when the infants re-encountered the toy in the dark at two years. We speculate that the nature of the state transformation was both cognitive and affective: a moment of recognition and accompanying surprise, joy, or efficacy. In Gunther's (cited in Stern, 1985) breast occlusion study, the state transformation occurred at the moment of difficulty in breathing. The transformation was one of physiological state, that is, less air, and also of affect, that is, distress. In the mobile experiment (Fagen et al., 1985), the state tranformation occurred at the moment the infants recognized that the second mobile contained fewer components than the first. The state transformation was a cognitive one, in the sense that an expectancy was violated when the infants recognized that the new mobile was not the same as the old one, and the remembering process was altered. It was also an affective transformation, since the infants became distressed and half of them cried. In the case of the infant who was burned (Casement, 1990), a state transformation occured at the moment of the burn. The transformation was a physiological one owing to the pain, and an affective one owing to the distress. We suggest that heightened moments are organizing because they effect a potentially powerful state transformation.

Integration of the Three Principles

The three principles of salience constitute criteria by which events are categorized over the course of the first year and beyond. These categories will be used to represent aspects of experience once the symbolic function is more developed. An infant's early presymbolic representational capacity will be used to store those interaction patterns which are salient by virtue of any of the three principles. Using all three organizing principles, the infant forms prototypes, that is, generalized categories, or models, of patterns of interactions, which become represented as the "rules" of the relationship. A self-regulatory style is represented within these prototypes of patterns of interaction.

Because all three principles interact, they need to be conceptualized together. If disruption is to occur, an ongoing pattern of regulation must first exist. The particular nature and sequence of disruption and repair in itself becomes an expected interaction pattern. Thus, its potential to organize experience derives both from the power of the repair and from the predictable, expected nature of the sequence. Furthermore, as Pine (1981) argued, heightened affective moments have a formative impact irrespective of their frequency or duration. But they do occur within an interactive context and sequence. Thus their structuring impact derives from both the predictable nature of the sequence and from the power of the heightened affective moment itself. Moreover, heightened affective moments, when positive, can repair disruptions. When disruptions are sufficiently severe, they lead to heightened negative affective states, which cascade and may traumatically disrupt self-regulation (E. Tronick, personal communication, May 18, 1993).

The facial mirroring interaction illustrates how all three principles interact. It fits an ongoing regulation model, since each partner influences the other to match the direction of affective change. In addition, at various points, both infant and mother hit peak, heightened, positive moments (Beebe, 1973). The notion of normative disjunction also applies, since at several moments the baby sobers and looks away, without distress. Although in general the mother matches the direction of affective change, occasionally she raises the intensity of her stimulation instead, calling to the infant, while the infant is still looking away. The infant's ability to reregulate his arousal, and the dyad's ability to return to the play encounter, will contribute to organizing the infant's experience.

The Three Principles and Affect

The use of all three principles yields a differentiated way of conceptualizing qualitative differences in the organization of infant experience. Specifically, affect is regulated within all three principles, but in different ways. Examples of the regulation of affect occurring during heightened affective moments include tantrums or falling asleep and melting into the mother's breast. These examples illustrate more global transformations of affective states.

Quite different are the subtle, moment-by-moment regulations of slight shifts of attention, affect, and arousal within the more narrow range typically described in face-to-face encounters. Here affect is a continually changing, subtle, incremental process. The ongoing *mis*regulation of attention, affect, and arousal will organize expectations of nonoptimal self- and interactive regulation. For example, infant overarousal or underarousal signals that the interactive regulation system has not succeeded in contributing to adequate infant self-regulation.

In sequences of disruption and repair, the *nature* of the affect regulation emphasizes a transformation of affect from positive to negative and back to positive. When expectancies are grossly violated, an infant may anticipate ruptures. When these ruptures are difficult to repair, the infant may develop an expectancy of nonrepair, such as has been documented in the infants of depressed mothers, which may contribute to later experiences of helplessness (see also Cohn et al., 1990; Tronick, 1989; Tronick and Cohn, 1989).

The Three Principles and Bodily Experiences

The three principles also provide a way to differentiate how bodily experiences are organized. Broadly speaking, the body is the subject of our entire discussion, since perception, cognition, affect, and arousal are all bodily experiences. However, more narrowly speaking, the regulation of bodily states has been addressed in each of the principles through the dimension of arousal. The infant represents bodily states as an aspect of all three principles of interaction patterns.

In the principle of ongoing regulations, bodily states organize experience insofar as they are repeated and expected. Processes of interactive and self-regulation shift with respect to which is in the foreground or background. Some urgent bodily needs, such as feeding, are of necessity regulated through the partner. Although adequate self-regulation is also necessary, these experiences tilt toward interactive regulation. Other experiences, such as the infant's control over elimination, emphasize self-regulation. Nevertheless, even these latter experiences are colored by the nature of the interactive regulation. Does the infant expect the comfort of being cleaned or a handling that is rough and constraining? Does the mother have postural, facial, and vocal responses of aversion, disgust, or withdrawal? What will be organized is the expectation that compelling bodily needs will or will not be adequately regulated with particular affect and arousal patterns.

The crucial role of the body is self-evident in the principle of heightened affective moments, since heightened affects are simultaneously heightened bodily states. Ekman (1983) has shown that patterns of physiological arousal closely correspond to facial-affective patterns (see also Beebe and Lachmann, 1988b).

Within the principle of disruption and repair, bodily experiences of disruption can be defined as those instances in which interactive regulation is inadequate to sustain self-regulation. Bodily experiences, such as hunger, cold, and fatigue then impinge on and overwhelm the self-regulatory process. When the partner is available for repair, however, the balance is shifted back toward more adequate interactive regulation. Following this principle, it is the expectation of a disruption of adequate bodily regulation that is organized. Or, with repair, the expectation is organized that a transformation of state will veer toward a more comfortable range.

Evidence that an infant will represent bodily states can be inferred from the treatments of children and adults. Recall Casement's (1990) description of an adult treatment in which the patient was preoccupied by having been severely burned at 11 months. Herzog (1983) described a toddler who continually expressed the wish to be hurt. This child had a history of multiple invasive medical procedures as an infant. The infant's experience in each of these cases can be seen as organized by transformations into heightened negative bodily states, with the disruption of the expectation of adequate bodily regulation. In addition, the infant's experience in the Herzog case can be seen as organized by the ongoing regulation of the expectation of repetitive painful bodily events and the expectation that protective interactive regulation fails.

The three principles of salience provide us with criteria to determine which aspects of experience will assume centrality and priority. Although we assume that an integration of all three principles of salience will be used to organize representations, individual differences in their emphasis and course of regulation will create different configurations or themes in the represention of the interrelatedness of self and other.

The Three Principles and Presymbolic Internalization

We have described the organization of presymbolic representations in the first year. This description can simultaneously illuminate processes of internalization. Although it has been argued that internalization is different from processes that establish the original representations of the internal and external world, we hold that internalization in the first year is a process not distinct from the organization of representations. Both Loewald (1962) and Schafer (1968) have pointed out the intimate connection between the first representations and the earliest forms of internalization.

The term *internalization* has generally been applied to processes after the first year; *secondary internalizations* (Loewald, 1962; Schafer, 1968) occur when symbolic levels of self- and object representations are in place. We are interested in applying the three principles of salience to a reconceptualization of processes in the first year that have been referred to as *primary internalizations*. We thus confine our discussion to the *presymbolic* origins of internalization.

Schafer (1968) defined internalization as "all those processes by which the subject transforms real or imagined regulatory interactions with his environment, and real or imagined characteristics of his environment, into inner regulations and characteristics" (p. 9). Because we are discussing the presymbolic origins of internalization, we are not referring to the "imagined" aspect of Schafer's definition.

Using Schafer's definition of inner, internalization proper can not be applied to the first year of life. In Schafer's view, "'inner' indicates that the stimulation and impact of the regulations does not depend on the actual presence, actions, or emotional position of the external object" (p. 10). In the first year, the infant is dependent on the actual presence of the object. In this sense, when we conceptualize the origins of internalization in the first year, we substantially change the concept.

Even in the first year, however, Schafer's term "inner regulation" has meaning. Two of the studies we cited, the still-face experiment (Tronick et al., 1978) and the study in which infants of depressed mothers acted depressed with a nondepressed adult (Field et al., 1988), provide evidence for inner organization. These experiments suggest that infants establish an interactive expectancy, with an associated self-regulatory style, which they can, under certain stressful circumstances, use in ways that are not dependent on immediate environmental input (E. Tronick, personal communication, May 18, 1993). In our view, the presymbolic origins of autonomy of inner regulations begin to evolve in the first year. The distinction between primary and secondary internalization thus begins to blur.

Furthermore, we argue that there is continuity between primary and secondary internalization. The presymbolically represented experiences of the first year bias the developmental trajectory in transformational ways (Sameroff, 1983; Sander, 1983; Sroufe and Fleeson, 1986; E. Tronick, personal communication, May 18, 1993). If these experiences are later encoded symbolically, they retain the impact of the first year.

Internalization and Interactive Regulation

There are remarkable parallels between the empirical infant literature, documenting the varieties of interactive regulation, and Schafer's (1968) notions of internalization, defined as regulatory interactions. Interactive regulation is the central concept in both. For this reason, we confine our discussion to Schafer's definition.

Schafer noted that Hartmann and Loewenstein's revision of Freud's definition of internalization "[shifted] the accent from *reactions* to *interacting regulations* [recognizing] both the importance of the developing organism's activity and the matrix of object relationship within which development takes place . . ." (p. 8, italics added). Schafer also noted that Loewald, like Erikson, had emphasized that it is relationships that are internalized. As Schafer put it, "the regulatory *interaction* has been interiorized" (p. 11). Infant research underlines and richly elaborates this interactive emphasis that was originally in Schafer's definition.

There is a further congruence between the experimental findings of infant research and Schafer's idea that what is regulated are behavior patterns involved in perceiving, remembering, and anticipating. Experimental infant perception research has by now documented remarkable early capacities for anticipation and memory (see chapter 5).

Although Schafer created an interactive model, he frequently lost sight of it in various one-way influence formulations that emphasize the effect of the environment on the child to the relative neglect of the effect of the child on the environment. For example, the environment provides the regulations of restraint, guidance, and mastery. It is the less well-modulated tendencies of the child or patient that are regulated. Similarly, in the formulation that it is the object's motives that are reproduced by the subject, the environment is seen to influence the child. Thus, there is a tension within Schafer's model. On one hand, it is an interactive model, so that internalization is based on what both the child and the environment co-construct. On the other hand, various one-way influence concepts are used in which the child receives the influence of the environment. In clinical practice and in much theorizing, the latter version of internalization has dominated our thinking. Only a fully bidirectional model can take into account the complexity of early interactive organization and the origins of internalization processes.

Interactive Regulation and Self-Regulation

There is a second essential difference between Schafer's formulations and our view. In Schafer's definition, "inner" regulations are assumed to result from the subject's transformation of regulatory interactions with the environment. We prefer the term self-regulation to inner regulation. Our position is that, from the very beginning of life, all regulatory interactions with the environment have simultaneous self-regulatory consequences. Thus, regulatory interaction with the environment does not become inner regulation in any linear fashion.

Regulatory interactions and self-regulation proceed hand in hand and shape each other. Rather than viewing interactive regulations as transformed *into* self regulations, existing self regulations are altered by, as well as alter, interactive regulations. Both infant and environment continuously construct, elaborate, and represent the regulations. Clearly, internalization is not an optimal metaphor (see also Goldberg, 1983). It inevitably carries the implications of transporting the outer to the inner and the suggestion that the internal increasingly supplants the external. Likewise, the idea of "taking in the functions of the other" has no place in our model, because the regulatory functions are always jointly constructed.

We are critical of the familiar formulation that outer becomes inner and that interactive regulations become inner regulations. Interactive regulations have always been inner. That is, infants have always participated in them and have always experienced them. Their self-regulations have always influenced, and have always been influenced by, the interactive regulations.

Whereas Schafer's (1968) inner organization is defined by a transformation of the outer, our "inner" organization is always jointly defined by self-regulation and the interactive regulations in which it is embedded. We concur with Schafer that what is at stake in the internalization process is the increasing relative autonomy from actual interactions with the environment. Such autonomy can begin only with the advance of symbol formation, when expectations of regulations are increasingly organized, elaborated, represented, and symbolized.

Internalization in the First Year

We suggest a view of the origins of internalization in the first year in which both partners bring to the interaction organized behavior and mutually construct modes of regulating their joint activity. These dyadic modes include interactive as well as self-regulation. *The expectation and representation of the dyadic modes of regulation constitute the internal organization* (see Beebe and Lachmann, 1994; Benjamin, 1988). With the advance of symbol formation, these modes are increasingly abstracted and depersonfied. That is, they become increasingly autonomous. This model puts the bidirectional nature of the regulation center stage. It further articulates the role of the subject in the regulation process, and it emphasizes the dyadic nature of the construction of experience.

Conclusion

We described a different view of how interactions function internally. In the principle of ongoing regulations, the way in which interactions typically proceed is expected and represented and defines the inner regulation. Generating, elaborating, anticipating, and representing the regulations that are jointly constructed constitutes the organizing process.

In the principle of disruption and repair, expectancies of a sequence of disequilibrium and righting constitute the inner regulation. What is organized is the dyad's management of the transformations back and forth across a range of greater or lesser degrees of coordination. Flexibility to manage the range is a consequence of this organization (Lachmann and Beebe, 1989). In disruption, experiences of contrast, disjunction, and difference are organized. Without repair, experiences of disruption organize expectancies of misregulation. With repair, coping, effectance, righting, and hope are organized. Since disruption and repair are both mutually regulated, infants represent their capacity to influence and be influenced by the righting process.

In the principle of heightened affective moments, powerful affective shifts that transform an infant's state constitute the inner regulation. These shifts may organize the transformation of bodily states where self-regulation is in the foreground. If the regulation is experienced positively, as with a pleasurable bowel movement or falling asleep and melting into the breast, these heightened moments organize experiences of control over one's own body, either actively or passively. If the regulation is experienced negatively, as with an intense crying jag, these heightened moments organize experiences of loss of control.

These heightened affective shifts may also accentuate dyadic regulations, in which self-regulation is in the background. If the shift is positive, such as it is in facial-mirroring interactions in which each face crescendos higher and higher, peak experiences of resonance, exhilaration, awe, and being "on the same wave length" with the partner are organized. If the shift is negative, for example when the infant arches his back as far away from the mother as he can possibly turn as the mother pulls his arm and tries to force a reorientation, state transformations of inundation, overarousal, impingement, and inability to escape are organized.

In summary, the three principles define a hierarchy of inner regulations at different levels of organization in time. They should be seen as a nested series in which each is a necessary context for the next. Thus, each principle is a distinct mode of organization, but each requires the others to describe the full range of experience. The three principles of salience simultaneously illuminate the presymbolic origins of representation and internalization in the first year. An integration of all three is necessary for a differentiated view of how representations and internalizations are formed in infancy.

8

THREE PRINCIPLES OF SALIENCE IN THE ORGANIZATION OF THE PATIENT–ANALYST INTERACTION

The Case of Clara

An empirical microanalysis of mother–infant interaction can deepen our understanding of the analyst–patient interaction. In the last chapter, we offered three organizing principles derived from infant research to describe how interactions are regulated, represented, and begin to be internalized in the first year of life. These principles are *ongoing regulations, disruption and repair* of ongoing regulations, and *heightened affective moments.* They further define the nature of self- and interactive regulation. They constitute hypotheses about how social interactions become patterned and salient in the first year. We now propose that these principles are applicable to the patterning of analyst–patient interactions and can specify modes of therapeutic action in adult treatment.

Although infant research has been construed as relevant to adult treatment in many ways (see, e.g., Horner, 1985; Stern, 1985, 1995; Sander, 1985; Emde, 1988; Osofsky, 1992; Soref, 1992; Seligman, 1994), in this chapter we explore the proposition that infant research is applicable to adult treatment through organizing principles of interaction. We view the dyad as a system within which self- and interactive regulation are integrated. The three salient principles of interactive regulation provide further specificity for conceptualizing how dyadic regulations may work and how internalizations may be co-constructed in adult treatment. These principles are relevant both to verbal and to nonverbal modes of regulation.

In reviewing the infant research literature in the last chapter, we conceptualized the three principles of salience in an attempt to organize different ways of viewing dyadic regulation. The three principles do not address the content of such clinical issues as oneness and separation or such motivational issues as needs or wishes. Rather, they address the process and patterning of interactions.

The model of development derived from infant research cannot, of course, be directly translated into the adult psychoanalytic situation. In adults, the capacity for symbolization, and the subjective or unconscious elaboration of experience in the form of fantasies, wishes, and defenses, further modify the organization and representation of interaction patterns. What makes this model appealing for adult treatment, however, is that it makes no assumptions about the dynamic content of adult experience. It focuses entirely on the *process* of interactive regulation. Thus, despite the many differences between mother–infant and patient–analyst interaction, we propose similarities with respect to how these three principles function to organize interactions. The three principles operate together and can be considered different angles of the camera in a foreground–background relationship.

The three principles are relevant to all sources of therapeutic action. Numerous well-established psychoanalytic concepts already cover the same terrain as do the three principles. Our integration is designed not to supplant these dynamic formulations but to provide analysts a differentiated view of the regulation of interactions and the organization of experience that goes beyond interpretation.

The Three Principles and the Analyst–Patient Interaction

Psychoanalysts have always paid attention to the issues covered by our three principles, albeit those issues have been known under other names. Ongoing regulations have been subsumed under discussions of patterns of transference and countertransference, the "holding environment" (Winnicott, 1965), and the "background of safety" (Sandler, 1987). Disruptions and their repair have been proposed as a basis for structure formation (Stechler and Kaplan, 1980; Kohut, 1984; Horner, 1985) and implicated in the analysis of resistance and the use of confrontation (Buie and Adler, 1973; Lachmann, 1990). Heightened affective moments (Strachey, 1934; Fenichel, 1938–1939; Pine, 1981, 1986) have been recognized as essential to making analysis emotionally meaningful.

Ongoing Regulations

The principle of ongoing regulations captures the characteristic, expectable pattern of repeated interactions in the treatment situation. Both partners actively contribute to the regulation of the exchange, moment by moment. The analyst has the greater range of flexibility in this process, but the actions of both partners are intimately linked in time, space, affect, and arousal. Expectations are organized that each partner either *can*, or *cannot*, affect and be affected by the other in specific ways. These expectations determine the nature of *interactive efficacy*. Both partners come to expect and represent these ongoing characteristic regulations and their unique interactive efficacy with this partner.

In the treatment situation, ongoing regulations range from subtle nonverbal behaviors, such as postural and facial interchanges, intonations and tone of voice, greeting and parting rituals, to verbal exchanges. Ongoing regulations include interactions where the patient narrates and discloses while the analyst attends, reflects, describes, and questions. The effects of such interactions are present throughout the treatment process. However, they can be most clearly illustrated in the phase of understanding (Kohut, 1984) and the processes of listening (Schwaber, 1981), exploring, and clarifying (Greenson, 1967). These patient–analyst interactions have generally been viewed as a preparatory phase. They have not been recognized as contributing *directly* to the formation of representations and internalization.

In these phases, repetitive themes of the patient, for example, expectations of nonresponse, indifference, or rejection, are engaged, potentially disconfirmed, and woven into the patient–analyst relationship. Through this process, these themes are altered, that is provided, as a matter of course, with a new context (Loewald, 1980; Modell, 1984). Thus, we propose that ongoing regulations can promote new expectations and constitute a mode of therapeutic action. Whereas the engagement and disconfirmation of expectations have been described as the interpretive work of analysis (Weiss and Sampson, 1986), they are also characteristic of ongoing regulations. That is, ongoing interactions that are never verbally explored or addressed can nevertheless potentially alter the patient's expectations.

The detailed study of ongoing regulations can further illuminate the processes of therapeutic action. The structure of the dialogue itself, irrespective of its verbal content, is the subject of study. Patient and analyst construct characteristic ways of asking each other questions, wondering aloud together, taking turns in the dialogue, and knowing when to pause and for how long. In this process both are constructing expectations and disconfirming fears of being ignored, steamrollered, intruded on, misunderstood, or criticized. These interactively organized expectations and disconfirmations are represented and internalized, whether or not they are ever verbalized. This process constitutes the therapeutic action of ongoing regulations.

Disruption and Repair

The disruption and repair of interactions is a specific extension of the principle of ongoing regulations. However, rather than emphasizing what is expectable in the interaction, disruption and repair organizes violations of expectancies and the ensuing efforts to resolve these breaches (Stechler and Kaplan, 1980; Horner, 1985; Tronick and Cohn, 1989; Beebe and Lachmann, 1994). Our review of infant research noted the wide range of disturbances encompassed by the term disruption. The continuum extends from the mild disjunctions, rapidly righted, that are typical of successful interactions, to severe ruptures. Although these mild disjunctions can be considered normative, more severe and frequent disruptions may prejudice development (Tronick, 1989).

Interactions of disruption and repair are most clearly evident during phases of explanation (Kohut, 1984) and during the processes of confrontation, working through, and interpretation (Greenson, 1967). Depending upon how, when, and where they occur, disruptions are variously understood. They may be seen as necessary for development, as emanating from the patient's resistance, or as due to the patient's inability to tolerate frustration. Others have ascribed disruptions to poor timing by the analyst, misunderstandings, specific transference–countertransference configurations, or the differently organized subjectivities of analyst and patient. Different notions of "repair" are associated with each of these views of "rupture" (Kohut, 1984; Blatt and Behrends, 1987; Stolorow et al., 1987).

The disruption and repair model lies at the heart of formulations of structure formation and therapeutic action in psychoanalysis. Structuralization has been variously assumed to result from the internalization of the lost object, frustration of drive derivatives, or optimal frustration whereby functions of the relationship that were disrupted are constructed within the psyche of the analysand (Freud, 1917; Tolpin, 1971; Klein, 1976; Loewald, 1980; Kohut, 1984; Blatt and Behrends, 1987).

We consider disruption and repair to be only one avenue of structuralization and therapeutic action and as operating during all phases of the treatment. Furthermore, it is an activity of the patient–analyst interaction. Disruptions are neither solely a consequence of the analyst's countertransference nor a result of the patient's "resistance." Repairs are also jointly constructed. The therapeutic action of disruption and repair lies in the organization of a flexibility in negotiating a range of coordination and miscoordination in the process of interactive and self-regulation (Beebe and Lachmann, 1994).

Heightened Affective Moments

The term heightened affective moments was originally defined by Pine (1981). In our elaboration, this principle refers to interactions that are organized when a person experiences a powerful state transformation, either positive or negative (Lachmann and Beebe, 1993; Beebe and Lachmann, 1994). State is used broadly to refer to arousal and activity level, facial and vocal affect, and cognition. Heightened affective moments in the context of the patient–analyst interaction can provide opportunities for new experiences, refinding old loves, or, potentially, retraumatization (Lachmann and Beebe, 1992, 1993, 1997). In the treatment of adults, we define affect broadly to include cognition and symbolic elaborations.

For an adult, the heightened moment may or may not include obvious nonverbal features and will include a symbolic context. For example, in the treatment (by Beatrice Beebe) of a highly intellectualized man who was dependent on a continuous verbal flow, a long, shared silence became a heightened moment. At this point in the interaction, the verbal content ushered in a new intimacy, which was then marked by a pause, which was much longer than usual. Both the patient and I extended the pause to savor this new experience. For this patient, the long moment of pausing was felt to be his first "direct" emotional communication to me, without words. It came to symbolize the possibility of a new kind of shared intimacy. This heightened affective moment ushered in a gradual transformation of his self-regulatory style. After this event, the patient had more access to a calmer state, where his verbal flow contained more pauses. There was more room for both my patient and me to reflect, absorb, and experience. In turn, the interactive regulation was altered. I was more present both for my patient and for myself. Both my patient and I increasingly came to be able to describe this altered interactive process in words.

In other treatments, moments of humor (Lachmann and Lichtenberg, 1992) and surprise (Reik, 1935; Lachmann and Beebe, 1993; Wolf, 1993) may organize heightened affects for both analyst and patient. For example, a patient (treated by Frank Lachmann) had been describing her slavish, obsessional attachment to a former boyfriend. He was a sadistic, exploitative man whom she had not seen in over a year. In the last minute of a session, she turned to me in desperation and pleaded, "I am like a deer, caught in the headlights of an oncoming car, unable to move. You have to help me get out of this state. Tell me something to help me!" Stymied, as her hand opened the door to leave, I said, "If you think of yourself as a deer, and you think of him as a car, think of him as a car without a driver." She turned, and for a split second we looked at each other. In the following session, she described her dramatic mood change after the comment. She said, "I thought of him as a suit of armor, without a knight." The patient had elaborated on my description of her image. Her state of helpless desperation was temporarily transformed.

This interaction became a heightened moment for the patient because she felt that I had joined her in sharing her imagery and rescuing her. Although I was stymied at first, it became a heightened moment for me because I succeeded in coming up with an elaboration of the patient's image just in the nick of time and was able to join her in a moment of shared relief from tension. This shared moment marked the beginning of a decrease in her rage at her ex-boyfriend and in her expectation that he rescue her.

Both vignettes illustrate key features of heightened affective moments. The moment is jointly constructed by both participants. An expectation of how the interaction will go is transformed for both analyst and patient. Simultaneously, the patient's state is dramatically transformed. These moments can be integrative, altering the transference. The therapeutic action of heightened affective moments is mediated through state transformations that potentially usher in opportunities for an expanded self-regulatory range and altered patterns of interactive regulation, thus new internalizations and therapeutic change.

In summary, new themes may be organized through all three principles of salience. All three principles alter the context of rigid themes and promote the development of new interactive expectations and thus new internalizations and therapeutic change. In the following case we examine the process of treatment in terms of these three principles to specify in greater detail the sources of therapeutic action. Rather than examining the three principles one-by-one, we weave them into the case.

Case Illustration

A 36-year-old divorced professional woman, who was seen on a three-session-per-week basis, began her fourth attempt at psychoanalytic therapy with me (Frank Lachmann) with a generally pessimistic feeling. Several years of previous treatments had not succeeded in diminishing her depressive outlook on life, her inability to enjoy herself in any endeavor, or her sense that nothing she was involved in was worthwhile. After the first month of treatment, Clara began her analytic hours with such questions as, How are *you* going to help me? How is *this* going to be any different? What *good* is this going to do?

The way this patient initially organized her experience in treatment was based on her long-standing and pervasive pessimism: nothing would make any difference. When this attitude was reflected to her, she responded that in her previous treatments she had been called "resistive." She was waiting to see when this label would be applied to her. Furthermore, she anticipated being accused of "masochism," of being "unwilling to help herself," and of being "unwilling to make use of the treatment situation." She expected to be blamed for not improving. In fact, she said that, if she were not blamed, it would only be because I was too nice, in fact pathologically nice, and had a problem with aggression. In that case I would also be unable to help her, and she might as well leave.

Cautious Hope and the Acceptance of Opposition

The patient recognized the importance to her of this grim belief (Weiss and Sampson, 1986) that she would not be helped and that she could not change. I had to monitor myself carefully—and not always successfully—so as not to impose on her a need to make herself an "easier" patient. After several months of exploration, a model scene was formulated based on a childhood experience (Lachmann and Lichtenberg, 1992).

The patient and her family lived on a farm in the Midwest. When she was eight years old she was given a horse as a present. Although she was told how to take care of it, she neglected to fol-

low the instructions, and the horse became incapacitated and had
to be killed. On the day that the horse was to be killed, her parents
told her that they were going to take her for a picnic. She knew that
the horse was to be killed and that the picnic was her parents'
attempt to spare her the pain of having to be there when the horse
was killed. Out of a sense of reponsibility, guilt, and loyalty, she
wanted to stay with her horse until the end. At the same time, she
believed that her parents needed to feel that they were protective
and caring. She gave in to her parents' need, betrayed her own ideals,
and went on the picnic. When she returned and the horse was
indeed gone, she felt ashamed.

This model scene—that is, collaborating with her parents' need
to appear "good" at the sacrifice of her integrity, acquiescing to going
to the picnic while her horse was killed—condensed many earlier,
dynamically similar experiences. It captured the way in which the
patient continued to organize her experience in adulthood, including the analytic relationship. To avoid further self-betrayal, the
patient strove to maintain self-respect by not allowing anyone, ever
again, to believe that they were doing anything for her or giving
anything to her.

The patient's depressive, pessimistic states, her inflexibility, her
"resistive" stance in the analysis, and the themes that organized her
model scene were explored and formulated as follows: "I must beware
of people trying to make me feel good. If I permit them to do so, I
run the risk of masking a painful but real event. A feeling of well-
being could turn out to be self-deceptive. When others want me to
feel good, or want to spare me pain, guilt, or anxiety, it is only out
of their own self-interest. My self-respect and integrity demand that
I not permit anyone to help me feel better. So long as I feel
depressed, guilty and despairing, I know I have maintained my
integrity." In fact, it became critical to the patient that she never
acknowledge that anyone could help her feel better. Only by feeling bad could she remain true to her horse. This picture defined the
nature of her self-regulation as she entered the treatment.

The joint construction of the model scene and its interpretation
became a heightened moment for me. All of a sudden I understood
the nature of her battle with me and the dire necessity for her

oppositionalism. However, she was not particularly impressed. She was mistrustful of the "Pollyanish" formulations. In this instance she did not share my heightened affective moment.

Acceptance of the patient's "resistive" stance as plausible and necessary did not yet alter her dread of reexperiencing her self-betrayal. It did, however, provide her with some sense of efficacy, since she had had an impact on me. It also organized an expectation of new possibilities with me as her new analyst despite her worry that I might be too nice. I noted a shift in her depressive state. She become cautiously hopeful in the face of this novel experience of acceptance. In addition, not expecting acquiescence minimized the likelihood of repeating her traumatic childhood experience in the treatment. Nevertheless, we continued to run into numerous severe but temporary impediments. Acceptance of her need to feel hopeless prevented the impediments from turning into impasses.

At this point in the treatment, the patient continued to feel endangered if she did not resist. If she were to reveal her longings to be understood and cared for, she might forfeit her integrity. Although the dread of self-betrayal persisted, we continued to investigate this theme. My acceptance of her "resistance" contributed to reorganizing and disconfirming her expectation that affirmation of my good work would be demanded.

This opening phase of the treatment illustrates the joint construction of a primary mode of ongoing regulation, her cautious hope and "the acceptance of opposition." My acceptance of the necessity of the patient's opposition and distrust and the patient's cautiously hopeful response became a new mode of interactive regulation.

This ongoing regulation can be evaluated in relation to the therapeutic dilemma that constrained the treatment. The dilemma was that the critical, contemptuous, confrontational, pessimistic stance of the patient, interwoven with hints of suicide, carried a continual possibility of my reacting with impatience, irritability, withdrawal, and blame. New modes of interactive regulation were required that nevertheless accommodated the limitations in the self-regulatory range of both the patient and me. On the patient's side, the self-regulatory issue was her need to shore up her self-protection so that she would not become engaged and trusting and then be betrayed. For my part, the self-regulatory issue was the management of anxiety and self-esteem in the face of these assaults. This underlying dilemma was never directly interpreted. To do so could only have been assimilated by the patient into her conviction that she was deeply flawed, irredeemable, and destructive. Instead it remained in the background as a dilemma that informed the interpretations and the ongoing interactive regulations of the treatment.

Loss and Intuitive Understanding

The patient had enjoyed an early relationship with a lively, adventuresome young housekeeper who helped take care of her from her birth until age three, when her sister was born. She preferred the housekeeper to her mother. The departure of the housekeeper left a void that ushered in a period of loneliness and hopelessness. When the patient was four-and-a-half years old, the housekeeper returned briefly. When the housekeeper left again after a few months, the patient was terribly disappointed. She believed that the housekeeper had come back to her to stay. She then attributed the housekeeper's departure to some inadequacy and badness on her part. The emotional responsiveness and subsequent loss of the housekeeper helped lay the groundwork for her ever-increasing state of pessimism.

The patient described the housekeeper's matter-of-fact manner as contrasting sharply with her mother's emotional shallowness and pretenses. The housekeeper's sudden, unexpected departure left her feeling uprooted and vulnerable. In the analysis, longings to find the housekeeper again and the dread of opening herself to a reexperience of loss were captured in the transference. A pervasive sense of depletion and depression fluctuated with her feeling responded to thoughtfully and "unpretentiously" by me.

A relatively stable mirroring selfobject tie, based on the early relationship with the housekeeper, enabled the patient to feel more alive, adequate, and valued. Gradually, she described feeling "better" during the analytic sessions. However, to reestablish this self-sustaining bond required that I infer, guess, deductively know, intuitively understand her feeling states and the meaning of images from dreams or other experiences, without her associations. More active collaboration with me carried the danger of her participating in a self-betrayal.

Thus, in this portion of the treatment, the usual analytic exploratory stance needed to be altered. For me to persist in inviting her to communicate her thoughts would lead her to feel endangered, enraged, and unable to function. However, to treat her without her associations might lead *me* to feel endangered, enraged, and unable to function. She was asking for the kind of intuitive understanding that she had experienced only in spurts from the housekeeper. She pinned all her hopes on my being able to revive her vitality. I implicitly confirmed the necessity for such intuitive understanding, which had apparently been a critical experience for her with the housekeeper.

At times her demands were irritating. I could dispell this feeling by relating it to my expectation that I should provide her with what she needed and my sense of inadequacy about not consistently providing it. It was important for me to accept how wrong I was when I guessed and to acknowledge how off I was when I tried to approximate what I thought she was feeling. My acknowledgment that I was off was more important than being correct. Even more important, I was willing to try. Expectations of being understood, of affecting me, and of being affected by me began to emerge as a silent background. She struggled to remain sufficiently engaged with me so as not to scuttle the treatment.

On some occasions the patient would say, "Yesterday I said something very important. Do you know what it was?" I would immediately draw a blank. Sometimes I would say, "I don't know." My response proved to her that, although she had thought we were connected at that moment in the previous session, in fact we had not been. She had been wrong. She would then feel devastated, and our tie would be disrupted. Gradually, I came to understand this interaction as her way of both severing a connection that had become too intimate and retaining it at a lower temperature. Eventually, her questions could be interpreted as her attempt to prove to herself that a shared intimacy had been false, an illusion. She thus attempted both to recreate and to avoid a repetition of the attachment–desertion sequence that had occurred with the housekeeper. On other occasions, when I guessed successfully, she would provide more clues and maintain the connection, which would be temporarily repaired.

When I felt that the connection had become attenuated and she was silent, I experimented by musing aloud about my sense of frustration and puzzlement at not being able to reach her. These were both self-regulatory efforts and attempts to reach her by a different route. I also speculated about what she might be feeling—anxious, angry, taking pleasure in tantalizing me, or experiencing a desperation about refinding the lost housekeeper. When I asked how she felt about my musing out loud, she expressed delight, saying that she felt important. This interaction constituted an important mode of repair as well as a shared heightened affective moment, an oasis in a desert, so to speak. It gave us both a glimpse of a more overtly shared bond.

This section of the treatment, "loss and intuitive understanding," illustrates the joint construction of a new ongoing regulation. With me, the analyst, the patient revived her dilemmas: longing to be cared for and dreading that her "badness" would result in her being abandoned; and needing to remain overtly unwilling to associate lest she betray herself again. Thus, the ordinary expectable participation of the patient was not available. Instead, she required an altered form of treatment in which I was the one who provided the "correct" associations. There was nothing playful about the patient's request. It was her rigidly held belief that nothing less would do. Eventually it became clear that she feared that, by talking, she would reveal her badness, alienate me, betray her integrity, and destroy the relationship.

I understood this phase of the treatment as a shift to the establishment (or re-establishment) of a nonverbal bond based on the expectation that the patient could feel accepted and not abandoned. When I failed to understand her, when I guessed wrong, I was met with contempt and rage. These reactions were eventually understood as her test to determine if the bond could tolerate her degree of "badness."

Thus a new ongoing regulation was constructed. The patient affected me by having me alter my usual way of working so that she could stay in treatment without betraying herself through overt participation. In turn, I affected the patient by attempting to provide her with the requisite conditions that might enable her to experience a degree of hope. There was a possibility of rekindling in her the feeling of being accepted by the housekeeper.

However, the treatment often hobbled from one potential stalemate to another. I interpreted that, on one hand, she was extremely brave to tolerate danger at every step; on the other hand, she was desperately self-protective. She remobilized her dread of refinding her "shallow" mother and her painful longings for the intuitive housekeeper. She feared that our intimacy might abruptly disappear. She was putting herself at risk to be with me, but her dread of retraumatization prevented her from taking advantage of this opportunity. This interpretive stance did not shift the intensity of her dread. We were continually on the verge of a disruption.

To extricate us from this dilemma, I had to alter my own self-regulation strategies. As she accused me of suffering from "terminal hopefulness," I had to dampen my enthusiasm and optimism. I concealed my expectation that I would actually help her. When I erred by misunderstanding her or by revealing my own "hope," she became enraged, sarcastic, and developed headaches. If I could tolerate her rage, we were back in business.

This section of the treatment demonstrates the delicate self- and interactive regulation required of both partners to be able to maintain this relationship. From the patient's side, mutual regulation was disrupted if she withdrew into physical complaints, or rages, which expressed only a small portion of the rage she claimed she felt. From my side, to avoid steering the treatment toward an impasse, I had to try to "guess," risk being wrong, tolerate feeling angry and inadequate, constrain my hope and enthusiasm, and acknowledge her fear that the intimacy had been false.

Complaints, Tests, and Acceptance

Approximately two years after the dread of self-betrayal was revealed in the analysis, the patient more and more frequently began her sessions by presenting a variety of complaints. The complaints illustrated both the presence of expectations of abandonment, apparently derived from the period after the departure of the housekeeper, as well as hopes for response.

The problematic aspects of her caregivers had contributed to these rigid expectations. The housekeeper had betrayed her through a sudden, unexpected departure. Her parents had betrayed her with their need that she affirm them as caring at the expense of her own integrity. Her younger sister had reveled in competitive triumphs over her. Nevertheless, her "complaints" in the analysis signaled that she retained some hope for responsiveness. Indeed, she feared that if she did not complain she might be taken for granted, found to be uninteresting, worthless, and then abandoned.

The patient complained that the analytic room was too hot, too cold, too stuffy, too bright, too dark. My chair was either too close or too far away. Or she would be unbearably thirsty or would suffer from a "migraine." Initially, these complaints were explored as communicating that she currently felt mishandled and anticipated further insensitivities. The patient's heightened sensitivity to variations in temperature, brightness, distance, or thirst states were understood as stirring up a sense of aloneness. She feared that she would be required to regulate her comfort on her own, by herself. I interpreted that she expected that now, just as in the past, she would be exposed to unresponsive, indifferent, intrusive, insensitive, or abandoning caregivers.

Before entering my office, the patient usually took her shoes off and left them in the waiting room. She explained that she felt more comfortable with her shoes off but worried that her feet smelled. Could I tolerate her with her smelly feet and her old, ugly, disgusting body? I realized that through this ritual she was revealing to me what she was most ashamed of. It was crucial that I recognize her silent question: Do you find me sexually repulsive? When she was silent during these sessions, it meant that she was waiting for me to ask her about her sexual feelings. This inquiry did not immediately provide insight into her unconscious fantasy life. Rather, the very fact that I inquired was pivotal. It meant to her that I was not turned off by her. In response, she would visibly relax. Through these interactions she felt that I was not avoiding intimacy with her. Memories of the lack of physical affection in her family then emerged, coupled with her own feelings of aversion toward her body.

The patient frequently brought a cup of water to the sessions. During one phase of the treatment it became clear that she wanted me to realize that she felt that she had to provide for herself. She stated that I had nothing to offer her. I learned that she was furious at me for offering her nothing but afraid to show me how enraged and sadistic she could be. She feared that I could not tolerate her rage.

Entering the analytic room shoeless and with a cup of water in her hand constituted a mutually organized ritual. My nonverbal acceptance of this pattern contributed to the stability of our connection. Acceptance required that I not interfere with any aspect of the ritual. Once, after she had arrived with the water a few times, I did question her about it. This inquiry was counterproductive. She told me that she would stop bringing the water if I was going to be so fussy.

My acceptance of the water, and of its meaning that I was not providing her with what she needed, made the subsequent dialogue possible. In retrospect, my acceptance of her ritual provided a necessary "background of safety" (Sandler, 1987). She required these concrete signs of acceptance of "unacceptable" aspects of herself. My noninterference in the ritual and my acceptance were my contribution to the interactive regulation. Her rituals were essential in maintaining her tenuous connection with me. They averted the danger of her retreating into sarcastic, despairing inaccessibility, with a suicidal potential. Over time the meaning of the various components changed, but the rituals continued.

In the earlier phases of understanding the meaning of the complaints, the patient had revealed the singular importance of my ability to guess, or to "know" intuitively, what she was concerned about without her associations. Any additional elaborations on my part were disruptive to her. When she felt "intuitively" responded to, she experienced a heightened sense of aliveness. Recognition of her needs, literal confirmation, and acceptance of her shame-ridden feelings constituted a central ongoing regulation. These literal confirmations were heightened affective moments for the patient. Her pessimistic state was momentarily transformed. She felt "known," "recognized," "remembered," "alive."

Later in the treatment there was a substantial shift in the nature of the transference. Her earlier requirement that I understand her intuitively was transformed into a new expectation. I was now required to make creative, illuminating, or even somewhat challenging or confrontational interpretations. Exploration of her request for this kind of intervention led to our understanding of a specific dynamic meaning. It was not the content of the interpretations that was important, but the fact that I could make them. Being the recipient of these creative and challenging interventions revived her experiences with her idealized, "phallic" father of prepuberty. Thus a new theme emerged in the ongoing regulations.

The "Castrated" Father and the "Phallic" Father

By the time the patient reached adolescence, her successful physician father had become a barbituate addict. From this time onward she viewed him as "castrated" and "devalued." These memories contrasted sharply with her earlier recollections of her energetic and "phallic" father. We inferred that she had turned to her father after the departure of the housekeeper. At that time her father had provided her with much-needed enthusiasm for some time until he, too, became a disappointment.

The "castrated" father assumed the foreground of the treatment when I failed to make illuminating and scintillating comments. In the analysis, she expressed her disappointment openly, but in her family she had held back her disappointment. She had not wanted to join her mother in denigrating and humiliating her father. She needed her father to be "tough." He had indicated that he wanted her to be "tough" by calling her "Rocky." Although she tried to provide him with the tough son she felt he wanted her to be, she failed. She felt that he was disappointed in her. She believed that her father's wish for a tough son reflected his "castrated" condition. Whenever she was able to experience me as distinct from her "castrated" father, she was relieved. Then she did not feel like a disappointment, nor was she obliged to become "tough" and sacrifice herself. Furthermore, she did not then need to prop me up, a replay of her struggle to restore her father to his previously idealized, phallic position.

The following vignette illustrates the working through of the "castrated" father transference. As a session was about to begin, the patient announced in the waiting room that there were no paper drinking cups in the bathroom. I took a package of paper cups from a closet and placed them in the bathroom. As the session began, the patient said that she was furious. Once again, I had failed her. As on various occasions in the past, she questioned my ability to treat her. Placing the paper cups in the bathroom meant to her that I was unable to deal with her rage. She said that if I had not provided the cups, I could have demonstrated my ability to deal with her rage at having been deprived of the cups. This incident constituted a disruption in the ongoing regulation of our relationship.

During an earlier time in the treatment, when I did not agree to remove a cinder from her eye, the patient had been reminded of her parents' indifference. My uncooperativeness had confirmed her belief that I found contact with her body disgusting. This time, I felt it was appropriate to respond to her need. However, in retrospect, I see that, at this point in the treatment, I was silently serving as a source of (phallic) strength from which she could derive a sense of safety and protection. This strength would relieve her of the burden of having to protect me from her rage. She indicated that a lack of response would have been a demonstration of my strength.

In contrast to past experiences, as synopsized in the "picnic," the patient was able to talk about her rage and her fears, disappointments and criticisms of me, thus participating actively in the repair process. My supplying her with the cups had ruptured the selfobject tie, leaving her feeling vulnerable. It confirmed her expectation that her rage could not be tolerated. Our understanding of the meaning of the rupture constituted its repair.

Integration of Interactive Process and Dynamic Interpretation

The three principles address the interactive process per se. This process can be attended to either verbally or nonverbally and will always be interwoven with dynamic themes and their interpretation. Although we have distinguished dynamic themes and the interactive process, this distinction is arbitrary since the content of the dynamic themes are themselves regulated in part through this interactive process. Nevertheless, we now turn to their integration.

In the clinical material just presented, we noted each principle separately, as it was relevant, to mark its unique contribution to therapeutic action. In any specific instance, however, the three principles may each be present to varying degrees. In the four examples from this case that follow, we integrate the three principles with the dynamic themes that they address.

Establishing a Dialogue: Ongoing Regulation of Engagement, Disruption, and Repair

The patient complains, and I appear too active, too concerned, too interested, too enmeshed in ameliorating the cause of her complaints. She feels that I cannot tolerate her anger. When I appear to be less active, she complains that I am too passive and incapable of helping her. I describe these sequences of distress, attempts at repair, and increased distress. Rather than our heading toward an impasse, a dialogue is established and the ongoing interaction is retained. I acknowledge the pattern of engagement and rupture. This acknowledgment constitutes a repair. I maintain an implicit, continued engagement with her, and she is then able to reengage.

Only later in the treatment were the associated dynamic themes clarified. The patient's sensitivity to these ruptures was organized through earlier experiences, such as the abandonment by the housekeeper, having to fend for herself unsupported and alone, or the disappointment in the "castrated" father.

The Mismatch Between Hope and Despair: Disruption and Repair

The patient is in despair and I am experienced as too hopeful. She becomes enraged and mistrustful. I acknowledge that my hopefulness may have been too jarring for her. My comment recognizes that an affective mismatch has occurred. She continues to feel hopeless and feels that she now has an analyst who may never under-stand her degree of hopelessness. I describe the whole sequence, and the ongoing regulation is retained.

Only later in the treatment could the dynamic content, the fam-ily stance toward the death of her horse, be linked to her experi-ence of the jarring effect of my hopefulness. By fostering a pretense about the fate of the horse, the family did not acknowldedge her despair. Making these connections too soon meant to her that I could not tolerate her despair and had to flee.

Heightened Affective Moments

The patient experiences states of rage or longing that she does not reveal. Intuitively, I correctly identify her state. She feels immensely gratified and hopeful. This sequence constitutes a heightened pos-itive moment for both of us. Her state transforms from despair to hope. However, she wonders whether her states are really accept-able. I worry silently whether I can ever do this again. My silent worry dampens my heightened affect. Only later in the treatment did I understand that my ability to intuit her state correctly was a refinding of the housekeeper.

At those all too rare moments in the analysis when her unver-balized expectations were met, she experienced a heightened sense of pleasure and satisfaction and felt deeply understood. These spe-cial moments were often based on my understanding of her yearn-ing to be found acceptable. It was important to her that I did not need her to be "tough." At other times, rageful, sadistic, vindictive intentions were at the heart of her complaints, dream images, or associations. My recognizing these states meant to her that I could accept aspects of her that were shameful and specifically censored within her family.

The Transformation of Ongoing Expectations

The patient feels hopeless and suicidal and threatens to quit treat-ment. I accept these feelings and do not flee. She feels understood and cared for. A complex interactive regulation is thus organized.

For my part, I match her distress, but at a level of intensity just under hers. Thus I stay in her distress state without upstaging her, that is, without drawing attention to my own state. I am moved by her despair, accept my discomfort, and stay with her feelings. For her part, she accepts this intervention, feels in contact with me and enlivened. Later we came to understand that in her suicidal threats she anticipated an abandonment. My active acceptance of her feelings, without my trying to change them, came to mean that the dreaded abandonment would not occur. Moreover, the groundwork has been laid for expectations of a new form of interactive regulation.

The Integration of Dynamic Content and Interactive Process

In considering the integration of the interactive process and dynamic themes, we came to understand that this patient could not engage in the treatment in the way it is ordinarily conducted. The patient's pessimism and "resistance" to change interfered with her participation in the usual verbal therapeutic dialogue. Her specific fears and hopes dictated a narrow range of responsiveness into which she assimilated my interventions. When I "accepted" the patient's rituals and made descriptive interventions, contact was restored. Without special attention to the *process* of the interactive regulation, as well as to dynamic content, this patient would have consistently experienced me as confirming her depressed and hopeless feelings and her resistive style. Attention to the process of the regulation was continually integrated with recognition of dynamic themes, such as her dread of participation due to fear of self-betrayal and shame. She needed to have shameful aspects of herself recognized and accepted without having to say what they were.

Attention to the interactive process as well as to dynamic interpretation is critical to all phases of every treatment, although their balance differs from case to case. The loss of the housekeeper and the "picnic" provided a dynamic basis for the interpretive dimension of the treatment. However, we hold that attention to the process of interactive regulation is more than a preparatory phase for later interpretation. Attention to the interactive process implicitly accepts, disconfirms, or alters aspects of the patient's expectations. It makes a major contribution to the patient's expectation of mutuality and being understood.

Although the dynamic interpretive activity made a substantial contribution, this patient was particularly responsive to the articulation of the interactive process. This articulation facilitated an increased self-regulatory capacity. Her manifest "complaints" became less intense and somewhat less frequent. She attempted to be more adventuresome in her life by permitting herself an occasional "extravagance" and in the analysis by increasingly revealing her shame-ridden fantasies. Most important, her ability to tolerate my lapses in understanding increased significantly.

At times this patient neither participated through her associations nor acknowledged my descriptive comments. Although she appeared to be "resistive," "unwilling to help herself," and "unwilling to make use of the treatment situation," we have shown that, instead, she was an active contributor to the process of change. Her continued engagement in the treatment was evidence of the success of this attention to the interactive process.

The clinical material described was drawn from the first five years of the treatment. At that point, toward the end of the fifth year, if the patient were asked what she had derived from her analysis to date, she would probably have answered, "Nothing." Yet her attendance was impeccable, and she was consistently responsive to me. Alterations in the schedule of analytic hours disorganized her and increased her sense of hopelessness, attesting to a viable self-object tie. Not until the seventh year of analysis was overt acknowledgment of its importance possible. Not until the eleventh year was termination possible.

Summary

In studying the dyad as well as the regulation of the individual, infant research brings to psychoanalysis the perspective of the system. This perspective explicates the individual's subjective experience within the dyad and the dyad's impact on the individual's experience. We used three principles of the organization of interactions from infant research to suggest a differentiated conceptualization of the analytic relationship and modes of therapeutic action. Using one case, we illustrated how attention to the interactive process through the three principles can be integrated with dynamic interpretations.

A central contribution of infant research is its description of interaction as a continuous, reciprocally influenced process, constructed moment to moment by both partners. The application of this concept of interaction to adult treatment enriches our view of therapeutic action. At every moment, there is the potential to organize expectations of mutuality, intimacy, trust, repair of disruptions, and hope, as well as to disconfirm rigid archaic expectations. At every moment, both analyst and patient contribute significantly to this organization. Everything the analyst does, interpretive and noninterpretive, verbal and nonverbal, exploratory and descriptive, potentially contributes to the organization of the patient's experience.

9

AN INTERACTIVE MODEL OF THE
MIND FOR ADULT TREATMENT

This chapter reviews the dimensions of a dyadic systems model and its implications for psychoanalysis. Several organizing principles of interaction can be derived from these dimensions:

(1) The distinction between explicit and implicit processing provides a new framework within which to integrate verbal and nonverbal communication in psychoanalysis.
(2) Patterns of expectation provide one definition of implicit procedural knowledge, which is a potent mode of therapeutic action.
(3) Therapeutic action can occur in an implicit form of processing without necessarily translating the communication into an explicit verbal mode.

In this chapter, we first provide a summary of the dimensions of a dyadic systems model. We then summarize our view on interaction in psychoanalysis, reviewing a number of organizing principles of interaction derived from infant research. In the next section, we suggest that the distinction between explicit and implicit processing provides a new framework within which to integrate verbal and nonverbal communication in psychoanalysis. Distinguishing

self-regulatory tilts and interactive tilts, we spell out some implications of our system model for adult treatment. We then use the systems model to reformulate several key concepts in psychoanalysis:
self and other, internalization, and mutuality versus autonomy.
Finally, we review recent experiments from dynamic systems theory on how the brain perceives and constructs its "maps." This
research further articulates two key themes of our book: the co-construction of experience and a transformational model of representations. The section on "The Mind That Updates Its Maps" further
explicates an interactive model of mind for psychoanalysis.

Dimensions of a Dyadic Systems Model

Communication Viewed as a Continuous, Moment-to-Moment Interactive Process

Variations in face, voice, and orientation provide an essential means
of sensing the partner. Moment-to-moment shifts can be considered to be the smallest unit, nested within larger units that are more
prolonged, such as discrete verbalizations. In the history of psychoanalysis, the concept of process has been most evident in the
careful tracking of patients' associations. Whereas tracking a patient's
associations uses an explicit, verbal mode of processing, the tracking of nonverbal shifts uses an implicit mode.

Interaction Organized Through Bidirectional "Influence" or Coordination

Since this term is so easily misunderstood, we reiterate that neither
causality nor mutuality is implied; rather, bidirectional coordination
(or "influence") refers to the probability that one person's behavioral
stream can be predicted from that of the other, and vice versa.
Positive as well as aversive interactions can be bidirectionally coordinated. The statistical concept of the probability that one person's
behavioral stream can be predicted from that of the other can be
translated into the idea that each person can sense whether or not

the partner's behavior is related in time to his or her own, that is, "coordinated." Sensing that the partner's behavior is coordinated with one's own provides the most fundamental layer of implicit relatedness. This sensing generally goes on out of awareness; it is most easily noticed when absent. But this sensing can be brought into awareness under certain conditions. This concept of bidirectional coordination defines one use of the term co-construction, that is, that all interactions are co-constructed by both people.

In translating the bidirectional model for psychoanalysis, it is important to articulate both the patient's experience of being influenced by the analyst as well as influencing the analyst, *and* the analyst's experience of being influenced by the patient as well as influencing the patient. Of these four vectors of experience (two for each partner), often one or two are privileged by patient and analyst.

Interactive Exchanges as a Product of the Integration of Self- and Interactive Regulation

Sander (1977) has argued that infants begin life with primary endogenous activity that must be coordinated with the partner. Included in this primary activity is an intrinsic motivation to order information, detect regularity, and generate and act on expectancies (Haith et al., 1988). In Sander's model, the way self-regulation is organized, in relation to the dyad, sets the stage for the sense of self as agent. A subjectivity of "one's own" is continually being organized, including access to, articulation of, and regard for one's inner states. But the inner process is enhanced or limited by the ongoing interaction.

This emphasis on self-regulation answers a current critique of relational and systems models as tilting too far toward environmental influences and neglecting endogneous influences (see Wilson, 1995). We thus return to one of Sander's most essential postulates: inner process is organized by both self- and interactive regulation. The individual can be fully described only in relation to the dyad. That self- and interactive regulation always affect each other defines our second use of "co-construction," the co-construction of inner and relational processes.

The co-construction view advanced here potentially alters our usual understanding of the analyst's subjectivity. Concerns about obfuscation or facilitation have dominated our understanding of the contribution of the analyst's subjectivity to the analytic process. The analyst's subjectivity is seen as potentially constraining, biasing, distorting, or facilitating the process. In contrast, using the co-construction model, each partner's subjective experience is an emergent process, continually affected by the interaction as well as by the person's own self-regulation.

Patterns of Expectations as Generated by Both Partners, Organized Through the Dimensions of Time, Space, Affect, and Arousal

The sequence of one's own actions in relation to those of the partner, and an associated self-regulatory range and style, come to be expected. Four-month-old infants detect regularity in spatiotemporal events, in both the self and the environment. Further, they develop expectancies based on these events, which implies some future-oriented mental process. This, in fact, is one definition of procedural knowledge of the social environment. In this book, we have used patterns of expectation to define presymbolic representations, which is one way of conceptualizing the initial organization of implicit procedural processing.

A Systems Model Uses a Constructivist View of Perception and Representation

Wilson (1995) has argued that a theory of representation is not adequate to map the mind. He suggests that the use of representations alone will lead to a model of the mind as "enslaved," as a mirror of nature. This view uses a copy theory of representation deriving from positivist/mechanist assumptions about the nature of perception (Reese and Overton, 1970). But a systems model uses constructivist assumptions about the nature of perception and representation. A positivist view assumes a one-to-one correspondence between the world and what we perceive in it. In contrast, a constructivist view assumes that there is no pure sensory event independent of the categories we bring, such as perceptual preferences, expectancies, and self-regulatory styles (see Kuhn, 1962; Reese and Overton, 1970; Lewis and Brooks, 1975). We actively construct and reconstruct all information, since what we perceive and represent is the result of an ongoing interaction between the environment and the categories we bring. Representations are thus "in process," open to being updated. The concept of representation shifts toward a continuously reorganizing process. Nevertheless, there are quasi-stable states of the system, patterns of expectancies. Much work remains to explicate the conditions under which systems do or do not transform, particularly when trauma enters the picture.

Interaction in Psychoanalysis

The foregoing dimensions of a systems model yield organizing principles of interactions for psychoanalysis, defining dimensions of an interactive model of mind. The most general of these principles entails the integration of self- and interactive regulation. An individual is continually affected by his or her own behavior as well as by that of the partner. Behavior is simultaneously communicative and self-regulatory (see Tronick, 1989). Self- and interactive regulation are simultaneous, complementary, and optimally in dynamic balance.

We have further differentiated three principles of salience: ongoing regulation, disruption and repair, and heightened affective moments, each of which further refines our understanding of the nature of self- and interactive regulation (see the case of Clara, chapter 8). The case of Karen (see chapter 3) was used to illustrate an experience of chronic mismatched interactive regulation which led to premature, drastic self-regulation.

Perceptual mechanisms linking the organization of inner and relational processes can be used to further explicate the nature of self- and interactive regulation. For example, through cross-modal matching we can link the behavior we see in the partner (for example, facial expression) and our own inner proprioception. The mere perception of a positive or negative expression in the partner creates a resonant emotional state in the perceiver. And, since a person's facial expression is associated with a particular physiological pattern, matching the expression of the partner creates in the onlooker a similar physiological state. These perceptual mechanisms illustrate our argument that internal processes and relational processes are inextricably coordinated and are organized concurrently (see chapter 2).

The general principle of interactive regulation can be further refined by the midrange model. We have reviewed research documenting a continuum of interactive regulation of vocal rhythm coordination, ranging from high to low, which predicted one-year attachment outcomes in a large study of mother–infant and stranger–infant interactions (Jaffe et al., 2001). Midrange coordination predicted secure attachment whereas scores outside the midrange predicted insecure attachment. High coordination was conceptualized as interactive vigilance; low coordination as an aspect of withdrawal or inhibition. Interactive vigilance and interactive inhibition further articulate forms of interactive regulation that can be used in adult treatment (see the case of Jennifer, chapter 6).

An elaboration of interactive vigilance can be seen in the chase-and-dodge pattern, in which not only are the two partners very highly coordinated, but there is an approach-withdrawal pattern as well. Sorter (1996) treated a young woman for whom a chase-and-dodge pattern had become a central organizing feature of her life. In the first session, that patient sat in a spot furthest away from Sorter. As Sorter rolled her chair slightly forward to a distance that was optimal for herself and usually acceptable for her patients, the patient's eyes became "as big as saucers" (p. 70) and she reared back. Sorter understood that she had violated the patient's space. As Sorter rolled her chair back, the patient visibly uncoiled. The movements seemed to happen in a flash and remained entirely nonverbal. As this pattern then gradually continued to unfold in the analytic dyad, Sorter was able to label it chase and dodge. Using it as a metaphor to understand their mutual engagement and disengagement processes became a powerful mode of therapeutic action.

The midrange balance model provides a more refined description of how self- and interactive regulation affect each other. Building on the midrange model, which described only interactive regulation, the midrange balance model posits a midrange optimum in both self- and interactive regulation. In the midrange, interactive coordination is present but not obligatory, and self-regulation is preserved but not excessive. Optimal social communication and development is hypothesized to occur with flexibility to move between self- and interactive regulation, yielding relatively optimal levels of attention, affect, and arousal. For each partner, operating outside the midrange may index an attempt to cope with a disturbance in the interaction. An excessive monitoring of the partner, at the expense of self-regulation, defines one pole of imbalance, interactive vigilance. Preoccupation with self-regulation, at the expense of interactive sensitivity, defines the other pole of imbalance, withdrawal or inhibition.

Implicit and Explicit Processing

The implicit mode of processing is beginning to be recognized as critical to psychoanalysis (see. e.g., Stern et al., 1998; Tronick et al., 1978). Lyon-Ruth (1998b) has defined implicit relational knowing as

> rule-based representations of how to proceed, of how to do things
> . . . with others . . . such as knowing how to joke around, express
> affection, or get attention . . . as much affective and interactive
> . . . as cognitive. . . . [It] begins to be represented long before the
> availability of language and continues to operate implicitly
> throughout life [p. 284].

It operates out of awareness and outside of verbal consciousness.

Whereas explicit memory refers to symbolically organized intentional recall for information and events, implicit memory includes procedural and emotional memory that is outside of awareness. Procedural memory refers to action sequences that are encoded nonsymbolically and influence the organizational processes that guide behavior (Squire and Cohen, 1985; Grigsby and Hartlaub, 1994). These action sequences are initially "intentional," both for the infant and the adult (Müler and Overton, 1998). Only after they become automatic with repeated practice are they "nonconscious" or out of awareness. They can again become the focus of awareness, particularly if these action sequences do not proceed as expected. Emotional memory includes aspects of the limbic system, such as the amygdala. For example, a facial change of the partner can be processed within four milliseconds and registered in a change in the amygdala, out of awareness. The explicit and implicit memory sytems are potentially dissociable.

The patterns of mother–infant interaction described in this book are examples of repetitive action sequences organized procedurally. An implicit "knowing how to proceed" can be illustrated by attention regulation patterns, such as who initiates looking, whether or not the partners mutually gaze at each other, how long it is comfortable to hold a mutual gaze, who looks away first, and how reactive either partner is to the other's looking away. The research on vocal rhythm provides another example of how to proceed moment by moment, that is, how each partner knows when it is his or her turn to speak, how easily the turn is exchanged, how tightly each partner "tracks" or coordinates with the other's vocal rhythm, and rules for interruption and joining. It is at the implicit procedural level, on a moment-to-moment basis, that powerful interactive "emotion schemes" (Bucci, 1997) of face, gaze, vocalization, and orientation are organized, shifts in degrees of coordination are played out, and disruption and repair are negotiated. In chapter 4 we argued that these patterns are encoded in infancy in a presymbolic representational format. In chapter 5 we described some of the research predicting attachment and cognition outcomes at one year from these repetitive action sequences at four months, illustrating how implicit processes can influence the ongoing developmental trajectory.

In psychoanalytic treatment the expectancies that regulate intimate relating can be reorganized in the implicit domain without necessarily reaching conscious awareness. Lyons-Ruth (1998b) notes that only a small area of a patient's implicit relational knowing will ever become the subject of verbal narrative or transference interpretation. By implication, the implicit mode is far more pervasive and potentially more powerfully organizing than is the explicit mode. The idea that therapeutic action can occur at the implicit level without verbalization is an important change for a theory of therapeutic action. This position is forcefully argued by Grigsby and Hartlaub (1994), Clyman (1991), Emde et al. (1991), Bucci (1997), Schore (1994, 1996), Morgan (1998), Pally (1998), Lyons-Ruth (1998b), and Stern et al. (1998) among others. Clyman (1991) has proposed that implicit procedural processing provides a measure of continuity from childhood to adulthood and organizes transference expectations.

Despite the importance of implicit relational knowing in potential continuities across the life span, we do not hold that early patterns necessarily become long-term, entrenched procedural memories that govern interaction in adult dyadic life (cf. Harris, 1997). Instead, we espouse a transformational view, along the lines of Sander (1977, 1995) and Sameroff (1983), that early patterns set a trajectory that can nevertheless transform. Only in pathology is there a relative loss of this transformational process.

The distinction between implicit and explicit processing provides a new framework for conceptualizing the integration of verbal and nonverbal communication in psychoanalysis (see also Lyons-Ruth, 1999; Pally, 2001; Stern et al., 1998; Tronick et al., 1978). Our approach takes into account both the symbolic representational level (explicit) and the action-perception level (implicit). The working assumption of psychoanalysis is that explicit symbolizable representations of self and other (conscious/unconscious) guide social behavior. In contrast, an implicit procedural view argues that social behavior is coordinated on a split-second basis, out of awareness, with such rapidity and density of information that central cognitive control or representation is not possible (Newtson, 1990). At the implicit action-perception level, the information sufficient to structure action is inherent in the person-partner relation (Gibson, 1979; Newtson, 1990; Fogel, 1992a, 1993; Thelen and Smith, 1994). In the latter view, actions contain information as an objective property, in contrast to the former view that information has no psychological reality until it is symbolically represented.

We note as a caveat that we are limiting the concept of nonverbal communication in psychoanalysis to the repetitive, rapid-action sequences that are largely out of awareness. Symbolic nonverbal gestures, such as a raised hand held flat and open, which is an explicit communication of "stop," are excluded from our discussion.

Stern (1995) has noted that there is a strong intellectual current against placing action at the center of an understanding of human behavior. He cites Gendlin's view that anything human depends on language. Stern suggests that "many modern strains of psychoanalysis privilege the narration or interpretation that stands behind . . . an act, . . . rather than the act itself" (p. 77) and that "what one experiences is not determined by the actions and interactions that make up the lived event, but rather by the later mental reconstruction of what happened" (p. 78).

These two levels, the implicit action sequence and the explicit symbolized narration, must be integrated for a fuller understanding of therapeutic action in psychoanalysis (see also Stem et al., 1998). These two levels potentially affect each other. The struggle to symbolize the implicit action level can be seen as one of the major goals of psychoanalysis (Bucci, 1985, 1997). The nature of the symbolization can then potentially affect the implicit action level. However, therapeutic action proceeds in both these modes, whether or not they are integrated.

Implications for Adult Treatment

With "difficult-to-reach" patients in particular, the interaction between analyst and patient requires close, continuous attention. These are the treatments where the critical cues that call for analytic attention go far beyond the usual verbal exchanges. These are the treatments for which terms like "parameters" (Eissler, 1953) and "noninterpretive interventions" (Lachmann and Beebe, 1996a, b; see also Stern et al., 1998) were coined. These are the treatments in which countertransference is seen either as an interference or as an analytic panacea, each introducing its own problems. These are the treatments in which attention to the system, the unfissionable unit (Kohut, 1984), and the moment-to-moment process carry the therapeutic leverage.

For infant and mother, as well as for patient and analyst, either person's self-regulation may disrupt or facilitate the interaction. For example, in the case of Paulina, who cried for the first three years of her treatment, as the analyst, I (Beatrice Beebe) might speak too quickly using a fast-paced style, in my eagerness to capture my thought. In this process, I came to understand that I could lose my patient, who went slowly, trying to make sure that she knew what she was feeling at every moment. If she followed my train of thought, she would warn me, she would lose her own. Thus, my racy style altered and potentially derailed the interactive process. These descriptions of what the analyst brings to the treatment, in self-regulatory style or interactive expectations, are usually understood in terms of countertransference. From a systems point of view, however, they are part-and-parcel of the interactive process. They are neither positive nor negative, they are unavoidable, and they influence the psychoanalytic encounter at every moment.

Specific nonverbal patterns can be observed in the therapeutic relationship. For example, an analyst may take note of particular patterns, such as Sorter's (1996) chase-and-dodge case, in which, as the analyst rolled her chair slightly toward the patient, the patient recoiled. These experiences are often very difficult to put into words. Neither the patient nor the analyst may be quite aware of them. For the patient, the history of these behaviors is also likely to be out of awareness. If the analyst can notice recurrent patterns or subtle shifts in nonverbal behaviors in either herself or the patient, these patterns may signal subtle difficulties in the engagement. These nonverbal patterns are particularly powerful because they occur in the here-and-now, possessing that special alive quality of something immediate for both.

Once such a pattern is noticed, much investigation is usually necessary to understand its history and meaning. It is important to note that a particular nonverbal pattern has no set meaning; its meaning can emerge only through the analytic process. Furthermore, months may go by before there is an appropriate moment to notice a particular pattern. And sometimes the analyst may choose never to bring it into the verbalized exchange.

Self-Regulatory Tilts

Specific patterns of self- and interactive regulation are highly visible in nonverbal behaviors. For example, we can observe the self-regulatory ranges that both patient and analyst bring. Is one rapid and one slow? What capability does this particular dyad generate to gain access to the patient's self-regulatory range and expand it? In chapter 3 we described the treatment of Karen where the analyst had to constrict his own "exuberant" tilt in order to make contact with Karen, who hid behind her coat. She remained immobile, visually avoidant, and barely audible. A particular patient may have a very different access to self-regulatory capacities with a different therapist. Similarly, with different patients, a therapist may experience different access to inner process and self-regulation. For example, some patients let the therapist pause and muse in the middle of a sentence and are not thrown by this behavior. Other patients cannot stand it and snap their fingers, asking "what's wrong?" In chapter 6 we described these patients as "hypervigilant," illustrated by Shumsky's (1996) treatment of Sandra, and as analogous to the disorganized attachment infants and mothers in the Jaffe et al. (2001) vocal rhythm study. Shumsky's patient monitored the analyst intently for microcues about her state and used communication primarily to protect the equilibrium of the analyst.

The details of these nonverbal regulations can refine an analyst's capacity to notice moment-by-moment self-regulatory shifts of both partners. These shifts are rooted in adaptive efforts to compromise between needs for engagement with the partner and needs to maintain organismic integrity, that is, arousal in a comfortable range. The shifts can inform both patient and analyst of the compromises that have been and continue to be necessary. We are not interested in pathologizing self-regulatory patterns nor necessarily drawing them into one theory of interpretation or another. Instead, we use these patterns to further explicate the nature of the interactive system.

Interactive Tilts

Stern (1983) has described maternal styles of joining (state sharing with similar timing, intensity, and contouring), in which affective empathy is the aim; altering (state transforming), in which attempting to transform the infant's state is the aim; and complementing (reciprocal completion of the behavior of the other), in which experiencing the other directly is the aim. His examples of complementing include vocal turn-taking, rolling a ball back and forth, and the infant's playing while mother is observing.

By analogy, does a therapist envision the analytic task as, for example, tracking and matching the patient's affect state (joining); stimulating or dampening the patient's affect and arousal (altering); engaging in give-and-take exchanges such as humor or maintaining an ongoing dialogue (complementing); or remaining "neutral"? How do patients respond to these different styles?

From the patient's side, if, for example, the unconscious goal is to make sure that the therapist does not intrude, or to obtain love and approval, or to attempt to find the therapist's own need for the patient, how do these different "goals" affect the patient's self-regulatory range and interactive patterns? And how does the therapist respond to these "tilts?" All therapists use a wide range of styles at different moments, and patients have a range of unconscious goals. Nonetheless, for illustrative purposes let us imagine the consequences of the predominance of any one of these styles or goals. Although any of the scenarios we describe may have "negative" consequences, we depict the potential benefit of each.

The midrange balance model described in chapter 5 provides a way of conceptualizing these tilts. Optimal social communication and development are hypothsized to occur in the midrange of self- and interactive regulation, with flexibility to move back and forth. Excessive monitoring by the partner, at the expense of self-regulation, tilts the system toward "interactive vigilance." Preoccupation with self-regulation at the expense of interactive sensitivity tilts the system toward the other pole of imbalance: withdrawal or "inhibition," on one hand, and escalating overarousal on the other.

Since this model was developed for infants, our examples illustrating these tilts for adult treatment consider more complex integrations of self- and interactive regulation. In adult treatment, simultaneous difficulties can occur at both poles of imbalance, such that preoccupation with both self- and interactive regulation can occur at the same time. For example, in Shumsky's (1996) treatment of Sandra, the patient's hypervigilance for cues to the analyst's discomfort functioned both to regulate the analyst's vulnerability and to maintain the bond (preoccupation with interactive tracking). In addition, Sandra's hypervigilance functioned to regulate her own vulnerability in case the analyst failed and the patient had to take over (preoccupation with self regulation). The analyst was initially preoccupied with maintaining her own self-regulation in the face of the patient's hypervigilance.

Joining patterns also illustrate the simultaneous organization of self- and interactive regulation. The therapist who envisions the analytic task as joining remains very interactive, carefully tracking and matching the patient's affect and arousal. Stern (1983, 1985) emphasizes that similarity of timing, intensity, and contouring brings two partners into a similar state, facilitating intimacy and attachment. This style affects the patient's self-regulation as well. Through nonverbal joining, the analyst communicates to the patient, "I am with you in this affective state." The therapist's joining behavior provides a nonverbal interactive background, heightening the attachment bond, while the patient remains in a particular state. Since the patient is no longer attempting to regulate this state completely alone, the attachment process may be facilitated. In addition, through joining experiences, the patient can undergo an interactive modulation of this state and, over time, experience more self-regulatory control. Thus, joining experiences tilt the system both toward intimacy and attachment, as Stern emphasized, and toward the interactive modulation of self-regulation and self-reflection. If, however, the analyst requires joining experiences for aspects of his or her own regulation, the patient may not be free to explore a sufficient range of experiences.

The therapist who envisions the analytic task as altering also remains very interactive, but the system is tilted toward the regulation of the patient's state. An obvious example of state transformation in infancy is the physical soothing of a distressed infant, with a dramatic transformation of arousal accruing to experiences of physical intimacy and trust (Stern, 1983). An analogous example in the adult psychoanalytic literature is the case of Bob, who was continually fired from his jobs owing to chronic, unmodulated rage states (Knoblauch, 1997). None of the "words" seem to help Bob. Knoblauch used the research example of Elliot (see chapter 5), in which Beebe joined Elliot's cry rhythm, and then gradually both slowed down. Knoblauch joined the agitated rhythm of Bob's rage state in the tempo and cadence, but not the volume, of his words. In this way, Bob gradually came to feel that his therapist "understood" him. This intervention facilitated Bob's ability to associate more freely about his history with his abusive father, his bosses, and his analyst. He gradually became less agitated.

Reformulating Three Key Concepts in Psychoanalysis

Self and Other

Within our systems perspective of the continual co-construction of experience, we prefer to use the terms self- and interactive regulation rather than the terms self and other. In a systems view, each component is defined in relation to the other. A systems view is critical of the position that self and other are initially separate, isolated individuals and that the task of development is their integration. In contrast, a systems view sees self and other as initially coordinated and interrelated, and the task of development is further elaboration, differentiation, and integration.

Since self-regulation and interactive regulation are continuously affecting each other, these terms also keep the focus on process. But it is not easy to maintain the dynamic tension between these two processes without tilting toward one or the other as the more dominant organizing principle. For example, when describing our position, Harris (1997) tilted toward the dyadic when she said that we were theorizing that "identity is given and elaborated through the interactive reaction of the other" (p. 202). This position does not preserve the equally important role of infant capacities, temperament, and, more generally, self-regulation style. In contrast, when discussing our work, Kulka (1997) tilted toward the self in holding that "the raison d'être of the human being is not interrelations but the creation of an experience of significant selfhood, even if this goal can be realized only within the contextual cradle of relations with an other" (p. 186).

Using the more traditional concepts of self and other, Tabin (1997) discussed our work in terms of a balancing process between individuality and mutuality. In our view, what is in balance is not "self" and "other," but, rather, the processes of self- and interactive regulation. Each person is always sensing and modulating her own state, while simultaneously sensing how she affects and is affected by her partner. What is in balance is the degree to which one can flexibly go back and forth, in foreground–background fashion, between both processes. If these two processes are in balance, attention, affect, and arousal can be regulated within an optimal range. The research by Jaffe et al. (2001) cited in chapter 5 showed that secure attachment at one year was predicted by midrange degrees of interactive regulation of vocal rhythms, which were interpreted as more flexible than either pole of high or low regulation. The midrange balance model recognizes that both self- and interactive regulation are always present, each affecting the other, and neither process is privileged over the other.

The balance model of self- and interactive regulation shifts the observing stance of the clinician. From this view, the clinician observes two processes in herself (self- and interactive regulation) and infers two in the patient. The analyst is actively involved in comparing her inferences about these two processes in the patient with the patient's own experience of them. Much work may be needed before the patient can articulate her experience of these two processes. Discrepancies between the therapist's inferences and the patient's experience are of particular interest. At the same time, the therapist attempts to maintain an ongoing observation of these two processes within herself.

The research on the regulation of interaction described in this book provides a basis for formulating "interactiveness" as a core psychoanalytic concept. Interactiveness can be defined as "a system whose processes are its essence" (Kulka, 1997, p. 184). Rather than conceiving of self as interacting with other, we conceptualize an ongoing co-construction of processes of self- and interactive regulation. Interactiveness is emergent, in a constant process of potential reorganization.

Internalization

Our systems view changes the concept of internalization. In proposing in chapter 7 that representation and internalization are not
distinct processes in the first year, we argued that the research artic-
ulating the presymbolic origins of representations speaks equally to
the origins of internalizations. Considering that infant research on
face-to-face interaction had barely begun in 1968, it is remarkable
that Schafer, in that year, defined internalization as regulatory interaction, with its striking parallel to the core metaphor of current
infant research on social interaction.

However, Schafer did not systematically play out the implications of this idea. Rather than viewing interactive regulations as
transformed *into* self regulations, which is the central concept in the
analytic literature, in our view regulatory interactions and self regulations proceed hand in hand and shape each other. Both the person and the environment continuously construct, elaborate, and
represent the regulations, which are simultaneously interactive and
self-regulatory. *The expectation and representation of the dyadic modes of regulation constitute the internal organization.*

We concur with Schafer that what is at stake in the internalization process is the increasing relative autonomy from actual interactions with the environment. With the advance of symbol
formation, modes of regulation are increasingly abstracted, depersonfied, and relatively autonomous. This model puts the bidirectional nature of the regulation center stage. It further articulates the
role of the subject in the regulation process, and it emphasizes the
dyadic nature of the construction of internalization.

Mutuality versus Autonomy: A Misunderstanding of the Systems Model

Mutuality and autonomy are frequently conceptualized as opposite
poles on a continuum. It is a misunderstanding of our model to
equate mutuality with interactive regulation and autonomy with
self-regulation. Both autonomy and mutuality require processes of

self- and interactive regulation. We reconceptualize autonomy as emerging from "good-enough" interactive regulation. Likewise, we see interactive regulation in the optimal range as emerging from "good-enough" self-regulation of both partners. Rather than seeing autonomy and relatedness as two separate poles, we see both as simultaneously co-constructed. They operate in a foreground–background format.

Even Tabin's (1997) elegant discussion of our work on the origins of self- and object representations nevertheless contained this frequent misunderstanding of our systems model. In discussing the chase-and-dodge interaction (see chapter 5) in terms of the infant's psychological autonomy, Tabin described this infant as "maintain(ing) his own affect" (p. 191) and "flout[ing] the mother's urgent effort" (p. 192). She described the chase-and-dodge sequence as "initiated and maintained by the infant" (p. 194).

On the contrary, what was so fascinating about the chase-and-dodge baby was his complex compromise between engagement and disengagement. The infant moved in a withdrawal direction but continued split-second responsiveness to his mother (as mother did to him). Before the mother had completed her loom movement into the infant's face, the infant had aleady begun to move away. And before the infant completed the head movement away, mother had already begun to move her head to the side, following the direction of the infant's head movement.

Thus, this infant was not on his own affective track or, in Tabin's language, maintaining his own affect. His attention, affect, and arousal were continuously linked to what the mother was doing and vice versa. To be so embedded in the split-second responsiveness of the dyad, while at the same time moving in the withdrawal direction, simply does not fit our traditional concepts of autonomy and separateness. Thus, the infant's withdrawal was an emergent dyadic property, reciprocally constructed by both partners. The infant's withdrawal had both interactive and self-regulatory functions.

Nevertheless, we retain the concept that an active infant has agency and potentially a different, conflicting agenda from that of the mother (see Slavin, 2000). However, in the chase-and-dodge infant, this agency did not result in efficacy. His own efforts at regulation (increasingly severe head and body orientations away from facing the mother and ultimately going limp) did not result in an optimal range of attention, affect, and arousal.

There is a second difficulty in equating mutuality with interactive regulation. Whereas mutuality carries a positive value, interactive regulation is neutral with respect to the success of the interaction. Positive and aversive patterns alike are interactively regulated, with both partners making reciprocal adjustments. For example, the chase-and-dodge pattern, although clearly aversive, is co-constructed by both partners, each affecting the other on a split-second basis.

The Mind That Updates Its Maps

In our first chapter, we showed how a systems view altered our thinking about the treatment of Burton. In chapter 2 we introduced our dyadic systems view, which integrates the contribution of the individual and that of the dyad to the organization of behavior and experience. In the course of this book, we have used this point of view to go back and forth between organizing principles of interactions in infant research, and in psychoanalysis.

In this final chapter, we have summarized the dimensions of a systems model that yields organizing principles of interaction for psychoanalysis. We have framed these organizing principles within the distinction between implicit and explicit processing, which allows for the integration of verbal and nonverbal communication in psychoanalysis. We have argued that the implicit and explicit levels must be integrated for a fuller understanding of therapeutic action and illustrated these ideas with examples from adult treatment describing self-regulatory tilts and interactive tilts. Now we look ahead to the connection of our work to burgeoning developments in broader systems views. The same general systems model informing our work has been generating research in other areas, particularly neuroscience, which further explicates an interactive model of mind.

Dynamic systems theory, drawing on the work of Edelman (1987, 1992; Tononi, Sporns, and Edelman, 1994), Freeman (1987, 1991), Thelen and Smith (1994), and others, has a critical contribution to make to an interactive model of mind for psychoanalysis through its empahasis on the question of how the brain perceives. Equal emphasis is placed on both sides of an interactive model: the brain influences behavior, but experience alters the brain. Tremendous neural diversity, with variability in size, shape, type and connections of cells, insures that every brain is different. Therefore, the con-nections between cells, the "wiring," is dependent on experience (Thelen and Smith, 1994; Schore, 1994). These connections among cells are continuously rewritten, remapped, as a function of ongo-ing experience. One implication of this model is that there is no fixed schema or representation of a stimulus. The representation of a stimulus is always being updated, "reassembled" as a function of organismic arousal, context, and experience. The mind updates its maps. Thus, brain and experience are co-constructed.

The Updating Process

An example of this updating process can be found in research on how the brain of a rabbit creates a "map" of the smell of sawdust (Freeman, 1987, 1991; Thelen and Smith, 1994). EEG patterns were recorded from 60 sites all over the olfactory bulb. The sawdust odor showed a particular pattern of amplitudes of EEGs in the brain of the rabbit, across the 60 sites. To study the updating process, the rabbit was then exposed to the smell of a banana. Then the same sawdust was returned and EEG patterns were again recorded. It was found that the sawdust map had been modified as a function of the interposed banana smell. Thus, extending the rabbit model to humans, what we perceive is continually updated in the light of the immediate context and the sum of our experiences up to that point.

This kind of research suggests that the mind is inherently rela-tional. The research provides an interactive model of how the brain creates perceptions, representations, or maps, and how these maps are continually updated by experience. This work has tremendous implications for the nature of representation in psychoanalysis. Although many theorists have emphasized the "process" rather than the "static" nature of representation, in this work, representations take on a more purely process character: they are continually updated as a function of experience. Thus, representation must be reconceptualized as a continually shifting process of emergent organization. However, quasi-stable states are posited by dynamic systems theorists. These states can be translated into the familiar concept of expectancies based on repetitive sequences. This work provides a model for the transformation of represenations and thus a model of therapeutic action for psychoanalysis. Nevertheless, much work is needed to explicate the conditions that interfere with the updating process, one of the central concerns of psychoanalysis. Trauma substantially alters the flexibility of the brain to update perception and representation. Healthy development may be characterized by an optimal degree of stability, which balances both predictability and transformation.

The Role of Context

The role of context is critical to understanding how representations form and transform, how the brain creates and updates its maps, how co-constructions reassemble. The way two people co-construct their dyadic process is very sensitive to context. The data on vocal rhythm coordination (Jaffe et al., 2001) show fascinating context sensitivities as a function of the particular partner, mother–infant or stranger–infant, and whether the dyad was filmed at home or in the lab. For example, vocal rhythms were more activated with novelty: from home to lab, and from mother–infant to stranger–infant interactions. The most novel context of stranger–infant in the lab showed more bidirectional vocal rhythm coordination than did the most familiar context of mother–infant at home.

Thelen and Smith (1994) have argued that it is context sensitivity which allows behavior its enormous flexibility and which allows for the possibility of change. They propose that a representation is not something we "have" but something we assemble and reassemble in the moment according to context and task. We hold that psychoanalysis must translate the notion of context into its own terms, identifying its own critical contexts, for example, separations and reunions, disruptions and their repair, moments of shifting affect, spatial orientation, or timing.

A Perturbation Theory of Change

A perturbation theory of change is proposed by nonlinear dynamic systems theorists. A key question for psychoanalysis is, how do systems change, create patterns, and transform patterns? The beginning assumption is that all action and knowledge is process. Patterns of activity in time arise in a certain context. They are inherently dynamic and changeable (Thelen, 1994, 1998; Thelen and Smith, 1994). Development is conceptualized as patterns of changing stability and instability. Some patterns are fairly stable in certain contexts; others are unstable, easily disrupted as a function of history and current context. In an optimally open system, there is a continual flow of information in and out, with the creation of temporarily stable patterns (expectancies). Because an open system is flexible and variable, it is open to exploration and responsive to perturbations, with new solutions.

Variability Is a Source of New Forms

For a pattern to change, some part of the system must disrupt the current stable pattern. New patterns then form as emergent properties of the system. These patterns are nonlinear: they cannot necessarily be predicted from what transpired before. When components are not too tightly coordinated, the system can explore and change. However, when coordination is too tight, it is harder for the system to shift and explore new solutions. In this case, if the system is perturbed, variability can emerge, and overly stable patterns can be pulled apart. In the example of vocal rhythm coordination (Jaffe et al., 2001), the tightest coordination was seen in the most insecure attachments (anxious-resistant and disorganized). Presumably the very tightly coupled dyads lost variability and flexibility. Shumsky's (1996) hypervigilant patient (see chapter 6) illustrated such a tightly organized pattern at the cost of any flexibility: every ripple portended disaster.

Redefinition of Pychopathology

The quality of interpersonal communication is related to the degree of coordination between the partners. Various theorists have suggested that high coordination is either optimal (Chapple, 1970) or not optimal (Gottman, 1979) for communication. Currently, nonlinear models of degree of coordination provide a more general view of its varying meaning (Cohn and Elmore, 1988; Lewis and Feiring, 1989; Thelen, 1998; Warner, 1988a; Watson, 1994). This nonlinear view argues that the person and the environment (partner or inanimate environment) are always coordinated in time; and that the tightness of coordination is flexible, changing according to context (Thelen, 1998). In situations of danger, such as speeding down the Los Angeles Freeway, we better be tightly coupled to the road. Similarly, situations of intense attention and concentration require high coordination. In relaxed contexts, such as meditation or with a very familiar partner, we may be loosely coordinated.

Thelen (1998) suggests that flexibility in the ability to change the strength of coordination provides one definition of adaptation. What is adaptive one second may not be adaptive the next. In an open system, degree of coordination is flexible, whereas loss of such flexibility is one hallmark of pathology.

We illustrated this concept with the work on mother–infant vocal rhythm and the prediction of attachment (Jaffe et al., 2001). Midrange coupling was optimal for secure attachment. At either end of the range, too tightly coupled or too loosely coupled, insecure attachments were predicted. We interpreted the tight range of coupling as vigilant, too predictable, too contingently responsive, presumably as a way of coping with stress or threat. We interpreted the low end of coupling as an inhibition, where the two partners were acting relatively independently of each other and the dyadic system had lost its coherence. Thus, preverbal vocal rhythms and their degree of coordination carry emotional "qualities" of interactions relevant to developing attachment. An extensive adult literature also shows that rhythmic coordination conveys emotional information regarding perceived warmth, similarity, and empathy of the speakers (see, e.g., Jaffe and Feldstein, 1970; Feldstein and Welkowitz, 1978; Warner, 1988a, b).

In conclusion, our purpose in this book has been to explicate the value of infant research and a systems view for psychoanalysis. The value of the research, however, goes beyond its application to adult treatment and an interactive model of mind. It provides a systematic view of the origins of the processes of relatedness itself.

REFERENCES

Adelmann, P. & Zajonc, R. (1989). Facial efference and the experience of emotion. *Annual Review of Psychology, 40,* 249–280.

Adler, G. & Buie, D. (1979). Aloneness and borderline psychopathology: The possible relevance of child development issues. *International Journal of Psycho-Analysis, 60,* 83–96.

Ainsworth, M., Blehar, M., Waters, E. & Wall, S. (1978). *Patterns of attachment.* Hillsdale, NJ: Lawrence Erlbaum Associates.

Allen, T., Walker, K., Symonds, L. & Marcell, M. (1977). Intrasensory and intersensory perception of temporal sequences during infancy. *Developmental Psychology, 13,* 225–229.

Als, H. & Brazelton, T. (1981). A new model of assessing the behavioral organization in preterm and fullterm infants. *Journal of the American Academy of Child Psychiatry, 20,* 239–263.

Alson, D. (1982). Maternal empathy in relation to infant affective engagement at four months. Unpublished doctoral dissertation, Yeshiva University, New York.

The American college dictionary (1962). New York: Random House.

Aron, L. (1996). *A meeting of minds.* Hillsdale, NJ: The Analytic Press.

Atwood, G. & Stolorow, R. (1984). *Structures of subjectivity.* Hillsdale, NJ: The Analytic Press.

Badalamenti, A. & Langs, R. (1990). An empirical investigation of human dyadic systems in the time and frequency domains. *Behavioral Science, 39,* 100–114.

Badalamenti, A. & Langs, R. (1992). Stochastic analysis of the duration of the speaker role in the psychotherapy of an AIDS patient. *American Journal of Psychotherapy, 46,* 207–225.

Bahrick, L. & Watson, J. (1985). Detection of intermodal proprioceptive visual contingency as a potential basis of self-perception in infancy. *Developmental Psychology, 21,* 963–973.

Bakeman, R., Adamson, L., Brown, J. & Eldridge, M. (1989). Can early interaction predict? How and how much? In M. Bornstein & N. Krasnegor (Eds.), *Stability and continuity in mental development* (pp. 235–248). Hillsdale, NJ: Lawrence Erlbaum Associates.

Bakeman, R. & Brown, J. (1977). Behavioral dialogues. *Child Development, 48,* 195–203.

Basch, M. (1988). *Understanding psychotherapy: The science behind the art.* New York: Basic Books.

Beebe, B. (1973). Ontogeny of positive affect in the third and fourth months of the life of one infant. (Doctoral dissertation, Columbia University, 1973). *Dissertation Abstracts International, 35* (2), 1014B.

Beebe, B. (1982). Micro-timing in mother–infant communication. In M. R. Key (Ed.), *Nonverbal communication today* (pp. 169–195). New York: Mouton.

Beebe, B. (1986). Mother–infant mutual influence and precursors of self and object representations. In J. Masling (Ed.), *Empirical studies of psychoanalytic theories, vol. 2* (pp. 27–48). Hillsdale, NJ: The Analytic Press.

Beebe, B. (1998). A procedural theory of therapeutic action: Commentary on symposium on Interventions that effect change in psychotherapy. *Infant Mental Health Journal, 19,* 333–340.

Beebe, B., Alson, D., Jaffe, J., Feldstein, S. & Crown, C. (1988). Vocal congruence in mother–infant play. *Journal of Psycholinguistic Research, 17,* 245–259.

Beebe, B. & Gerstman, L. (1980). The "packaging" of maternal stimulation in relation to infant facial-visual engagement: A case study at four months. *Merrill-Palmer Quarterly, 26,* 321–339.

Beebe, B. & Jaffe, J. (1992a). Mother–infant vocal dialogues. *Infant Behavior and Development, 15,* 48. International Conference on Infant Studies Abstracts Issue, May.

Beebe, B. & Jaffe, J. (1992b). The contribution of infant responsivity to the prediction of infant attachment. *Infant Behavior and Development, 15,* 113. International Conference on Infant Studies Abstracts Issue, May.

Beebe, B. & Jaffe, J. (1999). [Mother–infant regulation: Depression and attachment. NIMH Grant]. Unpublished raw data.

Beebe, B., Jaffe, J., Feldstein, S., Mays, K. & Alson, D. (1985). Interpersonal timing: The application of an adult dialogue model to mother–infant vocal and kinesic interactions. In T. Field & N. Fox (Eds.), *Social perception in infants* (pp. 217–247). Norwood, NJ: Ablex.

Beebe, B., Jaffe, J. & Lachmann, F. (1992). A dyadic systems view of communication. In N. Skolnick & S. Warshaw (Eds.), *Relational perspectives in psychoanalysis* (pp. 61–81). Hillsdale, NJ: The Analytic Press.

Beebe, B., Jaffe, J., Lachmann, F., Feldstein, S., Crown, C. & Jasnow, J. (2000). Systems models in development and psychoanalysis: The case of vocal rhythm coordination and attachment. *Infant Mental Health Journal, 21,* 99–122.

Beebe, B. & Kronen, J. (1988). Mutual regulation of affective matching in mother–infant face-to-face play. Unpublished manuscript.

Beebe, B. & Lachmann, F. (1988a). Mother–infant mutual influence and precursors of psychic structure. In A. Goldberg (Ed.), *Frontiers in self psychology: Progress in self psychology, vol. 3* (pp. 3–26). Hillsdale, NJ: The Analytic Press.

Beebe, B. & Lachmann, F. (1988b). The contribution of mother–infant mutual influence to the origins of self- and object representations. *Psychoanalytic Psychology, 5,* 305–337.

Beebe, B. & Lachmann, F. (1994). Representation and internalization in infancy: Three principles of salience. *Psychoanalytic Psychology, 11,* 127–165.

Beebe, B. & Lachmann, F. (1998). Co-constructing inner and relational processes: Self and mutual regulation in infant research and adult treatment. *Psychoanalytic Psychology, 15,* 1–37.

Beebe, B., Lachmann, F. & Jaffe, J. (1997). Mother–infant interaction structures and presymbolic self and object representations. *Psychoanalytic Dialogues, 7,* 133–182.

Beebe, B. & McCrorie, E. (1996). A model of love for the 21st century: Infant research, literature, romantic attachment, and psychoanalysis. Presented at 19th Annual Conference on the Psychology of the Self, Washington, DC.

Beebe, B. & McCrorie, E. (in press). A model of love for the 21st century: Literature, infant research, adult romantic attachment, and psychoanalysis. *Psychoanalytic Inquiry.*

Beebe, S. & Stern, D. (1977). Engagement-disengagement and early object experiences. In N. Freedman & S. Grand (Eds.), *Communicative structures and psychic structures* (pp. 35–55). New York: Plenum.

Beebe, B., Stern, D. & Jaffe, J. (1979). The kinesic rhythm of mother–infant interactions. In A. Siegman & S. Feldstein (Eds.), *Of speech and time* (pp. 23–34). Hillsdale, NJ: Lawrence Erlbaum Associates.

Behrends, R. & Blatt, S. (1985). Internalization and psychological development throughout the life cycle. In *The psychoanalytic study of the child, 40* (11–39). New Haven, CT: Yale University Press.

Bell, R. (1968). A reinterpretation of the direction of effects in studies of socialization. *Psychological Review, 75,* 81–95.

Bell, S. (1970). The development of the concept of the object as related to mother–infant attachment. *Child Development, 41,* 291–311.

Belsky, J., Rovine, M. & Taylor, D. (1984). The Pennsylvania infant and family development project III: The origins of individual differences in infant–mother attachment: Maternal and infant contributions. *Child Development, 55,* 718–728.

Benjamin, J. (1988). *The bonds of love: Psychoanalysis, feminism, and the problem of domination.* New York: Pantheon.

Benjamin, J. (1990). An outline of intersubjectivity: The development of recognition. *Psychoanalytic Psychology, 7,* 33–46.

Benjamin, J. (1995). *Like subjects, love objects.* New Haven, CT: Yale University Press.

Berg, C. & Sternberg, R. (1985). Response to novelty: Continuity vs. discontinuity in the developmental course of intelligence. In H. Reese (Ed.), *Advances in child development and behavior, vol. 19* (pp. 1–47). San Diego, CA: Academic Press.

Berlyne, D. (1966). Curiosity and exploration. *Science, 153,* 25–33.

Bernstein, A. & Blacher, R. (1967). The recovery of a memory from three months of age. In *The psychoanalytic study of the child, 22* (156–161). New York: International Universities Press.

Blatt, S. & Behrends, R. (1987). Internalization, separation-individuation, and the nature of therapeutic action. *International Journal of Psycho-Analysis, 68,* 279–297.

Blatt, S., D'Afflitti, J. & Quinlan, D. (1976). Experiences of depression in normal young adults. *Journal of Abnormal Psychology, 85,* 383–389.

Blatt, S., D'Afflitti, J. & Quinlan, D. (1979). Depressive experiences questionnaire. Unpublished manuscript, Department of Psychiatry, Yale University.

Bloom, L. (1993). *The transition from infancy to language.* New York: Cambridge University Press.

Blurton-Jones, N. (1972). *Ethological studies of child behavior.* Cambridge: Cambridge University Press.

Bornstein, M. (1979). Perceptual development: Stability and change in feature perception. In M. Bornstein & W. Kessen (Eds.), *Psychological development from infancy* (pp. 37–81). Hillsdale, NJ: Lawrence Erlbaum Associates.

Bornstein, M. (1985). Infant into adult: unity to diversity in the development of visual categorisation. In J. Mehler & R. Fox (Eds.), *Neonate cognition* (pp. 115–138). Hillsdale, NJ: Lawrence Erlbaum Associates.

Bower, T., Broughton, J. & Moore, M. (1970). Infant responses to approaching objects. *Perception and Psychophysics, 9,* 193–196.

Bowlby, J. (1958). The nature of the child's tie to his mother. *International Journal of Psycho-Analysis, 39,* 350–373.

Bowlby, J. (1969). *Attachment and loss, 1.* New York: Basic Books.

Bowlby, J. (1980). *Attachment and loss, 3.* New York: Basic Books.

Bromberg, P. (1998). *Standing in the spaces: Essays on clinical process, trauma, and dissociation.* Hillsdale, NJ: The Analytic Press.

Brazelton, T. B. (1973). Neonatal behavioral assessement scale. *Clinics in Behavioral Medicine, 50.* London: Heinemann Medical Books.

Brazelton, T. B. (1992). Touch and the fetus. Presented to Touch Research Institute, Miami, FL, May.

Brazelton, T. B., Koslowski, B. & Main, M. (1974). The origins of reciprocity. In M. Lewis & L. Rosenblum (Eds.), *The effects of the infant on its caregiver* (pp. 49–70). New York: Wiley-Interscience.

Brazelton, T. B., Tronick, E., Adamson, L., Als, H. & Wise, S. (1975). Early mother–infant reciprocity. In M. A. Hofer (Ed.), *The parent–infant relationship* (pp. 137–154). New York: Elsevier.

Bretherton, I. (1985). Attachment theory: Retrospect and prospect. In I. Bretherton & E. Waters (Eds.), *Growing points in attachment theory and research: Monographs of the Society for Research in Child Development, 50*(1–2) Serial No. 209, pp. 3–35.

Bromberg, P. (1998). *Standing in the spaces: Essays on clinical process, trauma, and dissociation.* Hillsdale, NJ: The Analytic Press.

Bruner, J. (1977). Early social interaction and language acquisition. In H. R. Schaffer (Ed.), *Studies in mother–infant interaction* (pp. 271–289). New York: Norton.

Bruner, J. (1983). *Child's talk: Learning to use language.* New York: Norton.

Bucci, W. (1985). Dual coding: A cognitive model for psychoanalytic research. *Journal of the American Psychoanalytic Association, 33,* 571–608.

Bucci, W. (1997). *Psychoanalysis and cognitive science.* New York: Guilford Press.

Buie, D. & Adler, G. (1973). The uses of confrontation in psychotherapy of borderline cases. In G. Adler & P. Myerson (Eds.), *Confrontation in psychotherapy* (pp. 123–146). New York: Science House.

Butterworth, G. (1990). Self-perception in infancy. In D.Cicchetti & M. Beeghly (Eds.), *The self in transition: From infancy to childhood* (pp. 119–137). Chicago: University of Chicago Press.

Byers, P. (1975). Biological rhythms as information channels in interpersonal communication behavior. In P. Klopfer & G. Bateson (Eds.), *Perspectives in ethology*. New York: Plenum.

Capella, J. (1981). Mutual influence in expressive behavior: Adult and infant-adult dyadic interaction. *Psychological Bulletin, 89*, 101–132.

Capella, J. (1991). The biological origins of automated patterns of human interaction. *Communication Theory, 1*, 4–35.

Casement, P. (1990). [Case report] Presented at meeting of American Psychoanalytic Association., Miami, FL, December.

Chance, M. & Larsen, R. (Eds.) (1996). *The social structure of attention*. New York: Wiley.

Chapple, E. (1970). *Culture and biological man*. New York: Holt, Rinehart & Winston.

Chatfield, C. (1982). *Analysis of time-series* (2nd ed.). London: Chapman & Hall.

Chevalnier-Skolnikoff, S. (1976). The ontogeny of primate intelligence and its implications for communicative potential: A preliminary report. *Annals of the New York Academy of Sciences, 280*, 173–211.

Clyman, R. (1991). The procedural organization of emotions: A contribution from cognitive science to the psychoanalytic theory of therapeutic action. *Journal of the American Psycohanalytic Association, 39*, 349–381.

Cohen, L., DeLoache, J. & Strauss, M. (1979). Infant visual perception. In J. Osofsky (Ed.), *Handbook of infant development* (pp. 393–438). New York: Wiley.

Cohen, L. & Gelber, E. (1975). Infant visual memory. In L. Cohen & P. Salapatek (Eds.), *Infant perception: From sensation to cognition, vol. I.* (pp. 347–403). New York: Academic Press.

Cohen, S. & Beckwith, L. (1979). Preterm infant interaction with the caregiver in the first year of life and competence at age two. *Child Development, 58*, 767–776.

Cohn, J. & Beebe, B. (1990). Sampling interval affects time-series regression estimates of mother–infant influence. *Infant Behavior and Development, Abstracts Issue, 13*, 317.

Cohn, J., Campbell, S., Matias, R. & Hopkins, J. (1990). Face-to-face inter-actions of partpartum depressed and nondepressed mother–infant pairs at two months. *Developmental Psychology, 26,* 15–23.

Cohn, J., Campbell, S. & Ross, S. (1991). Infant response in the still-face paradigm at 6 months predicts avoidant and secure attachments at 12 months. *Development and Psychopathology, 3,* 367–376.

Cohn, J. & Elmore, M. (1988). Effect of contingent changes in mothers' affective expression on the organization of behavior in 3-month-old infants. *Infant Behavior and Development, 11,* 493–505.

Cohn, J. & Tronick, E. (1983). Three-month-old infants' reaction to sim-ulated maternal depression. *Child Development, 54,* 185–93.

Cohn, J. & Tronick, E. (1988). Mother–infant face-to-face interaction: Influence is bidirectional and unrelated to periodic cycles in either partner's behavior. *Developmental Psychology, 24,* 386–392.

Cohn, J. & Tronick, E. (1989a). Specificity of infants' response to moth-ers' affective behavior. *Journal of the American Academy of Child and Adolescent Psychiatry, 28,* 242–248.

Cohn, J. & Tronick, E. (1989b). Mother–infant face-to-face interaction: The sequence of dyadic states at 3, 6, 9 months. *Developmental Psychology, 23,* 68–77.

Cormier, S. (1981). A match–mismatch theory of limbic system function. *Physiological Psychology, 9,* 3–36.

Crockenberg, S. (1983). Early mother and infant antecedents of Bayley skill performance at 21 months. *Developmental Psychology, 19,* 727–730.

Crown, C. (1991). Coordinated interpersonal timing of vision and voice as a function of interpersonal attraction. *Journal of Language and Social Psychology, 10,* 29–46.

Crown, C. (1992). Coordinated interpersonal timing. Presented to American Association for the Advancement of Science, Chicago, February.

Davidson, R. & Fox, N. (1982). Asymmetrical brain activity discriminates between positive versus negative affective stimuli in human infants. *Science, 218,* 1235–1237.

Davis, M. & Hadiks, D. (1990). Nonverbal behavior and client state changes during psychotherapy. *Journal of Clinical Psychology, 46,* 340–351.

Dawson, G. (1992a). Infants of mothers with depressive symptoms: Neurophysiological and behavioral findings related to attachment sta-tus. *Infant Behavior and Development, Abstracts Issue, 15,* 117.

Dawson, G. (1992b). Frontal lobe activity and affective behavior of infants of mothers with depressive symptoms. *Child Development, 63*, 725–737.

DeCasper, A. & Carstens, A. (1980). Contingencies of stimulation: Effects on learning and emotion in neonates. *Infant Behavior and Development, 4*, 19–36.

DeCasper, A. & Fifer, W. (1980). Of human bonding: Newborns prefer their mothers' voices. *Science, 208*, 1174.

DeCasper, A. & Spence, M. (1986). Prenatal maternal speech influences newborn's perception of speech sounds. *Infant Behavior and Development, 9*, 133–150.

Demos, V. (1983). Discussion of papers by Drs. Sander and Stern. In J. Lichtenberg & S. Kaplan (Eds.), *Reflections on self psychology* (pp. 105–112). Hillsdale, NJ: The Analytic Press.

Demos, V. (1984). Empathy and affect: Reflections on infant experience. In J. Lichtenberg, M. Bonnstein & D. Silver (Eds.), *Empathy, 2* (pp. 9–34). Hillsdale, NJ: The Analytic Press.

Dimburg, U., Thunberg, M. & Elmehed, K. (2000). Unconscious facial reactions to emotional facial expressions. *American Psychological Society, 11*, 86–89.

Donovan, W. & Leavitt, L. (1978). Early cognitive development and its relation to maternal physiologic and behavioral responsiveness. *Child Development, 49*, 1251–1254.

Edelman, G. (1987). *Neural Darwinism*. New York: Basic Books.

Edelman, G. (1992). *Bright air, brilliant fire*. New York: Basic Books.

Ehrenberg, D. (1992). *The intimate edge*. New York: Norton.

Eibl-Eibesfeldt, I. (1970). *Ethology: The biology of behavior*. New York: Holt, Rinehart & Winston.

Eimas, P. (1985). Constraints on a model of infant speech perception. In J. Mehler & R. Fox (Eds.), *Neonate cognition* (pp. 185–197). Hillsdale, NJ: Lawrence Erlbaum Associates.

Eissler, K. (1953). The effect of the structure of the ego on psychoanalytic technique. *Journal of the American Psychoanalytic Association, 1*, 104–143.

Ekman, P. (1983). Autonomic nervous system activity distinguishes among emotions. *Science, 221*, 1208–1210.

Ekman, P., Friesen, W. & Ancoli, S. (1980). Facial signs of emotional experience. *Journal of Personality and Social Psychology, 39*, 1125–1134.

Ekman, P., Levenson, R. & Friesen, W. (1983). Autonomic nervous system activity distinguishes among emotions. *Science, 221*, 1208–1210.

Ekman, P. & Oster, H. (1979). Facial expression of emotion. *Annual Review of Psychology, 30*, 527–554.

Emde, R. (1981). The prerepresentational self and its affective core. In *The psychoanalytic study of the child, 36,* 165–192. New Haven, CT: Yale University Press.

Emde, R. (1988). Development terminable and interminable. I. Innate and motivational factors. *International Journal of Psycho-Analysis, 69,* 23–42; II. Recent psychoanalytic theory and therapeutic considerations. *International Journal of Psycho-Analysis, 69,* 283–296.

Emde, R., Biringen, Z., Clyman, R. & Oppenheim, D. (1991). The moral self of infancy: Affective core and procedural knowledge. *Developmental Review, 11,* 251–270.

Fagan, J. (1974). Infant recognition memory: The effects of length of familiarization and type of discrimination task. *Child Development, 45,* 351–356.

Fagan, J. (1982). Infant memory. In T. Field, A. Huston, H. Quay, L. Troll & G. Finley (Eds.), *Review of human development* (pp. 72–92). New York: Wiley.

Fagen, J., Morrongiello, B., Rovee-Collier, C. & Gekoski, M. (1984). Expectancies and memory retrieval in three-month-old infants. *Child Development, 55,* 936–943.

Fagen, J., Ohr, P., Fleckenstein, L. & Ribner, D. (1985). The effect of crying on long-term memory in infancy. *Child Development, 56,* 1584–1592.

Fagen, J., Ohr, P., Singer, J. & Klein, S. (1989). Crying and retrograde amnesia in young infants. *Infant Behavior and Development, 12,* 13–24.

Fairbairn, W. R. D. (1952). *Psychoanalytic studies of the personality.* London: Routledge & Kegan Paul.

Fantz, R., Fagan, J. & Miranda, S. (1975). Early visual selectivity. In I. Cohen & P. Salapatek (Eds.), *Infant perception, vol. 1* (pp. 249–346). New York: Academic Press.

Fast, I. (1988). Interaction schemes in the establishment of psychic structure and therapeutic change. Unpublished manuscript.

Feldman, R. (1997). Affect regulation and synchrony in mother–infant play as precursors to the development of symbolic competence. *Infant Mental Health Journal, 18,* 4–23.

Feldstein, S. (1998). Some nonobvious consequences of monitoring time in conversation. In M. Palmer & G. Barnett (Eds.), *Mutual influence in interpersonal communication: Theory and research in cognition, affect, and behavior. Progress in communication sciences, vol. 14* (pp. 163–190). Norwood, NJ: Ablex.

Feldstein, S. & Welkowitz, J. (1978). A chronography of conversation: In defense of an objective approach. In A. W. Siegman & S. Feldstein (Eds.), *Nonverbal behavior and communication* (pp. 329–377). Hillsdale, NJ: Lawrence Erlbaum Associates.

Fenichel, O. (1938–1939). *Problems of psychoanalytic technique* (D. Brunswick, Trans.). New York: Psychoanalytic Quarterly Press, 1969.

Ferenczi, S. (1930). The principle of relaxation and neocatharsis. In *Final contributions to the problems and methods of psychoanalysis* (pp. 126–142). New York: Basic Books, 1955.

Fernald, A. (1987). Four-month-old infants prefer to listen to motherese. *Infant Behavior and Development, 8*, 181–195.

Fernald, A. & Kuhl, P. (1987). Acoustic determinants of infant preference for motherese speech. *Infant Behavior and Development, 10*, 279–293.

Field, T. (1981). Infant gaze aversion and heart rate during face-to-face interactions. *Infant Behavior and Development, 4*, 307–315.

Field, T., Healy, B., Goldstein, S. & Guthertz, M. (1990). Behavior-state matching and synchrony in mother–infant interactions of depressed and nondepressed dyads. *Developmental Psychology, 26*, 7–14.

Field, T., Healy, B., Goldstein, S., Perry, D., Bendell, D., Schanberg, S., Simmerman, E. & Kuhn, O. (1988). Infants of depressed mothers show "depressed" behavior even with non-depressed adults. *Child Development, 59*, 1569–1579.

Field, T., Woodson, R., Greenberg, R. & Cohen, D. (1982). Discrimination and imitation of facial expressions by neonates. *Science, 218*, 179–181.

Finkelstein, N. & Ramey, C. (1977). Learning to control the environment in infancy. *Child Development, 48*, 806–819.

Fogel, A. (1992a). Movement and communication in human infancy: The social dynamics of development. *Human Movement Science, 11*, 387–423.

Fogel, A. (1992b).Co-regulation, perception and action. *Human Movement Science, 11*, 505–523.

Fogel, A. (1993a). *Developing through relationships*. Chicago: University of Chicago Press.

Fogel, A. (1993b). Two principles of communication: Co-regulation and framing. In J. Nadel & L. Camaioni (Eds.), *New perspectives in early communicative development*. London: Routledge.

Fosshage, J. (2000). Interaction in psychoanalysis: A broadening horizon. *Psychoanalytic Dialogues, 5*, 459–478.

Fox, N. (1994). The development of emotion regulation: Introduction to part 3. In I. Bretherton & E. Waters (Eds.), *Growing points of attachment theory and research: Monographs of the Society for Research in Child Development, 50*(2–3) serial No. 240, pp. 189.

Freedman, N., Barroso, F., Bucci, W. & Grand, S. (1978). The bodily manifestations of listening. *Psychoanalysis and Contemporary Thought, 1*, 156–194.

Freeman, W. (1987). Simulation of chaotic EEG patterns with dynamic model of the olfactory system. *Biological Cybernetics, 56,* 139–150.

Freeman, W. (1991). The psychology of perception. *Scientific American, 264,* 78–85.

Freud, S. (1909). Notes upon a case of obsessional neurosis. *Standard Edition 10,* 153–318. London: Hogarth Press, 1955.

Freud, S. (1917). Mourning and melancholia. *Standard Edition 14,* 243–248. London: Hogarth Press, 1957.

Freud, S. (1938). An outline of psychoanalysis. *Standard Edition 23,* 139–207. London: Hogarth Press, 1964.

Frey, S., Hirsbrunner, H., Florin, A., Daw, W. & Crawford, R. (1983). A unified approach to the investigation of nonverbal and verbal behavior in communication research. In W. Doise & S. Moscovi (Eds.), *Current issues in European social psychology, vol. 1,* (pp. 143–199). New York: Cambridge University Press.

Gardner, J. & Karmel, B. (1984). Arousal effects on visual preferences in neonates. *Developmental Psychology, 20,* 374–377.

Gazzaniga, M. & LeDoux, J. (1978). *The integrated mind.* New York: Plenum.

Gendlin, E. (1992). The primacy of the body, not the primacy of perception. *Man and World, 25,* 341–353.

Gianino, A. & Tronick, E. (1988). The mutual regulation model: The infant's self and interactive regulation and coping and defensive capacities. In T. Field, P. McCabe & N. Schneiderman (Eds.), *Stress and coping* (pp. 47–68). Hillsdale, NJ: Lawrence Erlbaum Associates.

Gibson, J. (1966). *The senses considered as perceptual systems.* New York: Houghton Mifflin.

Gibson, J. (1979). *The ecological approach to visual perception.* Boston: Houghton Mifflin.

Gill, M. (1982). *Analysis of transference, vol. 1: Theory and technique.* New York: International Universities Press.

Goldberg, A. (1983). Self psychology and alternative perspectives on internalization. In J. Lichtenberg & S. Kaplan (Eds.), *Reflections on self psychology* (pp. 297–312). Hillsdale, NJ: The Analytic Press.

Goldstein, R. (1993). Modality and the regulation of mother–toddler attention. Doctoral dissertation. Ferkauf Graduate School of Psychology, Yeshiva University, New York.

Gottman, J. (1979). *Marital interactions.* New York: Academic Press.

Gottman, J. (1981). *Time-series analysis.* Cambridge: Cambridge University Press.

Gottman, J. & Ringland, J. (1981). Analysis of dominance and bi-directionality in social development. *Child Development, 52,* 393–412.

Greco, C., Rovee-Collier, C., Hayne, H., Griesler, P. & Early, L. (1986). Ontogeny of early event memory: 1. Forgetting and retrieval by 2- and 3-month olds. *Infant Behavior and Development, 9,* 441–460.

Greenberg, J. (1995). Psychoanalytic technique and the interactive matrix. *Psychoanalytic Quarterly, 64,* 1–22.

Greenson, R. (1967). *The technique and practice of psychoanalysis, vol. 1.* New York: International Universities Press.

Grigsby, J. & Hartlaub, G. (1994). Procedural learning and the development and stability of character. *Perceptual Motor Skills, 79,* 355–370.

Gunther, M. (1961). Infant behavior at the breast. In B. M. Foss (Ed.), *Determinants of infant behavior, vol. 2.* London: Methuen.

Habermas, J. (1979). *Communication and the evolution of society.* Boston: Beacon Press.

Hadley, J. (1983). The representational system: A bridging concept for psychoanalysis and neurophysiology. *International Review of Psycho-Analysis, 10,* 13–30.

Hadley, J. (1989).The neurobiology of motivational systems. In J. Lichtenberg (Ed.), *Psychoanalysis and motivation* (pp. 227–372). Hillsdale, NJ: The Analytic Press.

Haith, M. (1980). *Rules that babies look by.* Hillsdale, NJ: Lawrence Erlbaum Associates.

Haith, M., Hazan, C. & Goodman, G. (1988). Expectation and anticipation of dynamic visual events by 3.5 month old babies. *Child Development, 59,* 467–79.

Harris, A. (1991). Gender as contradiction. *Psychoanalytic Dialogues, 1,* 197–224.

Harris, A. (1997). The enduring encounter: Commentary on paper by Beebe, Lachmann, and Jaffe. *Psychoanalytic Dialogues, 7,* 197–206.

Hartmann, H. (1939). *Ego and the problem of adaption.* New York: International Universities Press.

Hayne, H., Greco, C., Earley, L., Griesler, P. & Rovee-Collier, C. (1986). Ontogeny of early event memory: II. Encoding and retrieval and 2- and 3-month-olds. *Infant Behavior and Development, 9,* 461–472.

Heller, M. & Haynal, V. (1997). A doctor's face: Mirror of his patient's suicidal projects. In J. Guimon (Ed.), *The body in psychotherapy.* Basel, Switzerland: Karger.

Herzog, J. (1983). A neonatal intensive care syndrome: A pain complex involving neuro-plasticity and psychic trauma. In J. Call, E. Galenson & R. Tyson (Eds.), *Frontiers of infant psychiatry* (pp. 291–299). New York: Basic Books.

Hirschfeld, N. & Beebe, B. (1987). Maternal intensity and infant disengagement in face-to-face play. Presented to Society for Research in Child Development, Baltimore, MD, April.

Hitchcock, D. (1991). Joint regulation of attention in mother–toddler, normal and risk dyads. Unpublished doctoral dissertation, Yeshiva University, New York.

Hofer, M. (1987). Early social relations: A psychobiologist's view. *Child Development*, 58, 633–647.

Hoffman, I. (1983). The patient as interpreter of the analyst's experience. *Contemporary Psychoanalysis*, 3, 389–422.

Hoffman, I. (1998). *Ritual and spontaneity in the psychoanalytic process: A dialectical-constructivist view*. Hillsdale, NJ: The Analytic Press.

Horner, T. (1985). The psychic life of the young infant: Review and critique of the psychoanalytic concepts of symbiosis and infantile omnipotence. *American Journal of Orthopsychiatry*, 55, 324–344.

Hunt, J. McV. (1965). Intrinsic motivation and its role in psychological development. In D. Levine (Ed.), *Nebraska symposium on motivation, vol. 13* (pp. 189–282). Lincoln: University of Nebraska Press.

Iberall, A. & McCullouch, W. (1969). The organizing principle of complex living systems. *Journal of Basic Engineering*, 91, 373–384.

Isabella, R. & Belsky, J. (1991). Interactional synchrony and the origins of infant-mother attachment: A replication study. *Child Development*, 62, 373–384.

Izard, C. (1979). *The maximally discriminative facial action coding system (MAX)*. Newark: University of Delaware Instructional Resources Center.

Jacobson, E. (1964). *The self and the object world*. New York: International Universities Press.

Jaffe, J., Beebe, B., Feldstein, S., Crown, C. & Jasnow, M. (2001). Rhythms of dialogue in early infancy. *Monographs of the society for research in child development*, 66(2) Serial No. 264, pp. 1–132.

Jaffe, J. & Feldstein, S. (1970). *Rhythms of dialogue*. New York: Academic Press.

Jaffe, J., Feldstein, S., Beebe, B., Crown, C., Jasnow, M., Fox, H., Anderson, S. & Gordon, S. (1991). [Final report for NIMH Grant No. MH41675.] Unpublished raw data.

Jasnow, M. (1983). Temporal accommodation in vocal behavior in mother–infant dyads. Unpublished doctoral dissertation, George Washington University, Washington, DC.

Jasnow, M. & Feldstein, S. (1986). Adult-like temporal characteristics of mother–infant vocal interactions. *Child Development*, 57, 754–761.

Jusczyk, P. (1985). On characterizing the development of speech perception. In J. Mehler & R. Fox (Eds.), *Neonatal cognition: Beyond the blooming buzzing confusion* (pp. 199–230). Hillsdale, NJ: Lawrence Erlbaum Associates.

Kagan, J. (1979). Structure and process in the human infant: The ontogeny of mental representation. In M. Bornstein & W. Kessen (Eds.), *Psychological development in infancy* (pp. 159–182). Hillsdale, NJ: Lawrence Erlbaum Associates.

Kagen, J. (1978). The enhancement of memory in infancy. *Newsletter of the Institute for Comparative Human Development*, 58–60.

Kaminer, T. (1999) *Maternal depression, maternal speech, and infant gaze at four months.* Unpublished doctoral dissertation, St. John's University, New York.

Kegan, R. (1982). *The evolving self.* Cambridge, MA: Harvard University Press.

Kiersky, S. & Beebe, B. (1994). The reconstruction of early nonverbal relatedness in the treatment of difficult patients: A special form of empathy. *Psychoanalytic Dialogues, 4,* 389–408.

Klein, G. (1967). Peremptory ideation: Structure and force in motivated ideas. In R. Holt (Ed.), *Motives and thought: Psychoanalytic essays in honor of David Rapaport* (pp. 80–182). New York: International Universities Press.

Klein, G. (1976). *Psychoanalytic theory: An exploration of essentials.* New York: International Universities Press.

Klinnert, M., Emde, R., Butterfield, P. & Campos, J. (1986). Social referencing. *Developmental Psychology, 22,* 427–432.

Knoblauch, S. (1997). Beyond the word in psychoanalysis: The unspoken dialogue. *Psychoanalytic Dialogues, 7,* 491–516.

Kohlberg, L. (1969). Stage and sequence: The cognitive developmental approach to socialization. In D. A. Goslin (Ed.), *Handbook of socialization theory and research* (pp. 347–480). Chicago: Rand-McNally.

Kohut, H. (1971). *The analysis of the self.* New York: International Universities Press.

Kohut, H. (1980). Selected problems in self psychological theory. *The search for the self, vol. 4* (P. Ornstein, Ed.) (pp. 489–523). New York: International Universities Press.

Kohut, H. (1984). *How does analysis cure?* (A. Goldberg & P. Stepansky, Eds.). Chicago: University of Chicago Press.

Korner, A. & Grobstein, R. (1976). Individual differences at birth. In E. Rexford, L. Sandler & T. Shapiro (Eds.), *Infant psychiatry* (pp. 67–78). New Haven, CT: Yale University Press.

Koulomzin, M. (1993). Attention, affect, self comfort and subsequent attachment in four-month-old infants. Doctoral dissertation, Yeshiva University, New York.

Koulomzin, M., Beebe, B., Jaffe, J. & Feldstein, S. (1993). Infant self comfort, disorganized scanning, facial distress, and bodily approach in face-to-face play at four months discriminate "A" vs. "B" attachment at one year. *Society for Research in Child Development Abstracts*, March 25–28, 1993, New Orleans, LA, p. 446.

Kronen, J. (1982). Maternal facial mirroring at four months. Doctoral dissertation, Yeshiva University, New York.

Kuhl, P. (1985). Methods in the study of infant speech perception. In G. Gottlieb & N. Krasnegor (Eds.), *Measurement of audition and vision in the first year of postnatal life: A methodological overview* (pp. 223–251). Norwood, NJ: Ablex.

Kuhn, T. (1962). *The structure of scientific revolutions.* Chicago: University of Chicago Press.

Kulka, R. (1997). Quantum selfhood commentaries on paper by Beebe, Lachmann, and Jaffe. *Psychoanalytic Dialogues, 7,* 183–188.

Lachmann, F. (1990). On some challenges to clinical theory in the treatment of character pathology. In A. Goldberg (Ed.), *The realities of transference: Progress in self psychology, vol. 6* (pp. 59–67). Hillsdale, NJ: The Analytic Press.

Lachmann, F. (1998). From narcissism to self pathology to . . . ? *Psychoanalysis and Psychotherapy, 15,* 5–27.

Lachmann, F. & Beebe, B. (1983). Consolidation of the self: A case study. *Dynamic Psychotherapy, 1,* 55–75.

Lachmann, F. & Beebe, B. (1989). Oneness fantasies revisited. *Psychoanalysis and Psychology, 6,* 137–148.

Lachmann, F. & Beebe, B. (1992). Representational and self-object transferences: A developmental perspective. In A. Goldberg (Ed.), *New therapeutic visions: Progress in self psychology, vol. 8* (pp. 3–15). Hillsdale, NJ: The Analytic Press.

Lachmann, F. & Beebe, B. (1993). Interpretation in a developmental perspective. In A. Goldberg (Ed.), *The widening scope of self psychology: Progress in self psychology, vol. 9* (pp. 45–52). Hillsdale, NJ: The Analytic Press.

Lachmann, F. & Beebe, B. (1996a). Three principles of salience in the organization of the patient-analyst interaction. *Psychoanalytic Psychology, 13,* 1–22.

Lachmann, F. & Beebe, B. (1996b). Self and mutual regulation in the patient–analyst interaction: A case illustration. In A. Goldberg, (Ed.), *Basic ideas reconsidered: Progress in self psychology, vol. 12* (pp. 123–140). Hillsdale, NJ: The Analytic Press.

Lachmann, F. & Beebe, B. (1997). Trauma, interpretation and self-state transformations. *Psychoanalysis and Contemporary Thought, 20,* 269–291.

Lachmann, F., Beebe, B. & Stolorow, R. (1987). Increments of separation. In J. & S. Bloom-Feshbach (Eds.), *The psychology of separation through the life span* (pp. 396–415). San Francisco: Jossey-Bass.

Lachmann, F. & Lichtenberg, J. (1992). Model scenes: Implications for psychoanalytic treatment. *Journal of the American Psychoanalytic Association, 40,* 117–137.

Laird, J. (1984). The real role of facial response in the experience of emotion. *Journal of Personality and Social Psychology, 47,* 909–917.

Lamb, M. (1981). The development of father–infant relationships. In M. E. Lamb (Ed.), *The role of the father in child development* (rev. ed.). New York: Wiley.

Langhorst, B. & Fogel, A. (1982). Cross-validation of microanalytic approaches to face-to-face interaction. International Conference on Infant Studies, Austin, TX.

Langs, R., Badalamenti, A. & Thompson, L. (1996). *The cosmic circle.* New York: Alliance.

Lashley, K. (1951). The problem of serial order in behavior. In L. A. Jefress (Ed.), *Cerebral mechanisms in behavior* (pp. 112–146). New York: Wiley.

Lenneberg, E. (1967). *Biological foundations of language.* New York: Wiley.

Lester, B. & Seifer, R.(1990). Antecedants of attachment. In T. Anders (Chair), The origins and nature of attachment in infants and mother. Symposium at Boston Institute for the Development of Infants and Parents, February.

Lewin, K. (1937). *Towards a dynamic theory of personality.* New York: McGraw-Hill.

Lewis, M. & Brooks, J. (1975). Infants' social perception: A constructionist view. In L. Cohen & P. Salapatek (Eds.), *Infant perception: From sensation to cognition, vol. 2* (pp. 101–148). New York: Wiley-Interscience.

Lewis, M. & Feiring, C. (1989). Infant–mother and mother–infant interaction behavior and subsequent attachment. *Child Development, 60,* 831–837.

Lewis, M., Feiring, C., McGuffog, C. & Jaskir, J. (1984). Predicting psychopathology in six year olds from early social relations. *Child Development, 55,* 123–136.

Lewis, M. & Goldberg, S. (1969). Perceptual-cognitive development in infancy: A generalized expectancy model as a function of the mother–infant interaction. *Merrill-Palmer Quarterly, 15,* 81–100.

Lewis, M. & Lee-Painter, S. (1974). An interactional approach to the mother–infant dyad. In M. Lewis & L. Rosenblum (Eds.), *The effect of the infant on its caregiver.* New York: Wiley-Interscience.

Lewis, M. & Rosenblum, L. (Eds.) (1974). *The effect of the infant on its caregiver* (pp. 49–76). New York: Wiley-Interscience.

Lewkowicz, D. (1989). The role of temporal factors in infant behavior and development. In I. Levin & D. Zakay (Eds.), *Time and human cognition: A life-span perspective.* Amsterdam: North-Holland.

Lewkowicz, D. & Turkewitz, G. (1980). Cross-modal equivalence in early infancy: Audio-visual intensity matching. *Developmental Psychology, 6,* 597–607.

Lichtenberg, J. (1983). *Psychoanalysis and infant research.* Hillsdale, NJ: The Analytic Press.

Lichtenberg, J. (1989). *Psychoanalysis and motivation.* Hillsdale, N.J. The Analytic Press.

Lichtenberg, J., Lachmann, F. & Fosshage, J. (1992). *Self and motivational systems.* Hillsdale, NJ: The Analytic Press.

Lindon, J. (1994). Gratification and provision in psychoanalysis: Should we get rid of the rule of abstinence? *Psychoanalytic Dialogues, 4,* 549–582.

Loewald, H. (1960). On the therapeutic action of psychoanalysis. In *Papers on psychoanalysis* (pp. 221–256). New Haven, CT: Yale University Press, 1980.

Loewald, H. (1962). Internalization, separation, mourning, and the superego. In *Papers on psychoanalysis* (pp. 257–276). New Haven, CT: Yale University Press, 1980.

Loewald, H. (1971). The transference neurosis: Comments on the concept and phenomenon. *Journal of the American Psychoanalytic Association, 19,* 54–66.

Loewald, H. (1980). *Papers on psychoanalysis.* New Haven, CT: Yale University Press.

Lyons-Ruth, K. (1991). Rapprochment or approchment: Mahler's theory reconsidered from the vantage point of recent research on early attachment relationships. *Psychoanalytic Psychology, 8,* 1–23.

Lyons-Ruth, K. (1998a). Attachment disorganization: Unresolved loss, relational violence, and lapses in behavioral and attentional strategies. In J. Cassidy & P. Shaver (Eds.), *Handbook of attachment theory and research* (pp. 520–554). New York: Guilford Press.

Lyons-Ruth, K. (1998b). Implicit relational knowing: Its role in development and psychoanalytic treatment. *Infant Mental Health Journal, 19,* 282–291.

MacFarlane, A. (1975). Olfaction in the development of social preferences in the human neonate. In M. Hofer (Ed.), *Parent–infant interaction.* Amsterdam: Elsevier.

Mahler, M., Pine, F. & Bergman, A. (1975). *The psychological birth of the human infant.* New York: Basic Books.

Main, M., Kaplan, N. & Cassidy, J. (1985). Security in infancy, childhood, and adulthood: A move to the level of representation. In I. Bretherton & E. Waters (Eds.), *Monographs of the Society for Research in Child Development,* 50 (1–2) Serial No. 209, pp. 66–104.

Malatesta, C., Culver, C., Tesman, J. & Shepard, B. (1989). The development of emotion expression during the first two years of life. *Monographs of the Society for Research in Child Development,* 54 (1–2) Serial No. 219, pp. 1–33.

Malatesta, C. & Haviland, J. (1983). Learning display rules: The socialization of emotion in infancy. *Child Development,* 53, 991–1003.

Mandler, J. (1988). How to build a baby: On the development of an accessible representation system. *Cognitive Development,* 3, 113–136.

Mandler, J. (1991). *The foundation of symbolic thought in infancy.* Presented to Society for Research in Child Development, Seattle, April.

Marler, P. (1965). Communication in monkeys and apes. In I. DeVore (Ed.), *Primate behavior.* New York: Holt, Rinehart & Winston.

Martin, J. (1981). A longitudinal study of consequences in early mother–infant interaction: A microanalytic approach. *Monographs of the Society for Research in Child Development,* 46(3) Serial No. 190, pp. 1–52.

Martin, G. & Clark, R. (1982). Distress crying in neonates: Species and peer specificity. *Developmental Psychology,* 18, 3–9.

Mast, V., Fagen, J., Rovee-Collier, C. & Sullivan, M. (1980). Immediate and long-term memory for reinforcement context: The development of learned expectancies in early infancy. *Child Development,* 51, 700–707.

Mays, K. (1984). Temporal accommodation in mother–infant and stranger–infant kinesic interactions at four months, Unpublished doctoral dissertation, Yeshiva University, New York.

McCall, R. (1979). Qualitative transitions in behavioral development in the first two years of life. In M. Bornstein & W. Kessen (Eds.), *Psychological development in infancy* (pp. 183–224). Hillsdale, NJ: Lawrence Erlbaum Associates.

McGrew, W. (1972). *An ethological study of children's behavior.* New York: Academic Press.

Mead, G. H. (1934). *Mind, self and society.* Chicago: University of Chicago Press.

Mehler, J. & Fox, R. (Eds.). (1995). *Neonate cognition*. Hillsdale, NJ: Lawrence Erlbaum Associates

Meissner, W. (1981). *Internalization and psychoanalysis*. New York: International Universities Press.

Meltzoff, A. (1985). The roots of social and cognitive development: Models of man's original nature. In T. Field & N. Fox (Eds.), *Social perception in infants* (pp. 1–30). Norwood, NJ: Ablex.

Meltzoff, A. (1990). Foundations for developing a concept of self: The role of imitation in relating self to other and the value of social mirroring, social modeling, and self practice in infancy. In D. Cicchetti & M. Beeghly (Eds.), *The self in transition: Infancy to childhood* (pp. 139–164). Chicago: University of Chicago Press.

Meltzoff, A. & Borton, R. (1979). Intermodal matching by human neonates. *Nature, 282,* 403–404.

Meltzoff, A. & Gopnik, A. (1993). The role of imitation in understanding persons and developing a theory of mind. In S. Baron-Cohen, H. Tager-Flusberg & D. Cohen (Eds.), *Understanding other minds* (pp. 335–366). New York: Oxford University Press.

Meltzoff, A. & Moore, M. (1977). Imitation of facial and manual gestures by human neonates. *Science, 198,* 75–78.

Meissner, W. (1981). *Internalization and psychoanalysis*. New York: International Universities Press.

Mitchell, S. (1988). *Relational concepts in psychoanalysis*. Cambridge, MA: Harvard University Press.

Mitchell, S. (1993). *Hope and dread in psychoanalysis*. New York: Basic Books.

Modell, A. (1984). *Psychoanalysis in a new context*. New York: International Universities Press.

Modell, A. (1992). *The private self*. Cambridge, MA: Harvard University Press.

Morgan, A. (1998). Moving along to things left undone. *Infant Mental Health Journal, 19,* 324–332.

Morris, C. (1934) Introduction. In G. H. Mead (Ed.), *Mind, self and society* (pp. ix–xxxv). Chicago: University of Chicago Press.

Müller, U. & Overton, W. (1998). How to grow a baby: A reevaluation of image-schema and Piagetian approaches to representation. *Human Development, 41,* 71–111.

Murray, L. (1991). Intersubjectivity, object relations theory, and empirical evidence from mother–infant interactions. *Infant Mental Health Journal, 12,* 219–232.

Murray, L. & Trevarthen, C. (1985). Emotion regulation of interactions between 2-month-old infants and their mothers. In T. Field & N. Fox (Eds.), *Social perception in infants* (pp. 137–154). Norwood, NJ: Ablex.

Newtson, D. (1990). Alternatives to representation or alternative representations: Comments on the ecological approach. *Contemporary Social Psychology, 14,* 163–174.

Ogden, T. (1989). *The primitive edge of experience.* Northvale, NJ: Aronson.

Orange, D. (in press). Why language matters to psychoanalysis. *Psychoanalytic Dialogues.*

Osofsky, J. (1992). Affective development and early relationships: Clinical implications. In J. Barron, M. Eagle & D. Wolitzky (Eds.), *Interface between psychoanalysis and psychology* (pp. 233–244). Washington, DC: American Psychological Association Press.

Oster, H. (1978). Facial expression and affect development. In M. Lewis & L. Rosenblum (Eds.), *The development of affect.* New York: Plenum Press.

Oster, H. & Ekman, P. (1977). Facial behavior in child development. In A. Collins (Ed.), *Minnesota symposium on child development, vol. 11* (pp. 231–276). New York: Crowell.

Pally, R. (1998). Emotional processing: The mind–body connection. *International Journal of Psycho-Analysis, 79,* 349–362.

Pally, R. (2001). *The mind-brain relationship.* London: Karnac Books.

Papousek, H. & Papousek, M. (1979). Early ontogeny of human social interaction. In M. Von Cranach, K. Koppa, W. Lelenies & P. Ploog (Eds.), *Human ethology: Claims and limits of a new discipline* (pp. 63–85). Cambridge: Cambridge University Press.

Peery, J. C. (1980). Neonate–adult head movement. *Developmental Psychology, 16,* 245–250.

Perris, E., Myers, N. & Clifton, R. (1990). Long-term memory for a single infancy experience. *Child Development, 61,* 1796–1807.

Perry, B. (1996). Childhood trauma, the neurobiology of adaptation, and "use-dependent" development of the brain: How "states" become "traits." *Infant Mental Health Journal, 16,* 271–291.

Piaget, J. (1937). *The construction of reality in the child* (M. Cook, trans.). New York: Basic Books, 1954.

Pine, F. (1981). In the beginning: Contributions to a psychoanalytic developmental psychology. *International Review of Psycho-Analysis, 8,* 15–33.

Pine, F. (1986). The "symbiotic phase" in the light of current infancy research. *Bulletin of the Menninger Clinic, 50,* 564–569.

Rapaport, D. (1960). *The structure of psychoanalytic theory: A systematizing attempt.* New York: International Universities Press.

Reese, H. & Overton, W. (1970). Models of development and theories of development. In L. Goulet & P. Baltes (Eds.), *Life-span developmental psychology* (pp. 115–145). New York: Academic Press.

Reik, T. (1935). *Surprise and the psychoanalyst: On the conjecture and comprehension of unconscious processes.* New York: Dutton.

Resch, R (1988). The later creation of a transitional object. *Psychoanalytic Psychology, 5,* 369–387.

Rioch, D. & Weinstein, E. (1964). *Disorders of communication. Proceedings of the association, December 7–8, 1962.* Baltimore, MD: Williams & Wilkins.

Robson, K. (1967). The role of eye-to-eye contact in maternal–infant attachment. *Journal of Child Psychological Psychiatry, 8,* 13–25.

Roe, K., McClure, A. & Roe, A. (1982). Vocal interaction at three months and cognitive skill at 12 years. *Developmental Psychology, 18,* 15–16.

Rose, S. (1979). Cross-modal transfer in infants: Relationship to prematurity and socioeconomic background. *Developmental Psychology, 14,* 643–682.

Ruff, H. (1980). The development of perception and recognition of objects. *Child Development, 51,* 981–992.

Sameroff, A. (1983). Developmental Systems: Contexts and evolution. In W. Kessen (Ed.), *Mussen's handbook of child psychology, vol. 1* (pp. 237–294). New York: Wiley.

Sameroff, A. & Chandler, M. (1976). Reproductive risk and the continuum of caretaking casualty. In F. D. Horowitz (Ed.), *Review of child development research, vol. 4* (pp. 187–244). Chicago: University of Chicago Press.

Sander, L. (1977). The regulation of exchange in the infant-caretaker system and some aspects of the context-content relationship. In M. Lewis & L. Rosenblum (Eds.), *Interaction, conversation, and the development of language* (pp. 133–156). New York: Wiley.

Sander, L. (1983). Polarity paradox, and the organizing process in development. In J. D. Call, E. Galenson & R. Tyson (Eds.), *Frontiers of infant psychiatry* (pp. 315–327). New York: Basic Books.

Sander, L. (1985). Toward a logic of organization in psycho-biological development. In K. Klar & L. Siever (Eds.), *Biologic response styles: Clinical implications* (pp. 20–36). Washington, DC: Monograph Series American Psychiatric Press.

Sander, L. (1995). Identity and the experience of specificity in a process of recognition. *Psychoanalytic Dialogues, 5,* 579–593.

Sander, L. (1998). Introductory comment in interventions that affect change in psychotherapy: A model based on infant research. *Infant Mental Health Journal, 19,* 280–281.

Sandler, J. (1987). *From safety to superego*. London: Karnac.

Sandler, J. & Sandler, A. (1978). On the development of object relations and affects. *International Journal of Psycho-Analysis, 59*, 285–296.

Sarro, S. (1993). The mutual regulation of mother–toddler attention. Doctoral dissertation. Yeshiva University, New York.

Schafer, R. (1968). *Aspects of internalization*. New York: International Universities Press.

Schore, A. (1994). *Affect regulation and the origin of the self: The neurobiology of emotional development*. Hillsdale, NJ: Lawrence Erlbaum Associates.

Schore, A. (1996). The experience-dependent maturation of a regulatory system in the orbital prefrontal cortex and the origin of developmental psychopathology. *Development and Psychopathology, 8*, 59–87.

Schore, A. (1997). Interdisciplinary developmental research and a source of clinical models. In M. Moskowitz, C. Monk & S. Ellman (Eds.), *The clinical significance of early development: Implications for psychoanalytic intervention* (pp. 1–72). Northvale, NJ: Aronson.

Schwaber, E. (1981). Empathy: A mode of analytic listening. *Psychoanalytic Inquiry, 1*, 357–392.

Seligman, S. (1994). Applying psychoanalysis in an unconventional context: Adapting infant–parent psychotherapy to a changing population. *The psychoanalytic study of the child, 49*, 481–510. New Haven, CT: Yale University Press.

Shane, M., Shane, E. & Gales, M. (1998). *Intimate attachments: Towards a new self psychology*. New York: Guilford Press.

Sherman, T. (1985). Categorization skills in infants. *Child Development, 56*, 1561–1573.

Shumsky, E. (1996). The house of mirrors: Self psychology and the exquisitely attuned patient. Presented to Association of Psychoanalytic Self Psychology, New York, November.

Shields, P. & Rovee-Collier, C. (1992). Long-term memory for context-specific category information at six months. *Child Development, 63*, 245–259.

Singer, J. & Fagen, J. (1992). Negative affect, emotional expression, and forgetting in young infants. *Developmental Psychology, 28*, 48–57.

Slavin, M. (2000). Hate, self-interest, and "good-enough" relating: An evolutionary-adaptive perspective. *Psychoanalytic Inquiry, 20*, 441–461.

Slavin, M. & Kriegman, D. (1998). Why the analyst needs to change: Toward a theory of conflict, negotiation and mutual influence in the therapeutic process. *Psychoanalytic Dialogues, 8*, 247–284.

Socarides, D. & Stolorow, R. (1984/1985). Affects and self-objects. *The annual of psychoanalysis, 12/13,* 105–120. New York: International Universities Press.

Sorce, J. & Emde, R. (1981). Mother's presence is not enough: The effect of emotional availability on infant exploration. *Developmental Psychology, 17,* 737–745.

Soref, A. (1992). The self, in and out of relatedness. *The annual of psychoanalysis, 20,* 25–48. Hillsdale, NJ: The Analytic Press.

Sorter, D. (1996). Chase and dodge: An organization of experience. *Psychoanalysis and Psychotherapy, 13,* 68–75.

Spelke, E. & Cortelyou, A. (1981). Perceptual aspects of social knowing. In M. Lamb & L. Sherrod (Eds.), *Infant social cognition* (pp. 61–84). Hillsdale, NJ: Lawrence Erlbaum Associates.

Spinelli, D. & Jensen, F. (1979). Plasticity: The mirror of experience. *Science, 203,* 75–79.

Spitz, R. (1983). The evolution of dialogue. In R. Emde (Ed.), *Rene A. Spitz: Dialogues from infancy, selected papers* (pp. 179–195). New York: International Universities Press.

Squire, L. & Cohen, N. (1984). Human memory and amnesia. In G. Lynch, J. McGaugh & N. Weinberger (Eds.), *Neurobiology of learning memory* (pp. 3–64). New York: Guilford.

Sroufe, A. & Fleeson, J. (1986). Attachment and the construction of relationships. In W. Hartup & Z. Rubin (Eds.), *Relationships and development* (pp. 51–71). New York: Cambridge University Press.

Sroufe, L. (1979a). The coherence of individual development. *American Psychologist, 34,* 834–841.

Sroufe, L. (1979b).The ontogenesis of emotion. In J. Osofsky (Ed.), *Handbook of infant development* (pp. 462–516). New York: Wiley.

Stechler, G. & Kaplan, S. (1980). The development of the self. *The psychoanalytic study of the child, 35,* 85–105. New Haven, CT: Yale University Press.

Stern, D. (1971). A microanalysis of the mother–infant interaction. *Journal of the American Academy of Child Psychiatry, 10,* 501–507.

Stern, D. (1974). Mother and infant at play: The dyadic interaction involving facial, vocal, and gaze behaviors. In M. Lewis & L. Rosenblum (Eds.), *The effect of the infant on its caregiver.* New York: Wiley.

Stern, D. (1977). *The first relationship.* Cambridge, MA: Harvard University Press.

Stern, D. (1981). Early transmission of affect. Presented to First International Congress on Infant Psychiatry, Cascais, Portugal.

Stern, D. (1982). Some interactive functions of rhythm changes between mother and infant. In M. Davis (Ed.), *Interaction rhythms* (pp. 101–117). New York: Human Sciences Press.

Stern, D. (1983). The early development of schemas of self, of other, and of "self with other." In J. Lichtenberg & S. Kaplan (Eds.), *Reflections on self psychology* (pp. 49–84). Hillsdale, NJ: The Analytic Press.

Stern, D. (1985). *The interpersonal world of the infant.* New York: Basic Books.

Stern, D. (1988). The dialectic between the "interpersonal" and the "intrapsychic": With particular emphasis on the role of memory and representation. *Psychoanalytic Inquiry, 8,* 505–512.

Stern, D. (1989). The representation of relational patterns: Developmental considerations. In A. Sameroff & R. Emde (Eds.), *Relationship disturbances in early childhood* (pp. 52–69). New York: Basic Books.

Stern, D. (1995). *The motherhood constellation.* New York: Basic Books.

Stern, D. (1997). *Unformulated experience: From dissociation to imagination in psychoanalysis.* Hillsdale, NJ: The Analytic Press.

Stern, D. (1998). The process of therapeutic change involving implicit knowledge: Some implications of developmental observations for adult psychotherapy. *Infant Mental Health Journal, 19,* 300–308.

Stern, D., Jaffe, J., Beebe, B. & Bennett, S. (1975). Vocalizing in unison and alternation: Two modes of communication within the mother–infant dyad. *Annals of the New York Academy of Science, 263,* 89–100.

Stern, D., Sander, L., Nahum, J., Harrison, A., Bruschweiler-Stern, N. & Tronick, E. (1998). Non-interpretative mechanisms in psychoanalytic therapy. *International Journal of Psycho-Analysis, 79,* 903–921.

Stolorow, R. (1997). Dynamic, dyadic, intersubjective systems: An evolving paradigm for psychoanalysis. *Psychoanalytic Psychology, 14,* 337–346.

Stolorow, R. & Atwood, G. (1992). *Contexts of being.* Hillsdale, NJ: The Analytic Press.

Storolow, R., Brandchaft, B. & Atwood, G. (1987). *Psychoanalytic treatment: An intersubjective approach.* Hillsdale, NJ: The Analytic Press.

Stolorow, R. & Lachmann, F. (1980). *Psychoanalysis of developmental arrests.* New York: International Universities Press.

Strachey, I. (1934). The nature of the therapeutic action of psycho-analysis. *International Journal of Psycho-Analysis, 15,* 127–159.

Strauss, M. (1979). Abstractions of proto-typical information by adults and 10 month old infants. *Journal of Experimental Psychology: Human Learning and Memory, 5,* 618–632.

Sucharov, M. (1994) Psychoanalysis, self psychology and intersubjectivity. In R. Stolorow, G. Atwood & B. Brandchaft (Eds.), *The intersubjective perspective* (pp. 187–202). Northvale, NJ: Aronson.

Sullivan, H. (1940). *Conceptions of modern psychiatry.* New York: Norton.

Sullivan, H. (1932). Socio-psychiatric research. In *Schizophrenia as a human process* (pp. 977–991). New York: Norton, 1962.

Sullivan, H. (1953). *The interpersonal theory of psychiatry.* New York: Norton.

Sullivan, H. (1964). *The illusion of personal identity: The fusion of psychiatry and social science.* New York: Norton.

Tabin, J. (1997). Catching up on babies, commentary on paper by Beebe, Lachmann & Jaffe. *Psychoanalytic Dialogues, 7,* 189–195.

Thelen, E. (1998). Presidential address. International Society for Infant Studies, Atlanta, GA, April.

Thelen, E. & Smith, L. (1994). *A dynamic systems approach to the development of cognition and action.* Cambridge, MA: MIT Press.

Thomas, E. & Malone, T. W. (1979). On the dynamics of two-person interactions. *Psychological Review, 86,* 331–360.

Thomas, E. & Martin, J. (1976). Analyses of parent-infant interaction. *Psychological Review, 83,* 141–155.

Thompson, R. (1994). Emotional regulation: A theme in search of definition. In N. Fox (Ed.), *The development of emotion regulation. Monographs of the Society for Research in Child Development, 59*(2–3) Serial No. 240, pp. 25–52.

Tobach, E. (1970).Some guidelines to the study of the evolution and development of emotion. In L. Aronson, E. Tobach, D. Lehrman & J. Rosenblatt (Eds.), *Development and evolution of behavior* (pp. 238–253). San Francisco: Freeman.

Tobias, K. (1995). The relation between maternal attachment and patterns of mother–infant interaction at four months. Doctoral dissertation, the City University of New York.

Tolpin, M. (1971). On the beginning of a cohesive self. In R. Eissler, A. Freud, M. Kris, S. Lustman & A. Solnit (Eds.), *The psychoanalytic study of the child, 26,* 316–354. New Haven, CT: Yale University Press.

Tomkins, S. (1962). *Affect, imagery and consciousness, vol. 1.* New York: Springer.

Tomkins, S. (1963). *Affect, imagery and consciousness, vol. 2.* New York: Springer.

Tomkins, S. (1980). Affect as amplification: Some modifications in theory. In R. Plutchik & H. Kellerman (Eds.), *Emotions: Theory, research and experience* (pp. 141–164). New York: Academic Press.

Tononi, J., Sporns, O. & Edelman, G. (1994). A measure of forebrain complexity: Relating functional segregation and integration in the nervous system. *Proceedings of the National Academy of Science (USA), 91*, 331–360.

Trevarthen, C. (1989). Development of early social interactions and the affective regulation of brain growth. In C. von Euier, H. Forssberg & H. Lagercrantz (Eds.), *Neurobiology of early infant behavior* (pp. 191–216). London: Macmillan.

Tronick, E. (1980). The primacy of social skills in infancy. In D. Sawin, R. Hawkins, L. Walker, & J. Penticuff (Eds.), *Exceptional infant, vol. 4* (pp. 144–158). New York: Bruner/Mazel.

Tronick, E. (1982). Affectivity and sharing. In E. Tronick (Ed.), *Social interchange in infancy* (pp. 1–8). Baltimore, MD: University Park Press.

Tronick, E. (1989). Emotions and emotional communication in infants. *American Psychologist, 44*, 112–119.

Tronick, E. (1996). *Dyadically expanded states of consciousness and the process of normal and abnormal development*. Presented to Colloque International de Psychiatrie Perinatal, Monaco, January.

Tronick, E. (1998). Dyadically expanded states of conscious and the process of therapeutic change. *Infant Mental Health Journal, 19*, 290–299.

Tronick, E., Als, H., Adamson, L., Wise, S. & Brazelton, T. (1978). The infant's response to entrapment between contradictory messages in face-to-face interaction. *Journal of the American Academy of Child and Adolescent Psychiatry, 17*, 1–13.

Tronick, E. & Cohn, J. (1989). Infant mother face-to-face interaction: Age and gender differences in coordination and miscoordination. *Child Development, 59*, 85–92.

Tronick, E. & Gianino, A. (1986). Interactive mismatch and repair: Challenges to the coping infant. *Zero to Three: Bulletin of the National Center Clinical Infant Program, 5*, 1–6.

Trout, D. & Rosenfeld, H. (1980). The effect of postural lean and body congruence on the judgement of psychotherapeutic rapport. *Journal of Nonverbal Behavior, 4*, 176–190.

von Bertalanffy, L. (1968). *General systems theory: Foundation, development, applications*. New York: Braziller.

Warner, R. (1988a). Rhythmic organization of social interaction and observer ratings of positive affect and involvement. *Journal of Nonverbal Behavior, 11*, 57–74.

Warner, R. (1988b). Rhythm in social interaction. In J. McGrath (Ed.), *The social psychology of time* (pp. 63–88). London: Sage.

Warner, R. (1996). Coordinated cycles in behavior and physiology during face-to-face social interactions. In J. Watt & C. VanLear (Eds.), *Dynamic patterns in communication processes* (pp. 327–352). Thousand Oaks, CA: Sage.

Warner, R., Malloy, D., Schneider, K., Knoth, R. & Wilder, B. (1987). Rhythmic organization of social interaction and observer ratings of positive affect and involvement. *Journal of Nonverbal Behavior, 11,* 57–74.

Watson, J. (1985). Contingency perception in early social development. In T. Field & N. Fox (Eds.), *Social perception in infants* (pp. 157–176). Norwood, NJ: Ablex.

Watson, J. (1994). Detection of self: The perfect algorithm. In S. Parker, R. Mitchell & M. Boccia (Eds.), *Self-awareness in animals and humans: Developmental perspectives* (pp. 131–148). New York: Cambridge University Press.

Weinberg, K. (1991). Sex differences in 6 month infants' behavior. Impact on maternal caregiving. Doctoral dissertation, University of Massachusetts, Amherst.

Weinberg, M., Tronick, E., Cohn, J. & Olson, K. (1999). Gender differences in emotional expressivity and self-regulation during early infancy. *Developmental Psychology, 35,* 175–188.

Weiss, P. (1970). Whither life or science? *American Scientist, 58,* 156–163.

Weiss, P. (1973). *The science of life.* Mt. Kisco, NY: Futura.

Weiss, J. & Sampson, H. (1986). *The Psychoanalytic Process.* New York: Guilford.

Werner, H. (1948). *The comparative psychology of mental development.* New York: International Universities Press.

Werner, H. & Kaplan, S. (1963). *Symbol formation.* New York: Wiley.

Wilson, A. (1995). Mapping the mind in relational psychoanalysis: Some critiques, questions and conjectures. *Psychoanalytic Psychology, 12,* 9–29.

Wilson, A. & Malatesta, C. (1989). Affect and the compulsion to repeat: Freud's repetition compulsion revisited. *Psychoanalysis and Contemporary Thought, 12,* 243–290.

Winnicott, D. (1957). *The child and the family.* London: Tavistock.

Winnicott, D. (1965). *Maturational processes and the facilitating environment.* New York: International Universities Press.

Winnicott, D. (1967). Mirror-role of mother and family in child development. *Playing and reality.* Middlesex, UK: Penguin, 1974.

Winton, W. (1986). The role of facial response in self-reports of emotion: A critique of Laird. *Journal of Personality and Social Psychology, 50,* 808–812.

Winton, W., Putnam, L. & Krauss, R. (1984). Facial and autonomic manifestations of the dimensional structure of emotion. *Journal of Experimental Social Psychology, 20,* 195–216.

Wolf, E. (1993). The role of interpretation in therapeutic change. In A. Goldberg (Ed.), *The widening scope of self psychology: Progress in self psychology, vol. 9* (pp. 151–130). Hillsdale, NJ: The Analytic Press.

Younger, B. & Cohen, L. (1985). How infants form categories. In G. Bower (Ed.), *The psychology of learning and motivation: Advances in research and theory* (pp. 211–247). New York: Academic Press.

Younger, B. & Gotlieb, S. (1988). Development of categorization skills: Changes in the nature or structure of form categories? *Developmental Psychology, 24,* 611–619.

Zajonc, R. (1985). Emotion and facial efference: A theory reclaimed. *Science, 228,* 15–22.

Zeanah, C., Anders, T., Seifer, R. & Stern, D. (1989). Implications of research on infant development for psychodynamic theory and practice. *Journal of the American Academy of Child and Adolescent Psychiatry, 28,* 657–668.

Zelner, S. (1982). The organization of vocalization and gaze in early mother–infant interactive regulation. Doctoral dissertation, Yeshiva University, New York.

Zelnick, L. & Bucholz, E. (1990). The concept of mental representations in light of recent infant research. *Psychoanalytic Psychology, 7,* 29–88.

Zicht, S. (1993). Attachment and the regulation of mother-toddler attention. Doctoral dissertation, Yeshiva University, New York.

INDEX